Energy and the English Industrial Revolution

The industrial revolution transformed the productive power of societies. It did so by vastly increasing individual productivity, thus delivering whole populations from poverty. In this new account by one of the world's acknowledged authorities the central issue is not simply how the revolution began but still more why it did not quickly end. The answer lay in the use of a new source of energy. Pre-industrial societies had access only to very limited energy supplies. As long as mechanical energy came principally from human or animal muscle and heat energy from wood, the maximum attainable level of productivity was bound to be low. Exploitation of a new source of energy in the form of coal provided an escape route from the constraints of an organic economy but also brought novel dangers. Since this happened first in England, its experience has a special fascination, though other countries rapidly followed suit.

SIR TONY WRIGLEY is a member and co-founder of the Cambridge Group for the History of Population and Social Structure and a former President of the British Academy. His previous publications include *Population and history* (1969), *People, cities and wealth* (1987), *Continuity, chance and change* (1988), *Poverty, progress, and population* (2004), and, with R. S. Schofield, *The population history of England 1541–1871* (1981).

Energy and the English Industrial Revolution

E. A. WRIGLEY

CAMBRIDGE
UNIVERSITY PRESS

CAMBRIDGE
UNIVERSITY PRESS

University Printing House, Cambridge CB2 8BS, United Kingdom

Cambridge University Press is part of the University of Cambridge.

It furthers the University's mission by disseminating knowledge in the pursuit of education, learning and research at the highest international levels of excellence.

www.cambridge.org
Information on this title: www.cambridge.org/9780521131858

First published 2010
3rd printing 2014

A catalogue record for this publication is available from the British Library

Library of Congress Cataloguing in Publication data
Wrigley, E. A. (Edward Anthony), 1931–
  Energy and the English Industrial Revolution / E.A. Wrigley.
  p.   cm.
  Includes bibliographical references and index.
  ISBN 978-0-521-76693-7 – ISBN 978-0-521-13185-8 (pbk.)
  1. Power resources–Great Britain–History.   2. The energy revolution–Great Britain–History.   3. Industrial revolution–Great Britain.   I. Title.
  HD9502.G72W75 2010
  333.790942′09034–dc22
  2010014620

ISBN 978-0-521-76693-7 Hardback
ISBN 978-0-521-13185-8 Paperback

For Marieke, Ave, Tamsin, and Rebecca

Contents

Figures

Tables

Acknowledgements

This book is dedicated to my children. It would not have been written if one of them had not remarked that it would be timely to abandon what might be termed the severely academic mode of writing and meet the challenge of communicating the same ideas less opaquely (though she expressed herself rather more pithily). They have each received earlier drafts of the book and commented on its strengths and weaknesses. As a result, the present text is much changed and much better than the original draft.

I am also indebted to two anonymous referees whose comments, I discovered with interest, sometimes paralleled those which I had received from my children.

I have benefited over many years from being a member of the Cambridge Group for the History of Population and Social Structure and this book owes much to the contacts and stimulus which this has afforded me. The Group has now been in existence for almost half a century. Although its personnel has changed greatly, its ethos has not. In addition to its core members, there have always been outstanding research students attached to the Group and a flow of eminent visiting scholars from all over the world. Those who have at any time been present at the Group in whatever capacity very frequently revisit us, the best kind of compliment. Coffee time at the Group often stretches out over three-quarters of an hour or more, and very often this is not only the most amusing but also the most intellectually rewarding part of the day.

One member of the Group, Max Satchell, made use of his expertise in GIS (geographical information systems) to produce the map of population growth in English hundreds in the period 1761 to 1851 which is to be found in figure 6.5. I am most grateful for his assistance. I have also benefited greatly from the help I have received from Phil Stickler whose expertise as a draughtsman and cartographer is reflected in all the other figures in this volume.

Introduction

Opening Pandora's jar

The story of Pandora exists in several versions which differ somewhat from each other. A summary of the most widely received version would run much as follows. Both Pandora herself and her jar were created at the command of Zeus who was hoping to punish Prometheus for having stolen fire from the sun to animate his man of clay. Pandora was made the personification of beauty and possessed many abilities. She was commanded to present her jar to the man whom she married. She was intended to captivate Prometheus but he was wary of accepting her and her jar. Instead she married Prometheus' brother, Epimetheus, who lacked his brother's caution. Despite receiving a warning about acting imprudently, Epimetheus, on being presented with the jar, opened it. In doing so he released into the world a host of evils but also hope which might, in some sense, offset them.

Any close analogy between this story and the industrial revolution might seem ludicrously far fetched. Yet in some respects there is a telling resemblance between the myth and the historical event. The industrial revolution was unexpected by contemporaries and many of the features of the period which have attracted so much attention with the benefit of hindsight went largely unnoticed at the time. Like Pandora and her husband when the jar was opened, nothing in their past experience had prepared people at the time for what was to follow. The possibility of a transformation which would radically enhance the productive powers of society was at the time generally dismissed as idle optimism. The nature of the new situation was acknowledged and understood only by a later generation and for a time any benefit from it was hotly disputed. Marx, for example, recognised the vastly enhanced power to produce which had come into existence but considered that the bulk of the population was condemned to receive little or no benefit from it, and was deeply angered by his assessment. Then

1

for more than a century an improvement in the material circumstances of whole populations appeared indisputable if uneven. More recently new uncertainties and misgivings have become increasingly prominent. The use of fossil fuels as the prime source of energy has vastly increased the power to produce of countries throughout the world but it is accompanied by environmental hazards which threaten disastrous consequences. If they are to be avoided speedy and radical action appears to be necessary. And the massive increase in the power to produce has been accompanied by an equally great rise in the power to destroy. There are able and well-informed observers who think that mankind as a species will be fortunate to survive to the end of the present century. The powers which were unleashed by the industrial revolution, in other words, have proved to possess the capacity to bestow blessings without earlier parallel but also to cause harm on a scale previously unknown. Once released from the jar they cannot be reconfined but it is reasonable still to remain in doubt whether the balance between their benefits and their dangers is favourable or malign.

It is said that Zhou Enlai, on being asked whether he considered the French revolution to have been a success, paused, and then replied that he thought it was a little early to tell. Most people if asked the same question in regard to the industrial revolution would probably reply positively, but the transformation of the capacity of societies to produce material goods brought about by the industrial revolution has brought with it matching dangers. The analogy with Pandora's jar may appear somewhat tenuous but the myth and the later reality are not without parallels. Many of the powers which were released by the industrial revolution have proved unambiguously beneficial but the attendant dangers are not trivial. The Cuban missile crisis was a stark reminder of how close to the edge of a precipice we stood and stand. The power to destroy and to pollute has risen in step with the power to produce. Any final verdict remains uncertain.

Overview of the nature and structure of the book

The England of 1850 was vastly different from the England of 1600. During the intervening quarter millennium it had been the setting for the beginning of one of the two greatest transformations of human society since hunter-gatherer days. And yet the pace of change throughout was more often measured than hectic. Many of the most widely used indicators of economic and social change have recorded far more rapid change in the century-and-a-half after 1850 than in the preceding period. The economy has expanded more rapidly, real incomes have risen at a faster pace, and expectation of life at birth has improved more quickly in the post-1850 period than in the two centuries which preceded it.

Everyone can name the transformation which took place, the change which makes this quarter millennium in England so central to world history. It is conventionally termed the industrial revolution and this term has been in common currency for so long and has become so deeply embedded in the general consciousness that it is idle to suggest that it should be replaced, even though both the adjective and the noun are somewhat misleading. Although everyone can name the transformation, neither its definition, nor its origins, nor its chronology, nor its relationship to other changes of the period are matters on which there is a wide consensus. And there is the further oddity that despite its profound significance (or perhaps, some might say, because of its profound significance) it was for the most part curiously and instructively imperceptible to contemporaries. The man in the street in the 1790s would be in no doubt about the occurrence of a revolution across the Channel in France but would have been astonished to learn that he was living in the middle of what future generations would also term a revolution and would regard as having far greater long-term importance. Nor was it just the man in the street who was unaware of the transformation in train. The three greatest of the framers of classical economics, Adam Smith, Thomas Malthus, and David Ricardo, not only were equally unaware of it, but were unanimous in dismissing the possibility of what later generations came to term an industrial revolution.[1]

In this book, I shall attempt to throw light on the developments which set the new age apart from the agricultural societies which had come into being because of the only earlier transformation of comparable magnitude, the neolithic food revolution.

One feature of my approach should be stressed immediately. It is conventional to focus on the question of how a breakthrough to more rapid growth, a 'take-off', was achieved; how it was possible to change the rate at which the economy expanded so markedly that for the first time in human history there was a prospect of vanquishing mass

---

[1] See below pp. 10–17 for a description of their views.

poverty. This approach tends to carry with it the implicit assumption that once the decisive acceleration had occurred, it was natural to expect it to continue. But this is to allow what actually happened to obscure a matter of fundamental importance. In my view the most important single issue on which to focus in trying to gain a clearer understanding of the industrial revolution is not how the period of more rapid growth began, but why it did not come to an end. All past experience appeared to justify the expectation that the very process of growth would set in train changes which would arrest and might well reverse the growth which had occurred. The faster the rate of growth achieved, the sooner and more abruptly it would cease. I hope to make clear the nature of the arrester mechanism which had always operated so powerfully before the industrial revolution and also to direct attention to those features of the growth process in England between the reigns of Elizabeth and Victoria which made it possible for the country for the first time to escape a similar fate.

There can be no single, 'true' account of the industrial revolution. Since its nature can be defined in different ways, it follows that a description and explanation which are satisfactory in the context implied by one definition are unlikely to carry conviction when the industrial revolution is differently defined. Even where there is agreement about definitions, the problem remains, partly because of the complexity of the *explicandum*, and partly because the limitations of much of the empirical evidence make conclusive proof (or, still more important, conclusive disproof) of a particular hypothesis elusive. What follows represents an attempt to provide good reasons for accepting a particular approach to the problem of making sense of the transformation which occurred. In developing my argument I shall hope to make clear the assumptions, the preconceptions, some may say the prejudices, which underlie my approach.

The book has a particular form. It marshals the discussion of the industrial revolution round a single, central theme, the history of energy availability and use. There are only glancing references to some aspects of change during the early modern period which are central to other interpretations of the events taking place. For many historians, for example, the absence of any extended discussion of the changing institutional and legal framework of society means missing the key background factor to the possibility of an industrial revolution occurring. Amongst other things, an independent and powerful judiciary implementing a legal code which affords protection to private assets was, it is argued, essential. The maxim *Quod principi placuit legis habet vigorem* does not provide a congenial setting for stable and consistent growth.[2] Or again, there is only passing reference to the striking scientific advances of the age which can reasonably be portrayed as having provided an insight into the nature of physical, chemical, and biological processes which cleared the way for a host of improvements across the whole range of productive activity. Perhaps even more important, it may be argued, was the way in which scientific progress produced a different mindset, seeking and finding explanations for every aspect of the functioning of the natural world without invoking the operation of divine providence.

These and other similar general explanations of the extraordinary transformation of traditional into modern economies have received much attention and it would be both presumptuous and mildly ridiculous to downplay their importance. A full and rounded account of the industrial revolution must incorporate them or find a compelling reason for failing to do so. But it is difficult to avoid a loss of clarity in seeking to be comprehensive. The problem in incorporating a full range of possible explanations of or contributory factors to the industrial revolution is that they are essentially incommensurable. The facility does not exist for weighing their relative importance. I have therefore, in a sense, chosen the easy way out. The topics treated in this book are not free from this problem but it is less prominent than in more inclusive treatments and I trust that there is a gain in clarity as a result. And, to repeat, the book has a more limited purpose than general treatments of the industrial revolution. It seeks above all to provide an explanation not for an acceleration in economic growth but for the absence of a subsequent deceleration. The choice of the topics selected should be judged in the light of this fact.

This book is divided into four parts. Part I consists of two chapters which describe the general thesis of the work, providing a background which should help to make clear the relevance of the topics discussed in the subsequent text. There are four chapters in Part II. Each considers the nature of the relationship between elements within the economy which promoted or accommodated change and growth,

---

[2] The maxim can be rendered as 'What is pleasing to the prince has the force of law.'

the type of relationship which is often referred to as one of positive feedback. These chapters should also clarify the nature of the changes taking place between the reigns of Elizabeth and Victoria which made it possible for growth to continue and even accelerate when past experience had always suggested that growth must give way to stagnation. In Part III there are two chapters. The first describes the timing and nature of the changes taking place during the industrial revolution. The second discusses the relevance of the concept of 'modernisation' to the changes which took place in England during this period; some of the issues involved are explored by a comparison of England and the Netherlands in the early modern period. Part IV is very short: it consists of a single chapter reviewing and restating some of the central theses of the earlier chapters.

It will be clear, therefore, that the book is neither a general history of the industrial revolution, nor a monograph presenting the findings arising from recent research, but rather an attempt to specify a particular interpretation of the key characteristics of the industrial revolution, supported by a series of essays dealing with the relevant aspects of changes taking place. Half a century ago in his inaugural lecture, F. J. Fisher, ever a plain speaker, said that the traditional monograph 'consisted of a thin rivulet of text meandering through wide and lush meadows of footnotes'. Whatever the drawbacks of this convention, however, they were clearly less objectionable, in his view, than what he termed the 'archetype of our modern fashion' in economic history 'in which a stream, often a less than limpid stream, of text tumbles from table to table and swirls round graph after graph'. He noted that his predecessor had asked for greater use to be made of statistics: 'The Almighty has answered his prayer, not with a shower, but with a deluge.'[3] I belong to that branch of historical enquiry which Fisher had in mind when amusing himself and his listeners and might be said to have been, at times, severely afflicted by a tendency to resort to quantification. For many purposes I believe firmly in its validity and value. Nevertheless I have done my best not to allow this weakness to figure too prominently in this book, without, however, failing to make use of quantification where it is effective either in description or in clarifying an argument.

---

[3] Fisher, 'The dark ages of English economic history', p. 184.

PART I

A sketch of the argument

1 | *The limits to growth in organic economies*

The neolithic agricultural revolution massively increased the quantity of food which could be produced from a given area of land and thereby made possible a matching growth in population. Whereas previously men and women had competed with other animals to secure a share of the natural products of the land, the development of agriculture, which was the defining feature of the change, meant that plant growth over vast areas was restricted to plants for human sustenance or to feed flocks of domesticated animals. This multiplied by orders of magnitude the capacity of each acre suitable for agriculture to support a human population.

All economies which developed in the wake of the neolithic food revolution may be termed organic. In organic economies not only was the land the source of food, it was also the source directly or indirectly of all the material products of use to man. All industrial production depended upon vegetable or animal raw materials. This is self-evidently true of industries such as woollen textile production or shoemaking but is also true of iron smelting or pottery manufacture, although their raw materials were mineral, since production was only possible by making use of a source of heat and this came from burning wood or charcoal. Thus the production horizon for all organic economies was set by the annual cycle of plant growth. This set physical and biological limits to the possible scale of production. Organic economies therefore differed fundamentally from economies transformed by the industrial revolution since many of the industries which grew most rapidly thereafter made little or no use of organic raw materials. Above all, access to a mineral rather than a vegetable energy source expanded the production horizon decisively. The significance of this distinction is the basic issue to be explored in this chapter.

The views of the classical economists

The writings of the classical economists provide an illuminating, in many respects a definitive, account of the reasons why it had seemed impossible to secure prolonged expansion of production at a rate which would allow the living standards of the mass of the population to rise progressively. There were, they argued, three factors involved in all material production: labour, capital, and land. The supply of the first two could, in favourable circumstances, expand as required. The supply of the third was fixed. This created a tension which must grow steadily greater in any period of expansion. More people meant more mouths to feed. An expansion in woollen textile production meant raising more sheep and therefore devoting more land to sheep pasture. A rise in iron output involved cutting down more wood to feed the furnaces and implied an increase in the area to be committed to forest. Each type of production was in competition with every other for access to the products of the land. Such pressures in turn must mean either taking land of inferior fertility into agricultural use, or working existing farmland more intensively, or, more probably, both simultaneously. The result must be a tendency for the return to both labour and capital to fall. Growth must slow and eventually come to a halt. Improvements in production techniques and institutional change might for a time offset the problems springing from the fixed supply of land. This might delay but could not indefinitely postpone the inevitable. In short, the very fact of growth, because of the nature of material production in an organic economy, must ensure that growth would grind to a halt. And this impasse was reached not because of human deficiencies, or of failure in political, social, or economic structures but for an ineluctable physical reason, the fixed supply of land.

Ricardo's chapter 'On profits' in the *Principles of political economy* contains a long discussion of the necessary tendency of the level of profit to fall over time replete with an arithmetic exposition of the process. He concludes with a summary in the following terms:

Whilst the land yields abundantly, wages may temporarily rise, and the producers may consume more than their accustomed proportion; but the stimulus which will thus be given to population, will speedily reduce the labourers to their usual consumption. But when poor lands are taken into cultivation, or when more capital and labour are expended on the old land, with a less return of produce, the effect must be permanent. A greater proportion of that part of the produce which remains to be divided, after paying rent, between the owners of stock and the labourers, will be apportioned to the latter. Each man may, and probably will, have a less absolute quantity; but as more labourers are employed in proportion to the whole produce retained by the farmer, the value of a greater proportion of the whole produce will be absorbed by wages, and consequently the value of a smaller proportion will be devoted to profits. This will necessarily be rendered permanent by the laws of nature, which have limited the productive powers of the land.[1]

Ricardo provided a particularly clear and pungent exposition of the dilemma facing all organic economies, but it did not differ greatly from the views of Adam Smith or Malthus.

Adam Smith identified the rate of return on capital as the proximate determinant of growth or stagnation. He had no doubt that the productivity of the land set the bounds to possible growth and that the return on capital declined steadily as the opportunities for profitable investment became rarer. For a time growth might be brisk and the demand for labour strong, leading to an increase in the prevailing level of wages and improving the living standards of the labouring poor, but such periods were bound to be transient:

In a country which had acquired that full complement of riches which the nature of its soil and climate, and its situation with respect to other countries, allowed it to acquire; which could, therefore, advance no further, and which was not going backwards, both the wages of labour and the profits of stock would probably be very low. In a country fully peopled in proportion to what either its territory could maintain or its stock employ, the competition for employment would necessarily be so great as to reduce the wages of labour to what was barely sufficient to keep up the number of labourers, and, the country being already fully peopled, the number could never be augmented. In a country fully stocked in proportion to all the business it had to transact, as great a quantity of stock would be employed in every particular branch as the nature and extent of the trade would admit. The competition, therefore, would everywhere be as great, and consequently the ordinary profit as low as possible.[2]

[1] Ricardo, *Principles of political economy*, pp. 125–6.
[2] Smith, *Wealth of nations*, I, p. 106.

Malthus provided a further consideration to reinforce these conclusions. Like Adam Smith he regarded it as self-evident that a rise in real wages would tend both to reduce mortality and to increase fertility through encouraging earlier marriage. A fall would produce the opposite effect. In the first version of his *Essay on population*, published in 1798, he found a telling argument with which to drive home the implications of the link between economic circumstance and demographic behaviour.[3] He argued that a population unchecked by deteriorating economic circumstances would grow geometrically. In contrast, the best that could be expected of material production was that it would grow arithmetically.[4] The former, therefore, because of the nature of the two series, must always tend to outstrip the latter, bringing increasing misery to the labouring classes.[5] Eventually population growth would be brought to a halt, primarily as a result of what Malthus termed the 'positive check' (that is, through higher mortality). Even though periods of relatively rapid economic growth might occur, relieving pressure on the labouring poor for a time, there could be no escape from the tendency of the wage to revert to a conventional minimum which in some societies might be close to bare subsistence. Malthus's invocation of the contrast between arithmetic and geometric progressions was an ingenious and highly effective way of highlighting the intractable nature of the problem. But it is worth noting that even if economic growth could also grow geometrically, in the circumstances of an organic economy the problem would not be resolved. Even in the most favourable circumstances improvements in

---

[3] In the later editions of the *Essay* he modified his initial views substantially. Indeed the sophistication of his final position is often overlooked in descriptions of his work.

[4] An arithmetic progression goes 1, 2, 3, 4, 5; a geometric progression goes 1, 2, 4, 8, 16.

[5] Although Malthus supposed the preventive check (principally marrying late or not at all) operated in some degree at all levels, he believed in 1798 that it was clear that the positive check (a rise in the death rate) was the main factor preventing population growth among the labouring classes who formed the bulk of the population. Malnutrition among the poor classes was widespread and sometimes severe. 'The sons and daughters of peasants will not be found such rosy cherubs in real life, as they are described to be in romances. It cannot fail to be remarked by those who live much in the country, that the sons of labourers are very apt to be stunted in their growth, and are a long while in arriving at maturity. Boys that you would guess to be fourteen or fifteen, are upon inquiry, frequently found to be eighteen or nineteen.' Malthus, *Essay on population* [1798], pp. 29–30.

technology were highly unlikely to produce a long-term growth rate as high as, say, 0.5 per cent per annum.[6] Population growth could match this without difficulty.

It follows from the stance taken by the classical economists that there is a further consideration which must prohibit progressive growth. If the wages of the bulk of the population must in the long run necessarily drift towards a conventional minimum, it follows that the structure of aggregate demand must take a form which rules out beneficial change.[7] The demand for necessities of life, above all food, but including shelter, clothing, and fuel, will dominate. The scale of the demand for what the classical economists termed comforts and luxuries will be limited and hence the inducement to invest in their production will be slight. Such demand as there might be for any but the most basic of commodities will come from a tiny minority of the privileged and wealthy and will be met from the workshops of small groups of specialist craftsmen. In the absence of large-scale demand for standard industrial products there will be no large-scale production and therefore little incentive to introduce or invest in new techniques of production. The great bulk of the labour force will be employed on the land and many of the rest in producing simple textiles and in basic construction.

The energy constraint

The argument advanced by the classical economists for ruling out of court the possibility of sustained growth and rising living standards for the population as a whole can be restated in a related form which leads to the same conclusion. All types of material production involve the expenditure of energy. Wielding a spade or driving a plough, mining copper ore, operating a loom, smelting iron, or baking bricks all mean making use of either heat or mechanical energy. The same is true of many other aspects of economic activity. The transport of raw materials and finished products, for example, is as much a part of the production process as a whole as is farming or manufacture. Transport often involves a large expenditure of energy, and, although

[6] In practice a sustained rate of growth in output as high as 0.5 per cent annually was probably unknown in a fully settled organic economy. Such a rate means doubling in about 140 years and a twelvefold rise over 500 years.

[7] Aggregate demand simply means the sum of all individual demands added together.

the quantity of energy needed may be smaller, many other service industries also require some energy expenditure. In all organic economies this fact necessarily limited the opportunity for growth.

The total quantity of energy arriving each year on the surface of the earth from the sun is enormous, far exceeding the amount of energy expended each year across the world today, but in organic economies human access to this superabundant flow of energy was principally through plant photosynthesis. Plant growth was the sole source of sustenance for both people and animals, whether herbivores, carnivores, or omnivores. Plant photosynthesis is the food base of all living organisms. This is as true of a pride of lions as of a herd of antelopes. Photosynthesis, however, is an inefficient process. Estimates of its efficiency in converting the incoming stream of energy from the sun normally lie only in the range between 0.1 and 0.4 per cent of the energy arriving on a given surface. Moreover, insufficient or excessive rainfall and very high or low temperature may prohibit or greatly limit plant growth over large areas. It has been estimated that the annual solar energy receipt of the United Kingdom is equivalent to the energy contained in approximately 23 billion tons of coal. Thus, on these estimates, photosynthesis is only capable of capturing energy equivalent to between c.20 and c.80 million tons of coal at best from the surface of the United Kingdom.[8] Since a significant fraction of vegetable growth is consumed directly or indirectly by wildlife or plays no part in the human economy, the amount of energy which was effectively available for human use while England was an organic economy must have fallen well short of the figures just quoted. Yet in an organic economy plant photosynthesis was by far the most important source of energy, both mechanical and thermal. Wind and water power added little to what was secured via photosynthesis.[9] Mechanical power was principally provided by human and animal muscle. Thermal energy came from burning wood or charcoal. Each may be considered in turn.

---

[8] White and Plaskett. *Biomass as fuel*, pp. 2, 12; Pimentel, 'Energy flow in the food system', p. 2.

[9] Warde estimates that even at its peak early in the nineteenth century wind and water power combined (including the energy captured from the wind by sailing vessels) did not exceed 3 per cent of the total energy consumed in England and Wales, though if coal is excluded from the calculation the contribution of wind and water rises to about 12 per cent of the total. Warde, *Energy consumption in England and Wales*, app.1, tab. 2, pp. 123–30.

The mechanical energy derived from muscle power was only a limited fraction of the calories consumed in food and fodder because men and women in common with all warm-blooded creatures must devote a large part of their food intake to basic body maintenance. For example, about 1,500 kilocalories are needed daily to keep a man alive even if no work is performed. Thus if the daily food intake is 2,500 kilocalories only 40 per cent of the energy consumed is available for productive work. It follows that the amount of useful work that each man could perform might vary substantially according to the prevailing levels of food intake per head. With a daily intake of 3,500 kilocalories a man could undertake double the amount of physical effort which he could perform if his intake was 2,500 (3,500 − 1,500 = 2,000: 2,500 − 1,500 = 1,000). The same basic point applies to draught animals just as to man. Ill-fed animals will use a high proportion of their food intake to stay alive, leaving only a small proportion of their energy intake to drag a plough or pull a cart.

A factor of great significance in organic economies was the ratio of available animal muscle to human muscle. In many societies the amount of energy at the disposal of each man was determined much more by this ratio than by the level of human nutrition. When employed in agricultural work, for example, a horse can carry out about six times as much work as a man and where horses or oxen were abundant the quantity of useful work which each man performed was in effect greatly magnified.[10] As an example, three-quarters of a century ago maize was cultivated in Mexico both solely by hand and by using oxen. Without the assistance of oxen 1,140 man hours were needed to till and cultivate a hectare of maize. Where oxen were used the number of man hours involved fell to 380, though in addition 200 hours of work by oxen was needed.[11] Assigning large areas of land for animal pasture meant reducing the area which could be used for growing human food and therefore limited the size of the human population which could be supported, but, on the other hand, it could raise output per head in agriculture substantially by increasing the quantity of useful work which each man could perform.

Animal muscle power also normally provided the bulk of the energy needed in land transport, and could make a significant difference to

[10] Wrigley, *Continuity, chance and change*, p. 39.
[11] Pimentel, 'Energy flow in the food system', pp. 5–6.

output per head in many industrial and mining activities. Difference in the draught animal/worker ratio is, therefore, one of the factors which could cause the conventional minimum standard of living to differ significantly in different organic economies.

Heat energy like muscle energy depended on plant photosynthesis. Burning wood provided the great bulk of the heat energy consumed. Many industrial processes required large quantities of heat energy. Glass manufacture, brickmaking, beer brewing, textile dyeing, metal smelting and working, lime burning, and many similar processes required much heat energy. Wood was the dominant, indeed in most organic economies virtually the sole source of heat energy. But on a sustained-yield basis an acre of woodland could normally produce only 1–2 tons of dry wood per annum.[12] Two tons of dry wood yields the same amount of heat as one ton of coal.[13] To produce a ton of bar iron in seventeenth-century England involved consuming about 30 tons of dry wood.[14] If half the land surface of Britain had been covered with woodland, it would only have sufficed to produce perhaps 1¼ million tons of bar iron on a sustained-yield basis. Simple arithmetic, therefore, makes it clear that it was physically impossible to produce iron and steel on the scale needed to create a modern railway system, or to construct large fleets of steel ships, or to enable each family to have a car, if the heat energy needed to smelt and process the iron and steel came from wood and charcoal. By the late 1830s the production of pig iron in Britain had already reached the level just quoted for bar iron, but by then, of course, wood had given way to coal as the source of the heat required in its production. By the first

---

[12] The heat output from the combustion of dry wood is 4,200 kcal/kg compared with 8,000 kcal/kg in the case of bituminous coal. White and Plaskett, *Biomass as fuel*, tab. 1, p. 12. Forests in northern Europe today yield between 3 and 8 tons of bone-dry wood per hectare annually on a sustained-yield basis, or 1.2 to 3.2 tons per acre. *Ibid.*, p. 125. It is unlikely that yields were as high as this in the past.

[13] Wrigley, *Continuity, chance and change*, pp. 54–5.

[14] Hammersley quotes a figure of 2,100 cu. ft of wood to produce a ton of bar iron. Hammersley, 'The charcoal iron industry', p. 605. Dr Paul Warde, to whose extensive knowledge of every aspect of woodland management and exploitation I am deeply indebted, reckons that this volume of wood would weigh about 28 tons. He stresses, however, that there are many plausible estimates of the tonnage of wood needed to produce 1 ton of bar iron, ranging between 25 and 50 tons.

decade of the twentieth century it had reached 10 million tons, far beyond the maximum which could have been produced using traditional fuels.[15] In any case, because it was necessary to devote the bulk of the land surface to the production of so many other commodities, the effective ceiling on production was far lower than the notional figure of 1¼ million tons of bar iron just quoted. In a modern economy the large-scale production of iron and steel is a *sine qua non* of industrial expansion. In 2008 China produced 500 million tons of steel in her drive to transform her productive potential. No organic economy could have produced even a tiny fraction of this total.

It is true, no doubt, that the constraints on material output in any one country could be alleviated in some degree by international trade but the basic problem remained. As Ricardo had noted, the limits to growth were set by physical and biological factors which appeared to be beyond human capacity to modify other than marginally. As long as supplies of both mechanical and heat energy were conditioned by the annual quantum of insolation and the efficiency of plant photosynthesis in capturing incoming solar radiation, it was idle to expect a radical improvement in the material conditions of the bulk of mankind.

Production and reproduction

All forms of production in an organic economy were ultimately conditioned and constrained by the character of the process of photosynthesis in plants. As Malthus argued, however, the economic circumstances of a given community were strongly conditioned by reproduction no less than by production, and especially by the character of the interaction between the two. Figure 1.1 may serve to introduce the issues involved by presenting a simplified picture of the relationships in question.

In the top half of the figure the vertical axis plots fertility and mortality while the horizontal axis plots population size. In an organic economy population growth cannot continue indefinitely. At some point growth will cease and therefore fertility and mortality will be in balance. In the case of F_1 fertility is high and does not change

---

[15] Mitchell, *British historical statistics*, ch. 5, tab. 2, pp. 280–5.

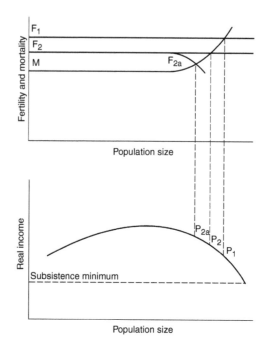

Figure 1.1 *Fertility, mortality, and living standards*

as population increases. This might be the situation, for example, in a community where all women are married at the time they reach sexual maturity and fertility within marriage is not deliberately controlled. Mortality represented by the M line is initially much lower than fertility and the population therefore increases quickly, but as population density rises economic circumstances deteriorate and mortality begins to rise as the standard of living falls and with it nutritional levels. Eventually mortality rises to the same level as fertility and growth ceases. The lower half of the figure plots the relationship between population size, again shown on the horizontal axis, and real income. The line representing this relationship rises for a while as population increases. Greater specialisation of function is possible and some forms of capital investment, for example in the construction of roads and bridges, which are not profitable where population densities are low, become feasible and serve to raise the prevailing standard of living. Real incomes rise to a peak at an optimum population size but then decline gradually as population rises more rapidly than the output available to support it, eventually reaching bare subsistence when population increases to the maximum attainable. In the least favourable case shown in the figure the dotted line which drops from the point where F_1 and M intersect meets the real income curve at P_1, indicating that the resulting level of average real income is modest in a community with these demographic characteristics, not very far above the subsistence minimum.

Two other possibilities are shown in the figure. The level of fertility shown by F_2 may be lower than in the first case considered because, say, marriage takes place later or a difference in breast feeding practice leads to longer birth intervals, but, like F_1, it is shown as invariant with increasing population. This assumption implies a somewhat higher average real wage, shown at P_2 in the lower half of the figure because the M line intersects with F_2 at a lower population total than in the case of F_1. A further variant form, shown as F_{2a}, is also shown. F_{2a} embodies the assumption that fertility no less than mortality is sensitive to increasing population pressure, perhaps because the age at marriage rises and the proportion of men and women who never marry increases with deteriorating economic circumstances. As a result population growth is arrested earlier and average real income, indicated by P_{2a} in the lower section of the figure, is maintained at a higher level than in either of the other two possibilities shown.[16] This might be termed an example of a *low-pressure* system where the less favourable F_1 situation represents a *high-pressure* system. The two extremes imply substantially different average living standards and growth possibilities.

Figure 1.1 is artificially simple. In 'real life' situations the interplay of fertility and mortality is usually far more complex. The figure does, however, serve to illustrate the point that, by influencing demographic behaviour, different social conventions and institutional structures may help to determine living standards in organic societies. It should be noted that the location of a given society on the real income curve shown in the bottom half of the figure has important implications for the structure of aggregate demand in that society. Where demographic conditions push real incomes close to the subsistence minimum the bulk of demand will be for the four necessities of life: food, shelter, clothing, and fuel (it is convenient to express the situation in

---

[16] See also, for example, Schofield, 'Demographic structure and environment'.

terms appropriate to market economies, but the effect is the same in economies where market exchange is limited; poor peasants, buying little for cash and selling only a fraction of what they produce, labour primarily to provide for basic wants). Lack of demand for comforts and luxuries will restrict the opportunity for the development of a wider range of secondary industries (manufactures) and discourage innovation and technological change. Where real incomes are higher the situation is different. The income elasticity of demand for the basic necessities is less than unity but for most other goods it is above unity, which means that the structure of aggregate demand may change substantially as a result of comparatively minor changes in the level of real incomes. As an illustration of the idea underlying this jargon, suppose a household which enjoys an income of 100 units and must spend 75 of the units on necessities is fortunate enough to increase its income by a half to 150 units. The household will then spend a greater absolute amount on necessities but a reduced fraction of its total income. Thus expenditure on necessities may rise to, say, 100 units, an increase of one third, but the margin available for other purchases will rise much faster from 25 units to 50 units, a doubling of the amount available to be spent on comforts and luxuries. This type of development is a major element in the changes which are transforming countries such as India and China today.

The arithmetic illustration of the effect of a rise in income is arbitrary and simplistic but it highlights a point of importance. The structure of aggregate demand will be mirrored by the occupational structure of the community. Where real incomes are low agricultural employment will dominate. The typical household may spend three-quarters or more of its income on food and a comparable proportion of the workforce will be engaged in agriculture. Where real incomes are higher a larger part of the labour force will be employed off the land, satisfying the demand for 'comforts', such as better clothing and footwear, furniture and household utensils, floor coverings, tableware, and better housing. The service sector will also benefit, with a rising demand for transport facilities, greater wholesale and retail trading activity, and wider opportunities for the legal, educational, administrative, medical, and religious professions. The contrast between, say, the Netherlands and Finland in the eighteenth century illustrates the extent of the range of possibilities among organic economies. In the former it has been estimated that in the later eighteenth century the percentage distribution of the workforce was as follows: agriculture 41; industry 32; trade and transport 16; other 11. The comparable percentages in Finland in 1769 were 80, 4, 1, and 15.[17] Both sets of data are based on fragmentary information and should not be taken as reliable, nor as directly comparable, but the contrast is nonetheless massive. One set reflects the nature of an advanced organic economy; the other that of a much poorer and simpler economy. The wide differences between Finland and the Netherlands were certainly not due solely, perhaps not even primarily, to differences of the sort captured by figure 1.1 but equally the importance of the interplay between production and reproduction where overall economic growth is necessarily limited should not be underestimated.

Conclusion

The distinction between necessary and sufficient conditions may be helpful in considering the characteristics of the organic economy and the escape from its constraints. It is likely always to prove elusive to identify with confidence a sufficient cause or combination of causes to explain the transition which occurred. This is so for reasons that exemplify the difference between the study of societies and work in many branches of the natural sciences. It is not possible to conduct a series of controlled experiments in which, for example, England is reconstituted as it was in 1600 but then its characteristics are modified to test, say, whether its development would have differed significantly if age at marriage and proportions marrying did *not* change with changing economic circumstances. This characteristic of analysis in the social sciences limits the confidence with which assertions can be made about the relative importance of a given factor in affecting the pattern of change. But it may be possible to make a claim of a different type – that *without* the presence of a given factor the change in question would have been impossible. I suggest that one necessary condition for the escape from the constraints of an organic economy was success in gaining access to an energy source which was not subject to the limitations of the annual cycle of insolation and the nature of plant photosynthesis.

---

[17] De Vries and van der Woude, *The first modern economy*, p. 524; Mitchell, *European historical statistics*, tab. C1, p. 163.

The classical economists made much of the importance of capital accumulation in facilitating economic growth (though they commonly used the term stock rather than capital). The accumulation of capital facilitated the division of labour which was the key to improved productivity. As Adam Smith remarked, 'As the accumulation of stock must, in the nature of things, be previous to the division of labour, so labour can be more and more subdivided in proportion only as stock is previously more and more accumulated.'[18] Equally necessary, however, for success in the long run was a different type of capital accumulation. In the Carboniferous era over many millions of years a proportion of the annual plant growth in some swampy areas became part of an energy store by the process which has given rise to the presence of coal measures in all the continents. A massive capital store of energy was slowly brought into being by setting aside a small proportion of the products of photosynthesis over a geological era.[19]

The store of energy present in coal measures is, of course, finite. Each ton of coal consumed means a ton less available in the future, whereas a ton of wood cut from a forest conducted on a sustained-yield basis does not reduce the quantity of wood which can be cut in subsequent years. The difference between wood and coal as energy sources reflects the distinction made by medieval philosophers and theologians between a fungible and a consumptible. A field is a fungible. Its use to produce a crop of hay in one year does not prevent its use for a similar or a different purpose in the next year. The same is true of an area of woodland. A fruit cake is a consumptible. Once it is eaten its value is lost. Coal is a consumptible. A ton of coal burnt is a ton less of fossil fuel remaining to meet future needs. But the total amount of energy present in accessible coal measures is very large when compared with annual consumption. If societies thought and acted in terms of millennia rather than decades the limitations of coal as an energy source (and still more of oil and gas) would be evident, but in the short run coal offers a means of escape from the constraints of organic economies which photosynthesis does not. But because coal and other fossil fuels are consumptibles, the energy base of industrialised economies is less stable than was the case in organic economies. They cannot ensure the continuance of societal affluence in the longer

---

[18] Smith, *Wealth of nations*, I, pp. 291–2.
[19] Wrigley, 'Two kinds of capitalism'.

term. There are, of course, alternative sources of energy which may resolve the difficulty. If, for example, a means can be found of trapping the incoming stream of solar energy much more efficiently than by photosynthesis the problem will retreat. Similarly, tapping into the heat energy in the rocks beneath our feet is another possible escape route. Though developments such as these may solve the problem, it is as yet dangerous to assume that success is certain.

The importance of the absolute size of an energy store built up by 'saving' a small part of the products of each annual cycle of insolation is illustrated by comparing coal with peat. The Netherlands in the Dutch golden age of the 'long' seventeenth century made extensive use of peat as an energy source but the quantity of heat energy present even in the richest of peat deposits is trivially small when compared to that in coal measures and therefore peat can only provide an escape from the normal energy problems of an organic economy for a relatively brief period of time.[20]

The switch to coal may be regarded as a necessary condition for the industrial revolution but it was not in itself a sufficient cause. The status of a favourable demographic structure is more uncertain. It would be difficult to demonstrate beyond doubt that it was a necessary condition for the change but it may be thought an invaluable contributory factor. If the conventions governing marriage are such that the age at which marriage takes place and the proportion of each rising generation who marry are both sensitive to economic circumstances, this greatly reduces the danger that excessive population growth will force living standards down close to the subsistence level. In protecting relatively high real incomes it will favour a different occupational structure because of its impact on the structure of aggregate demand. The relative importance of primary, secondary, and tertiary activities within the economy is altered and the prospects for further growth and change are enhanced.[21]

---

[20] The stagnation which overcame the Dutch economy in the eighteenth century was not primarily due to a decline in the size of local peat reserves but the problem of the limited scale of the reserves would have become increasingly serious in a matter of decades rather than centuries as in the case of coal.

[21] Primary activities are those, like agriculture, which produce raw materials; secondary activities comprise manufacturing industry which converts the primary materials into finished goods; tertiary activities comprise service industries, such as retail and wholesale dealing, the professions, or transport. This system of classification derives from the work of Colin Clark, *The conditions of economic progress*.

Organic economies were essentially fungible in nature. A field may be tilled to grow wheat in a given year but the taking of the crop does not prevent the field being available to grow barley in the following year. Organic economies were entirely dependent upon the use of the land to provide food and raw materials. This meant that they suffered from the limitations of which the classical economists were so conscious. Growth possibilities were necessarily limited. Land was in fixed supply and set limits to the extent to which output could be expanded for the reasons which the classical economists made vividly plain. On the other hand, the nature of the land as a fungible guaranteed that a roughly similar level of production could be maintained year after year. It was in this respect a stable world. The potential for securing energy for human use was limited but could be maintained indefinitely.

In contrast the energy-intensive mineral-based economies created in the wake of the industrial revolution were on a different footing. They had gained access to a vast store of energy bequeathed to them by events which had taken place hundreds of millions of years earlier. But, as a result, their economies were consumptible rather than fungible in character. A ton of coal, like a slice if cake, once consumed cannot then be consumed again. Fossil fuel deposits constitute a very large cake but if they remain the principal source of energy they will be exhausted in decades or at most centuries rather than millennia. There are, as we have noted, other potential energy sources which have a fungible rather than consumptible character. If means are found to transfer to sources such as these to replace fossil fuel the potential problems inherent in dependence on fossil fuel may disappear. Yet it remains true that the initial character of the economies created by the industrial revolution makes them vulnerable in the medium term to a degree unknown in organic economies.

The course of the industrial revolution therefore has something of the character of the opening of Pandora's jar. Extraordinary new powers of production were released which both offered the possibility of ridding mankind of the curse of poverty and its attendant evils but at the same time created new dangers and sources of anxiety. When in the middle decades of the nineteenth century it became clear that the limits to growth inherent in organic economies no longer constrained productive capacity, initial fears centred on the possibility that the benefits of this new capacity would be confined to a tiny minority. *Das Kapital* embodied this fear and encapsulated the anger which moved millions in much of the twentieth century. In the event Marx's forebodings proved to be based on a partial misjudgement of the way capitalist economies would develop but other fears related to the new world created by the industrial revolution have arisen which may prove to be better grounded. The immense increase in the energy available for human use now means, when harnessed for destructive purposes, that mass slaughter on a scale previously unimaginable can be brought about by a touch on a metaphorical button. And the burning of fossil fuels threatens to raise prevailing temperatures with consequences which remain unpredictable and could prove dire.

The degree to which the arguments advanced in this chapter are convincing will turn on the consideration of the history of England in the early modern period. This is the subject of the next chapter which represents an initial review of a range of topics which are considered in greater detail later in the book.

2 | The transition from an organic to an energy-rich economy

There was a notable contrast between England and her near neighbours both in the sixteenth and in the nineteenth century but the nature of the contrast changed fundamentally. At the beginning of the period England was a laggard economy. It was one of the least urbanised countries in Europe in the sixteenth century.[1] In Tudor times when an attempt was made to create a new mining or industrial venture it frequently involved attracting expert advice and craftsmen from the continent.[2] Financial expertise in London did not compare with that in Italy or the Low Countries. In international trade England was a source of raw material or simple manufacture; wool and woollen cloth had long dominated the export trade.[3] Improvements in agriculture consisted chiefly of the adoption of methods first introduced elsewhere, especially in the Low Countries. The population of the country was probably smaller than it had been at its peak before the Black Death and did not rival those of several continental countries.[4] If a comparison is made in terms of political influence or military strength it is clear that England fell some way short of the major powers of the day, notably Spain and France. Writing of seventeenth-century

---

[1] Using as his criterion the proportion of the population living in cities with 10,000 or more inhabitants, de Vries estimated the following percentages in 1550: England and Wales 3.5; the Netherlands 15.3, Belgium 22.7; Germany 3.8; France 4.3; northern Italy 15.1; Spain 8.6; Portugal 11.5: de Vries, *European urbanization*, tab. 3.7, p. 39.

[2] Coleman remarked, 'Over a range of industries – paper, linen, silk, leather-working, hosiery, iron-founding, glass-making – English inferiority to French, Spanish, Italian, Flemish, or German products was manifest.' He added, 'The import of continental skills and techniques, via immigrant labour and, in some cases, capital, is one of the major themes of Tudor and Stuart industrial history': Coleman, *The economy of England*, pp. 69–70.

[3] As late as 1699–1701 woollen textiles accounted for 69 per cent of the value of domestic exports, and even in the mid-eighteenth century the comparable figure was 47 per cent. *Ibid.*, tab. 14, p. 139.

[4] See tab. 6.1, p. 141.

England, Wilson remarked: 'Almost everywhere, and especially in the remoter parts of the countryside, there survived the remains of an ancient and unspecialized economy in which many people lived a more or less self-sufficient life, growing a substantial proportion of the food they ate or drank, making their own clothes and footwear, cutting their own fuel, boiling their own soap, and so on.'[5]

Two centuries later the contrasts were largely in the opposite direction. At the time of the Great Exhibition in 1851 England had become the most urbanised country in Europe, with London as its biggest city.[6] London was the largest and most influential single centre of commercial expertise and the chief vehicle for international investment, the hub of world trade. Approximately two-thirds of the European production of cotton textiles took place in the UK.[7] The comparable percentages for iron production and coal output were 64 and 76 per cent.[8] The percentages for England alone would, of course, be lower, though still well over half of the European total. Steam engines were more widely employed than elsewhere to provide power in a rapidly widening range of industrial and transport uses. The total of installed steam engine horsepower was far larger than on the continent. In 1840, 75 per cent of the combined total capacity of stationary steam engines in Britain, France, Prussia, and Belgium was in Britain alone (the other three countries accounted for the great bulk of installed capacity on the continent).[9]

Some years later Levasseur, commenting on the rapid increase in the total of steam engines in France, noted that one steam horsepower performed work equivalent to twenty-one labourers and memorably

[5] Wilson, *England's apprenticeship*, p. 67.
[6] The population of Greater London in 1851 was 2,685,000. The only other European city with more than a million inhabitants was Paris, with 1,053,000. Mitchell, *European historical statistics*, tab. B4, pp. 86–9. For urban percentages at this date, de Vries, *European urbanization*, tab. 3.8, pp. 45–7.
[7] There are series both for raw cotton consumption and for spindles in the cotton industry in Mitchell, *European historical statistics*, tabs. E14 and E15. After making allowances for countries which were already significant producers but whose series began only from a later date, the cotton consumption figures suggest a UK percentage of some 59 per cent, while the cotton spindles totals suggest a figure of some 68 per cent.
[8] *Ibid.*, tabs. E8 and E2. The coal production totals exclude brown coal production. All the quoted percentages may very slightly overstate English percentages since there are no data for some countries. In none of them, however, was production of cotton, iron, or coal other than of marginal significance.
[9] Allen, *The British industrial revolution*, tab. 7.2, p. 179.

remarked that whereas in 1840 installed steam engines were carrying out work that would otherwise have required the exertions of just over 1 million men, by the middle 1880s this figure had risen to the equivalent of 98 million men. Steam engines were 'de véritables esclaves, les plus sobres, les plus dociles, les plus infatigables que l'imagination puisse rêver'.[10] England benefited from possessing vast numbers of such 'slaves' from an early date to assist in the production process and to reduce the cost of manufacture.

By the early nineteenth century the flow of experts and expertise in industrial and agricultural techniques was predominantly in the opposite direction to that prevailing in the sixteenth century. The population of England was still smaller than that of several other European countries but growth had been faster than elsewhere and as a result the relative differences had shrunk as may be seen in table 6.1. The British navy lacked a serious rival which, in combination with its commercial power, enabled the country to exert a powerful influence on events worldwide. Though the lives of many families were made harsh by poverty and uncertain by the trade cycle, it is probably true that living standards were, on average, higher than in any other European country and that the lives of the least fortunate, though miserable, were no more and may well have been less oppressed by hunger, cramped accommodation, and disease than was the case with their equivalents elsewhere in Europe.[11]

Agricultural change, industrial growth, and transport improvements

Such a striking transformation in relative fortune is rare to a degree. How did it come about? Consider first what was possible within the context of an organic economy. Of necessity in such economies the key to progress must lie in agriculture since the land provided both

[10] Levasseur, *La population française*, III, p. 74 (true slaves, the most sober, manageable, and tireless imaginable).

[11] For example, mortality in Stockholm was considerably higher than in any of the big industrial cities in Britain in the early nineteenth century. Stockholm was an extreme case but urban death rates in much of Europe were higher than in Britain in this period: Söderberg, Jonsson, and Persson, *A stagnating metropolis*, pp. 171–200. They comment: 'British cities like Manchester, Liverpool, and Glasgow, under pressure of an uncontrolled urbanization, had far lower death rates than Stockholm.' *Ibid.*, p. 175.

food and the raw materials used in secondary industry. If there was no significant change in agricultural output, and especially if there was no significant change in output per head in agriculture, there could be little scope for economic growth. A major element in the growing success of the English economy was the notable advance which occurred in agricultural production. Gross cereal output per acre roughly doubled between the late sixteenth and early nineteenth centuries, but the scale of the increase is understated if measured by gross yield.[12] For example, if the gross yield of wheat rises from 10 to 20 bushels per acre, the net yield rises from 8 to 18 bushels because the amount of wheat needed for seed is unchanged at 2 bushels. Thus although gross yield rises by 100 per cent, net yield rises by 125 per cent.[13] There was also a significant reduction in the proportion of the arable acreage in fallow. At the beginning of the period perhaps 30 per cent of arable fields grew only weeds each year. By 1800 the figure had fallen to about 16 per cent. This implies that, even without taking into consideration any new land brought into cultivation, the effective arable area increased by 20 per cent.[14] Taking both these changes into account, output of wheat per acre rose by 170 per cent over the two centuries.[15] The output of other cereals rose comparably. The productive capacity of arable agriculture was transformed.

The pastoral sector enjoyed progress comparable to that in the arable sector. Animals were better fed and matured more swiftly. The latter point meant that the proportion of a herd of beef cattle which could be slaughtered each year rose. This, combined with an increase

[12] Overton, *Agricultural revolution*, tab. 3.7(c), p. 77 and, more generally, ch. 3.

[13] There is a fuller discussion of this issue in Wrigley, 'Corn yields and prices', esp. pp. 111–13.

[14] Overton estimated the percentage of arable land in fallow as 20 per cent c.1700 and 16 per cent c.1800: Overton, *Agricultural revolution*, tab. 3.6, p. 76. Allen, basing his estimate on the work of Gregory King, suggested a figure of 30 per cent for 1700: Allen, 'Agriculture during the industrial revolution', tab. 5.6, p. 112. In c.1300, it is reasonable to suppose the fallow percentage was a little over a third of the arable area: Wrigley, 'Advanced organic economy', pp. 440–2. The suggested figure for the late sixteenth century is therefore at best a rough approximation.

[15] At the beginning of the period, of 100 acres of arable land available for wheat growing 30 acres would have been fallow and the remaining 70 acres would have produced a net yield of 560 bushels (70 × 8 bushels). At the end of the period only 16 of the acres would have been in fallow, and with a net yield of 18 bushels per acre the total output would have risen to 1,512 bushels (84 × 18).

in slaughter weights and an increase in the number of beef cattle, meant that meat production rose significantly.[16] There were parallel improvements in milk yields in dairy herds and in the wool clip produced on average by each sheep.[17] The introduction of crop rotations which included legumes such as clover and sainfoin both improved the soil by raising nitrogen levels, facilitated the reduction in fallow, and increased fodder output substantially, which in turn increased the volume of manure which could be spread on arable land.[18] Crop yields benefited from the larger quantities of animal manure, and the comparative abundance of draught animals made it feasible to spread huge quantities of lime and marl to improve soil quality.

The rising demand for the products of the arable and pastoral sectors stemmed not merely from the food needs of a growing population but also from the expansion in the economy generally. Industrial growth was as striking as agricultural expansion in the seventeenth and eighteenth centuries. Such growth meant a rising demand for raw materials, and these were almost exclusively the product of the soil: wool, leather, flax, tallow, hair, bones, bark, wood. Employment in industry probably grew at least fourfold between the beginning of the seventeenth and the end of the eighteenth century, implying a commensurate increase in the demand for industrial raw materials.[19]

The rising scale of output in both primary and secondary industries produced an even greater proportionate increase in the demand for transport services. Division of labour, which Adam Smith placed at the heart of the growth process, implies that this must be a leading

[16] As an illustrative but hypothetical exercise, if it were the case that average age at slaughter fell from five years to four, that the number of beef cattle rose by a half, and that their average weight at slaughter rose by three-quarters, the quantity of meat produced annually would have risen more than threefold over the two centuries. This may appear a dramatic increase but is roughly consonant with other estimates. See below p. 85 n. 58.

[17] Hard evidence is largely absent on changes in the productivity of livestock. Clark accepts estimates which suggest very large increases over the long term but with no indication of the phasing of change. Overton inclines to a less optimistic view over the early modern period, notably in regard to cattle. Turner, Beckett, and Afton present data which suggest a rising trend but with wide margins of uncertainty. Clark, 'Labour productivity', tab. 8.3, p. 216; Overton, *Agricultural revolution*, pp. 111–16; Turner, Beckett, and Afton, *Farm production in England*, ch. 6.

[18] This, however, is a complex matter: Brunt, 'Where there's muck, there's brass'.

[19] See below p. 33 for the basis of the estimate of the fourfold increase.

feature of change, because it implies that the distance a good is carried on average between producer and final consumer will rise. A pin 'manufactory' could, he argued, produce tens of thousands of pins each day but production on such a large scale implies a need to market the product over a considerable area.[20] Pins incur only trivial transport costs, but for products of greater bulk and weight a similar development, exploiting the greater efficiency which could be achieved by division of labour, was feasible only if there was improvement in transport facilities to match the new need.

It is significant, therefore, that while the output of all cereal crops rose markedly between late medieval times and the early nineteenth century, oats outstripped other grains both in the percentage rise in total production and in the percentage rise in output per acre.[21] The dominant use of oats was to feed horses. The energy output of a horse well supplied with oats was substantially greater than that of a largely grass fed animal. This was helpful not only in a farm context but also in the economy generally. There was a massive rise in the scale of road transport in the later seventeenth and eighteenth centuries, facilitated by the rapid increase in the mileage of turnpike roads, and therefore a parallel rise in the need to employ more horses. Ville has reported estimates, for example, showing that over the period 1681–1840 the annual rate of growth of goods traffic by road between London and the provinces was in excess of 1 per cent, which would imply a roughly sixfold cumulative growth over the period. Passenger traffic was rising even more rapidly. Between 1715 and 1840 the rate of growth probably exceeded 2 per cent annually, implying that by the end of the period the traffic was twelve times larger than at the beginning.[22] Gerhold, focusing on productivity growth rather than total output, came to comparable conclusions:

productivity in road transport before the railways increased much more impressively than has generally been implied – between two and a half- or three-fold in long-distance carrying between about 1690 and 1840, without taking account of reduced journey times, and four-fold in stage coaching between 1658 and 1820, without fully taking into account reduced journey times.[23]

---

[20] See below p. 110 for a description of Smith's account of the benefits of the division of labour in pin manufacture.
[21] See below tab. 3.4, p. 79 and p. 83.
[22] Ville, 'Transport', p. 297.
[23] Gerhold, 'Productivity change in road transport', p. 511.

Partway through this period, in 1787 Arthur Young approached Paris in a post-chaise and wrote in his journal: 'The last ten miles I was eagerly on the watch for that throng of carriages which near London impede the traveller. I watched in vain; for the road, quite to the gates, is, on comparison, a perfect desert.'[24]

Other large towns also became the focus for networks of turn-pike roads with effects on transport provision similar to that which occurred through the growth of London. The intimate connection between urban growth and transport provision was stressed by Stobart in his study of economic growth in Lancashire and Cheshire: 'In general, the strength and diversity of inter-town linkages was quite closely associated with urban dynamism. The best-linked towns grew at more than three times the rate of those with the poorest links and increased their share of the urban population of the region from one third to one half.'[25]

There was a parallel development in inland water transport, though later in date than the surge in turnpike creation. In the later eighteenth century many new canals were built. Canal barges also depended on horses for motive power, thus adding further to the need for a plentiful supply of fodder. The fact that agriculture was able to meet the 'fuel' needs of a growing population of horses engaged in transport and industry is testimony to the absence of pressure aris-ing from the need to meet human food requirements in England in the 'long' eighteenth century despite the very rapid growth of popu-lation in its latter half. England, it should be noted, remained largely self-sufficient in foodstuffs until the early decades of the nineteenth century, apart from those which could not be grown in a temperate climate.[26]

---

[24] Young, *Travels in France and Italy*, p. 13.

[25] Stobart, *The first industrial region*, p. 203. He was referring to the first half of the eighteenth century.

[26] Precision is out of reach on this point. Jones concluded, tentatively, that 'something of the approximate order' of 90 per cent of the British population was fed from domestic sources c.1800. Brinley Thomas estimated that in 1814–16 the value of imports of grains, meat, and butter from all sources represented 6.4 per cent of the total income of British agriculture, fishing, and forestry. The comparable figure for England alone would presumably be somewhat higher. Jones, 'Agriculture 1700–1800', p. 68: Thomas, 'Escaping from constraints', tab. 2, p. 743.

Manpower productivity in agriculture

The rise in agricultural output per acre in England set her apart from much of the continent, but her case was not unique. The advances taking place in England were paralleled in the Low Countries. Crop yields in Belgium in the early modern period, for example, appear to have risen by a comparable amount, and the introduction of crop rotations and the use of legumes followed a similar pattern. But there was one feature of English agriculture which was without parallel elsewhere. Output per head rose broadly in parallel with the increase in gross output. The workforce in agriculture was little changed in 1800 or indeed in 1850 from what it had been in 1600, whereas in Belgium rising output per acre conformed to a Ricardian paradigm in that the agricultural workforce grew faster than agricultural production and output per head declined.[27] The population of England increased substantially between 1600 and 1800 which meant, given the absence of any major change in employment in agriculture, that the proportion of the labour force working on the land fell sharply from c.70 per cent to less than 40 per cent.[28] This implies, of course, that the proportion of the labour force engaged in secondary and tertiary activities doubled from c.30 to more than 60 per cent during these two centuries and the absolute number increased far more dramatically since population was rising fast. In 1600 the population was 4.2 million; in 1800 8.7 million.[29] If for simplicity we take the population as doubling and the percentage engaged outside agriculture as doubling also, this implies that the total employment in the secondary and tertiary sectors quadrupled over the period, a change which can fairly be termed sensational. The growth in absolute numbers was much faster in the eighteenth than in the seventeenth century since population growth accelerated in the later century, but the change in occupational structure was probably in train throughout the whole period.

[27] Dejongh and Thoen, 'Arable productivity in Flanders'.
[28] There can be little doubt about the accuracy of the second percentage. The first is subject to much wider margins of error but is unlikely to be seriously at fault. Wrigley, 'Men on the land', pp. 332–6, and 'Urban growth and agricultural change', p. 169. Work currently in train at the Cambridge Group for the History of Population and Social Structure will provide regional and local information on all aspects of the occupational structure of England during the nineteenth century and comparable, if less complete data for earlier periods.
[29] Wrigley *et al.*, *English population history*, tab. A9.1, pp. 614–15.

Without the striking gains in manpower productivity in agriculture which took place in early modern England it is very doubtful whether the industrial revolution would have occurred. Rural England had both to provide a large part of the growing non-agricultural labour force by losing a fraction of each rising generation to industrial and commercial centres and to raise output sufficiently to cover the food needs of town and country alike. Moreover, it had to meet the massive growth in demand for industrial raw materials. To meet all these differing demands without excessive strain was possible only if output per head in agriculture was rising substantially.[30]

It is ironic that for two centuries beforehand the home country of the classical economists should have been experiencing change which ran contrary to the view set out so clearly by Ricardo, but common to all three. One of them was afforded an opportunity to modify his initial stance as new evidence became available. Malthus reformulated his initial concept of the behaviour of populations when the first census was published. In the first edition of the *Essay on population*, published in 1798, he had argued from first principles that population growth must either cease or become very slight as numbers increased and the pressure on resources grew more pronounced. The Parish Register Abstracts which were published as part of the 1801 census left no room for doubt that population growth had been rapid for much of the eighteenth century and was accelerating. As a result of the census, and also of his extensive inquiries about events in other countries, Malthus's model of economic and demographic change became less simplistic. He came to place much greater emphasis on the importance of the preventive check (essentially marriage behaviour) in determining population growth rates and less on the positive check (mortality), at least in some European populations. He also came to recognise that, because demographic regimes might differ markedly, a wider range of outcomes than he had originally envisaged was possible, some of which were compatible with relatively comfortable circumstances for the bulk of the population.[31]

---

[30] See below pp. 86–7 for estimates of the scale of the growth in the output of some of the industries using animal and vegetable raw materials.

[31] 'From high real wages, or the power of commanding a large portion of the necessaries of life, two very different results may follow; one, that of a rapid increase of population, in which case the high wages are chiefly spent in the maintenance of large and frequent families; and the other, that of a decided improvement in the modes of subsistence, and the comforts and

Ricardo was less fortunate. If he had known that the national population had doubled over the two preceding centuries while remaining largely self-sufficient in food, and that over the same period the size of the agricultural labour force had remained much the same, he might have been tempted to modify his exposition of the inexorable effects of the fact that the supply of land could not be expanded like the supply of labour or capital.

What happened in English agriculture in this period was clearly most unusual. Periods of rapid population growth after a country had been fully settled for many centuries frequently followed the pattern which Ricardo's analysis would suggest. Poorer land was taken into cultivation, holdings became subdivided, and the process which Geertz termed agricultural involution was likely to take place.[32] How was it that the same did not happen in seventeenth- and eighteenth-century England? Two features of the period may go some way towards answering this question. The first is the interplay between agricultural change and urban growth, a topic which is explored at length in the next chapter. It was true both that an increasing urban sector provided a valuable stimulus to agriculture and, equally, that urban growth was contingent upon the ability of the agriculture to meet the food needs of the increasing proportion of the population which no longer worked on the land.

The beneficial feedback between urban growth and agricultural change was of great importance, but it had been evident in other times and places without making it possible to break the bonds common to all organic economies. It was a second feature of the English economy in the early modern period that was decisive in making escape possible. As background to the appreciation of timing, scale, and nature of this second feature, consider first why it might have seemed inevitable that there would be increasing stresses within the economy during the seventeenth and eighteenth centuries in addition to those associated with the increasing demand for food resulting from a rapidly rising population.

If non-agricultural employment was four times as large in 1800 as in 1600, it follows that there must have been a massive increase

conveniences enjoyed, without a proportionate acceleration in the rate of increase': Malthus, *Principles of political economy*, p. 183.
[32] Geertz, *Agricultural involution*.

in the demand for industrial raw materials. Industrial raw materials in an organic economy were almost exclusively animal or vegetable in character. In one of the industries in which growth was very rapid towards the end of the period the raw material came exclusively from overseas. Cotton, however, was unusual. In industry generally the bulk of the raw material consumed was domestically produced until the end of the eighteenth century. This was true, for example, both of the woollen and worsted industries and of the industries which used leather as their principal raw material. Woollen and leather industries were two of the most important industries c.1800. Crafts's estimates suggest that the four largest British industries by value added in 1801 were cotton, wool, building, and leather. Between them they accounted for 68 per cent of the total of value added in British industry as a whole and they were of roughly equal size.[33] The wool and hides which formed the raw material input of two of these four industries were very largely home produced in 1800.[34] Some tertiary activities also made a large claim on agricultural output. Inland transport expanded very rapidly and with it, at least until the advent of the railway, the demand for fodder since horses provided the mechanical energy needed to pull wagons and canal barges. It is probable that demand for non-food agricultural products was rising substantially faster than that for food. This combination of circumstances might be expected to have given rise to all the problems which Ricardo had in mind in insisting that growth in an organic economy will eventually arrest itself. Plainly this did not happen in England and the absence or comparative feebleness of the usual arrester mechanism was a prerequisite for the industrial revolution. Why should England have been so fortunate in this regard?

The energy revolution

It is in this context that the effect of the steady expansion in the coal industry deserves particular attention. Table 2.1 contains estimates of coal output in England, Wales, and Scotland and for the three combined at intervals between the 1560s and 1850. It also shows at each date the component elements of energy consumption in England and

---

[33] Crafts, *British economic growth*, tab. 2.3, p. 22.
[34] See below pp. 86–7.

Table 2.1 *Coal production in England, Wales, and Scotland ('000 tons) and related statistics*

	(1)	(2)	(3)	(4)	(5)
	1560s	*1700–9*	*1750–9*	*1800–9*	*1850–9*
Coal production ('000 tons)					
England	177	2,200	4,295	11,195	51,650
Wales	20	140	220	1,850	13,400
Scotland	30	300	715	2,000	9,000
Total	227	2,640	5,230	15,045	74,050
Energy consumption, England and Wales (petajoules)					
Draught animals	21.1	32.8	33.6	34.3	50.1
Population	14.9	27.3	29.7	41.8	67.8
Firewood	21.5	22.5	22.6	18.5	2.2
Wind	0.2	1.4	2.8	12.7	24.4
Water	0.6	1.0	1.3	1.1	1.7
Coal	6.9	84.0	140.8	408.7	1,689.1
Total	65.1	168.9	230.9	517.1	1,835.3
Total less coal	58.2	84.9	90.1	108.4	146.2
Other related energy estimates, England and Wales					
Coal as a percentage of total energy consumption	10.6	49.7	61.0	79.0	92.0
Per caput energy consumption (gigajoules)	20.5	29.6	35.1	52.3	96.5

Note. The 1850–9 firewood figure refers to 1840–9 rather than the next decade. Warde stopped the series after the 1840–9 decade because firewood usage had by then reached a very low level. The coal production totals, other than the total for 1850–9, refer to an individual year or years rather than the whole decade.

Sources. Coal output. Cols. 1 and 2, Hatcher, *British coal industry*, I, tab. 4.1, p. 68; cols. 3 and 4, Flinn, *British coal industry*, II, tab. 1.2, p. 26; col. 5, Church, *British coal industry*, III, tab. 1.1, p. 3. Energy consumption, England and Wales. Warde, *Energy consumption in England and Wales,* app. 1, tabs. 1, 2, and 3, pp. 115–36.

Wales; the percentage of the total energy consumption which was provided by coal; and energy consumption per head. The energy consumption data in the second section of the table apart from that for coal are made up of estimates of the calories represented by fodder consumed by draught animals, and by the food eaten by the human population, plus the energy drawn from wind and water power and from firewood. The notable growth in the consumption of wind power arises because it includes estimates of the energy used in driving sailing ships, an energy use which grew rapidly over the three centuries in question. All estimates are energy 'inputs', not 'outputs'. Thus, for example, the energy contained in the fodder consumed by draught animals is measured. Much of this went in bodily maintenance so that their work output represented a much lower energy total than their food intake.

In the middle of the sixteenth century, energy consumption per head in England was little different from that in other European countries[35] but this changed progressively with the growth of coal production. By the latter part of the eighteenth century the contrast with the rest of Europe was pronounced and this remained the case until the middle of the following century,[36] though by 1900 the gap between England and other leading economies was closing fast.

In the mid-sixteenth century, coal, though it already supplied a tenth of English energy consumption, was substantially less important than human and animal muscle power, and firewood was the prime source of heat energy. By 1700 about half of the total energy consumption of England came from coal. At the end of the eighteenth century the proportion exceeded three-quarters, and by 1850 was over 90 per cent. Much coal was consumed for domestic purposes. Until the end of the seventeenth century it is likely that domestic heating and cooking accounted for more than half the total consumption, but by the early nineteenth century this figure appears to have declined to roughly one third of the total.[37] Note first the implication of the growth in coal use for the Ricardian analysis of organic economies. Coal provided 'ghost acres' on a

---

[35] Apart from the Netherlands, where energy consumption levels were much higher because of the widespread use of peat.

[36] See Malanima, *Pre-modern European economy*, figs. 12 and 14, pp. 89 and 92.

[37] Hatcher, *British coal industry*, I, p. 409 and more generally ch. 12; Flinn, *British coal industry*, II, tab. 7.13, pp. 252–3.

huge scale.[38] For example, in 1700, when the English coal output is estimated at about 2.2 million tons, to have provided the same heat energy from wood on a sustained-yield basis would have required devoting 2 or 3 million acres to woodland.[39] This assumption may well underestimate the area required but is unlikely to overestimate it. By 1800, on the same assumption, 11 million acres of woodland would have been needed. This would have meant devoting more than a third of the surface area of the country to provide the quantity of energy in question.[40]

In the absence of coal as an energy source, Ricardian pressures would have become acute. Even to cover domestic heating needs as the population rose with increasing speed would have been a severe challenge, and industrial expansion would have faltered at some point because of the strength of competition for other products of the land. The supply of fuel to London may illustrate the severity of the problem which would have arisen in the absence of a rising output of coal.

The small Danish town of Odense, which had about 5,000 inhabitants in the later eighteenth century, received roughly 15,000 cartloads of firewood and 12,000 cartloads of peat each year to cover its domestic heating and industrial needs.[41] A city a hundred times larger, like London towards the end of the seventeenth century, even if for climatic reasons the fuel requirement per head were somewhat lower, would by analogy have needed perhaps 2 million cartloads of firewood each year at a conservative estimate to cover its heating needs in the absence of coal. This level of consumption is roughly equivalent to 1.5 tons of firewood per head of the population of London.[42] It would have required

[38] The phrase 'ghost acres' is used to refer to the area outside the boundaries of a given state which enable it to overcome a production limit which would otherwise have inhibited domestic growth. Pomeranz makes much of this concept in seeking to explain European success. Europe, he claims, 'was able to escape the proto-industrial cul de sac and transfer handicraft workers into modern industries as the technology became available. It could do this, in large part, because the exploitation of the New World made it unnecessary to mobilize the huge numbers of additional workers who would have been needed to use Europe's own land in much more intensive and ecologically sustainable ways.' Pomeranz, *The great divergence*, p. 264.

[39] Wrigley, *Continuity, chance and change*, pp. 54–5.

[40] The surface area of England is 32 million acres, or 50,000 square miles.

[41] Van der Woude, Hayami, and de Vries, eds., *Urbanization in history*, p. 13, n.7.

[42] Medieval London is estimated to have consumed 1.76 tons of dry wood per head of population each year. Galloway, Keene, and Murphy, 'Fuelling the city', p. 455.

setting aside a very large acreage to produce the firewood in question (approximately 1,250 square miles or 3,500 square kilometres), but in addition still more land would have been required to provide fodder for the large number of horses needed to bring the firewood overland, either direct to London or to a suitable shipping point. In contrast, coal made only a minimal claim on land for its production and animal haulage was required only in getting the coal from the pithead to the coal staithe on the Tyne and from the dockside on the Thames to the consumer (London's coal supply came almost exclusively from Tyneside collieries until the railway age). When discussing England in a wide-ranging survey of urban growth in the past van der Woude, Hayami, and de Vries posed a question: 'what was the key to the rapid urbaniza-tion of England, where 20 per cent of the population lived in cities with more than 10,000 inhabitants by 1800, and, even more remarkably, Europe's first city of one million inhabitants emerged in the form of London?' They also provided an answer: 'Both features of England's urbanization – its rapid growth and its concentration in one great city – appear to be related to the character of its energy supply.'[43] They went on to discuss the coal trade supplying London from Tyneside.

Cheap heat energy from coal not only was a desirable if dirty means of meeting domestic needs in London but also provided the heat energy needed in a wide range of industries. When Daniel Defoe's Colonel Jack was a poor lad adrift in London he could sleep comfortably at nights by lying in a hole close to the warmth radiating out from one of the glass furnaces along the banks of the Thames.[44] Glass manufacture required a source of abundant heat. The banks of the Thames were a good location for glass manufacture because Newcastle coal was read-ily available. It was indirectly because of the existence of cheap and abundant energy from coal that when later in the eighteenth century Arthur Young chronicled his travels in France he was much struck by the rarity of window glass in the places he visited, noting that it was seldom found even in the more substantial houses. 'Pass an extraordin-ary spectacle for English eyes', he wrote, 'of many houses too good to be called cottages, without any glass windows.'[45] For the same reason, towns became brick built in early modern England wherever cheap coal was available locally to fire the clay.

---

[43] Van der Woude *et al.*, eds., *Urbanization in history*, p. 12.
[44] Defoe, *Colonel Jack*, p. 26.
[45] Young, *Travels in France and Italy*, p. 22.

An extensive range of industries switched to coal to provide the heat energy needed in their production process during the seventeenth century, influenced in part by differential price movements. For example, Hatcher noted that in London and Cambridge the price of coal scarcely altered between the 1580s and the 1610s but that over the same period the price paid by the abbey college in Westminster for a bundle of firewood rose by more than 80 per cent.[46] Allen has described the role of coal as 'backstop' technology and the way in which in London, once it had become the dominant energy source, the price of coal came to determine also the price of wood and charcoal.[47] By the end of the seventeenth century the switch to coal was largely complete in brewing, lime burning, salt production, dye industries, brick and tile making, glassmaking, alum boiling, sugar and soap production, smithying, and a wide range of metal processing trades. Summarising his detailed description of the increasing use of coal in industrial processes, Hatcher wrote, 'By 1700 coal was the preferred fuel of almost all fuel-consuming industries, and access to coal supplies had already begun to exert a determining influence over industrial location.'[48] The change was simplest where there was a physical barrier between the burning fuel and the object to be heated as in the boiling of salt in a salt pan.[49] Where there was no such barrier, the problem of the transmission of chemical impurities might complicate matters. It was only after many decades of trial and error that it proved possible to use the new fuel successfully to smelt iron ore, and lesser problems occurred in many industries on switching to coal, but by the later eighteenth century across a wide range of industries any remaining problems were minor.

The switch to coal as a source of heat made it possible to prolong the benefits flowing from a 'Smithian' economy in which the 'hidden hand' helped to ensure that capital was used profitably and economically and with benefit also to those who were dependent on wages for

---

[46] Hatcher, *British coal industry*, I, p. 6.
[47] Allen, *The British industrial revolution*, pp. 87–90.
[48] Hatcher, *British coal industry*, I, p. 458.
[49] However, even with salt boiling there could be complications. The Cheshire 'wiches' were handicapped in competition with other areas such as Tyneside because their pans were traditionally made of lead which melted if coal was used as a heat source, unlike the iron pans which were used on Tyneside. Foster, *Capital and innovation*, pp. 186–7.

a livelihood. But to secure a definitive break from the constraints of an organic economy it was necessary to find a means of paralleling for mechanical energy what had earlier been achieved for heat energy. As long as the mechanical energy needed in most industrial processes and many forms of transport was secured from human or animal muscle power, there was a comparatively low ceiling to the level of productivity per head that could be attained. The final step in the process by which the use of fossil fuel broke the bonds of the organic economy was taken with the discovery of ways of using the energy in steam to extend the breakthrough in the availability of heat energy to overcome the mechanical energy bottleneck also. It made Newcomen and Watt central figures in the conventional histories of the industrial revolution. The steam engine became the iconic symbol of the new age. Mokyr described it as 'conceptually one of the most radical inventions ever made'. Referring to heat and mechanical energy, he added: 'The equivalence of the two forms was not suspected by people in the eighteenth century; the notion that a horse pulling a treadmill and a coal fire heating a lime kiln were in some sense doing the same thing would have appeared absurd to them.'[50]

A steady growth in the scale of material production no longer implied making demands upon the productivity of the land that could not be met. Not only was the pressure on the land much reduced but in due course agricultural productivity could reach new heights. Previously, for example, it would have been nonsensical to expend greater energy in the course of agricultural production than was embodied in the final product. But in the circumstances of the new era chemical fertilisers produced by using the capital stock of energy laid down in earlier geological ages could be employed to boost agricultural yields even though this involved breaking one of the iron rules of all organic economies.

Switching to coal as an energy source produced two further benefits of great importance. The first relates to investment in transport facilities. The production of coal is punctiform, that is each coal mine may be regarded as a point, occupying very little ground. The output of a single mine, however, could run into tens of thousands of tons each year. In contrast, production of wood is areal. To produce

---

[50] Mokyr, 'Editor's introduction', pp. 19–20.

an equivalent amount of energy from wood a very large acreage of woodland must be felled. Coal production, because of its punctiform character, creates a powerful incentive to improve transport facilities. A large capital investment in transport improvement to facilitate the movement of coal from a colliery in Worsley to its market in Manchester, or from a pithead in Northumberland to a staithe on the Tyne, could offer an excellent return on expenditure. The same was not true of the movement of products of the soil where the pattern of the road system must be dendritic to match the areal nature of vegetable and animal production. The road system bringing such products to a large town must resemble the catchment area drained by a river, with large tributaries of the main river being fed in turn by ever smaller streams. In contrast the transport link between a large town and a coal mine will be linear; a single route suffices. Heavy investment in the bulk of the road system was uneconomic in organic economies because the density of traffic was generally too low to justify improvement. Pack horses remained in widespread use in early modern England because road surfaces were often so unsuitable for wagons. Keeping the roads in good order might involve expense not justified by easier traffic movement because the volume of traffic was too small to result in an adequate return on investment.

It is no accident that the railway gauge in England, and as a result in much of the rest of the world, is an odd-sounding 4 feet 8½ inches. Trial and error had shown that flanged iron wheels running on iron rails fixed to wooden sleepers greatly increased the ton-miles which each horse and coal cart could perform when dragging a load of coal from the pithead to the coal staithe and it was natural to use the same track dimension when steam engines replaced draught horses. George Stephenson, when constructing the Stockton and Darlington railway, the first public railway using steam locomotives, was influenced by his earlier experience in working for Durham coal mines. The prevailing gauge used by the local collieries was half an inch less, but he added the further half inch to reduce binding on the curves in the line, which was built primarily to carry coal to the wharves at Stockton.

The rise in the volume of coal production created an incentive not only to invest in more efficient land transport but also to construct canals. A large proportion of the traffic on most canals consisted of coal. Much of the final cost of coal to the consumer, whether domestic or industrial, represented the cost of moving it from the pithead to the place of consumption. The market for coal expanded rapidly wherever its price fell because of canal construction. In later decades rail construction had a similar effect. Without benefit of canal or rail transport the price of coal carried overland doubled within ten miles of the pithead, which meant that before canal and railway facilities existed much of the country had no access to coal at an economic price.

The second benefit associated with the increasing importance of coal as an energy source may have been of even greater significance. The size of *accessible* coal reserves in early modern England was a function of drainage technology since water accumulated in every mine and became an increasingly severe problem as the depth of working increased. Having reviewed the use of adits or soughs where circumstances made it possible to use gravity to evacuate the water, and the use of wind, water, and horse power to combat the problem where pumping was unavoidable, Flinn concluded as follows:

Gravity, wind-, water- and horse-power, then, were capable of only a very modest contribution to the drainage of mines. If drainage technology were to stand still at the point reached at the beginning of the eighteenth century, mining in Britain could scarcely have expanded and must probably have begun to show diminishing returns. At depths of between ninety and 150 feet the influx of water almost invariably created problems insoluble by the technology of the day, so that when seams of lesser depths were exhausted mining must cease. Most British coal-reserves, of course, lay at greater depths. There was a future for mining in Britain only if some more efficient drainage techniques were available.[51]

The contemporary recognition that improving access to deeper coal measures was crucial to many industries is reflected in the fact that in the first three decades after the Restoration more than two-fifths of all the patents granted were for steam engines to pump water out of mines and for methods of using coal instead of charcoal to smelt metals.[52] As already noted, the development of the steam engine was arguably the single most important technical advance of the whole industrial revolution period. Coal had been very widely used as a source of heat energy. It overcame the bottleneck in providing heat

[51] Flinn, *British coal industry*, II, p. 114.
[52] Thomas, *The industrial revolution*, p. 105.

energy which was inherent in dependence on wood. But without a parallel breakthrough in the provision of mechanical energy to solve the comparable problem associated with dependence on human or animal muscle to supply motive power in industry and transport, energy problems would have continued to frustrate efforts to raise manpower productivity.

The link between the drainage problem in mines and the development of a reliable steam engine was intimate. A successful solution promised great rewards. No other industry was presented with a similar problem in such an acute form. Moreover, only where coal was available at a very low cost could the early engines have been put to economic use since both the Savery and the Newcomen engines were very inefficient in their use of coal. Only a tiny fraction of the potential energy was harnessed. The cost of providing coal on the scale needed to operate such engines was prohibitive away from a coalfield, given the transport costs involved. At a pithead, however, even a very inefficient coal-fired engine could be employed since the coal was consumed at the place of production.[53]

The Newcomen engine became the standard means of pit drainage in the course of the eighteenth century. It made it possible to mine coal at much greater depths than was possible with horse power, which had been the commonest power source in mine drainage previously. It was not until Watt developed a more economical steam engine using a separate condenser, patented in 1769, that the steam engine began to appear in other industries, and a further half-century elapsed before steam engines became widespread wherever a reliable source of motive power was needed on a large scale. It is, of course, impossible to be certain that an effective steam engine would not have been developed outside the peculiar context of coal mining and its drainage problems, but in the English industrial revolution it is evident that there was a close association between the problems experienced in mining coal and the discovery of a satisfactory solution to the problem of providing mechanical energy on a greatly enlarged scale and at much reduced cost.

---

[53] In the early eighteenth century a Newcomen engine consumed 45 lb of coal per horsepower-hour, roughly 20 times as much as was needed a century later with a Watt steam engine. Allen, *The British industrial revolution*, pp. 164–8.

Even though far more steam engines were in use in Britain than elsewhere in Europe in the early and middle decades of the nineteenth century, it is easy to exaggerate the importance of the steam engine as a power source before the second half of the nineteenth century. By far the largest user of steam engines in the first half of the century was the cotton industry, and this probably remained true even as late as 1870.[54] Musson concluded a careful review of the limited available evidence by suggesting that the total of industrial steam power in 1850 was no more than 300,000 horsepower, of which the textile industry alone accounted for more than one third, overwhelmingly concentrated in the cotton industry, though he noted that it was especially difficult to achieve an accurate estimate for coal mining.[55] Church in a similar review inclined to a somewhat higher figure than Musson, endorsing Kanefsky's estimate of 400,000 horsepower for steam engines c.1840. Later in the century the steam engine became perhaps the most important single consumer of coal. By 1870 steam engines consumed an estimated 30 per cent of UK coal production.[56]

It is one of the minor paradoxes of the industrial revolution that, although the increasing use of coal was central to the solution of the problem which had made protracted growth impossible in organic economies, there was no revolutionary change in productivity within the coal industry itself. In the course of a year a coal miner in the seventeenth century probably dug about 200 tons of coal. At the time of the Great Exhibition in 1851 this figure had increased to perhaps 300 tons.[57] There were, of course, a host of industries in which manpower productivity increased by a far larger factor. Coal mining remained an occupation involving much hard physical labour with limited opportunities to substitute machinery for men. At one remove, however, its role in magnifying what each worker could produce was central to the overall gain in physical output per head.

---

[54] Musson, 'Industrial motive power', appendix.
[55] *Ibid.*, p. 435.
[56] Church, *British coal industry*, III, pp. 17–18.
[57] Flinn, *British coal industry*, II, pp. 361–6; Church, *British coal industry*, III, tab. 6.1, p. 472.

Conclusion

The changes which were taking place in England between the reigns of Elizabeth and Victoria transformed first England itself and soon thereafter much of the rest of Europe and North America. By the end of the nineteenth century the country which at the time of the Great Exhibition in 1851 dominated many branches of industrial production and commerce was arguably no longer even *primus inter pares*.[58] After a further century had elapsed the whole world was caught up in the same transforming process. Both its nature and its importance are now obvious. Yet in England itself until at least the middle of the nineteenth century the attributes of the new world were far from clear. The classical economists did not sense either the nature or the importance of the changes which were already well advanced in their lifetimes. Adam Smith had indeed referred to the importance of location on a coalfield but for a very different reason from that which had gained general currency by the time Jevons published *The coal question*, written a century later. Smith wrote:

In a country where the winters are so cold as in Great Britain, fuel is, during that season, in the strictest sense of the word, a necessary of life, not only for the purpose of dressing victuals, but for the comfortable subsistence of many different sorts of workmen who work within doors; and coals are the cheapest of all fuel. The price of coal has so important an influence upon that of labour, that all over Great Britain manufactures have confined themselves principally to the coal countries; other parts of the country, on account of the high price of this necessary article, not being able to work so cheap.[59]

---

[58] Coleman, referring to the later twentieth century, made the following valedictory comment on the final upshot of these changes: 'By the '70s, as the country's decline in manufacturing competitiveness accelerated, so hundreds of old industrial plants came to a stop. The one-time glory of Lancashire's cotton industry finally departed; textile mills closed by the dozen. In iron and steel, blast furnaces fell derelict and rolling mills were abandoned. Ancient shipyards and engineering works, venerable docks and rural railways: all and more went the same way. Nostalgia took them, or at any rate some of them, into her welcoming arms. The relics of Britain's industrial past were transformed into tourist shrines. Thus did *the* Industrial Revolution and its heroic achievements enter Valhalla.' Coleman, *Myth, history and the industrial revolution*, p. 32.

[59] Smith, *Wealth of nations*, II, p. 404.

The importance of reduced labour costs in enhancing competitiveness was clear to him but the significance of overcoming the limitation to productive potential inherent to dependence upon energy derived from plant photosynthesis was not. Even in the middle decades of the nineteenth century John Stuart Mill was dubious about the possibility of surmounting the barrier to a long-term improvement in real incomes which Ricardo had identified.[60]

Though the forebodings of the classical economists turned out to be unjustified, it was not until the later decades of the nineteenth century that it became generally accepted that a radically new era had arrived. Arnold Toynbee's concerns, when he published his *Lectures on the industrial revolution* in 1884, were very different from those of Mill. Toynbee is often credited with establishing the expression 'industrial revolution' as the standard term for referring to the changes which brought into being a new era in world history, though the term had been used sporadically for several decades before his lectures were published. It may have gained currency when it did because by the 1880s it was widely understood that the productive powers of societies had indeed been placed on a new basis. Ever since the term industrial revolution came into general use it has, of course, been a central concern of economic historians to describe it and, if possible, to explain its origin and nature. But Toynbee, and the same is true of many of his successors in subsequent generations of economic historians, was more concerned with the injustices of the new situation than its genesis.

Toynbee was able to take for granted the transformation in productive capacity which had taken place. This could ensure increasing comfort for all, but he feared that a misplaced understanding of the rules which should govern economic life was confining the benefits of the new situation to a favoured few. Toynbee was only 30 years old at the time of this death in 1883 and most of the text of *The industrial revolution* is based on the collation by others of notes for the lectures which he had delivered as a very young man. The book is a testimony to the strength of his revulsion at the worst features of the English society and economy of the day. Given the circumstances under which the text was put together it is hardly surprising that it is somewhat

[60] See below p. 246.

disjointed and perhaps less balanced than the work he might have written had he lived longer. He wrote:

The essence of the Industrial Revolution is the substitution of competition for the mediaeval regulations which had previously controlled the production and distribution of wealth. On this account it is not only one of the most important facts of English history, but Europe owes to it the growth of two great systems of thought – Economic Science, and its antithesis, Socialism.[61]

He was bitterly opposed to the deductive type of political economy epitomised by Ricardo's writings and appalled by the effects of a blind acceptance of the benefits of *laissez-faire* and unrestricted competition.

It is next assumed that this struggle for existence is a law of nature, and that therefore all human interference with it is wrong. To that I answer that the whole meaning of civilisation is interference with this brute struggle. We intend to modify the violence of the fight, and to prevent the weak being trampled under foot.[62]

Toynbee saw it as essential to hold a balance between the two extremes of political economy and socialism:

Not admitting, with the socialist, the natural right of all men to an equal share in the benefits of civilisation, not proposing, with the socialist, to stamp out competition, and substitute a community of goods, we yet plead for the right of all to equal opportunities of development, according to their nature. Competition we now recognise to be a thing neither good nor bad; we look upon it as resembling a great physical force which cannot be destroyed but must be controlled and modified. As the cultivator embanks a stream and distributes its waters to irrigate his fields, so we control competition by positive laws and institutions.[63]

By the 1880s at the latest, therefore, it had become evident that the world had changed. It was abundantly clear that the capacity to

---

[61] Toynbee, *The industrial revolution*, p. 64.
[62] *Ibid.*, p. 66.
[63] *Ibid.*, p. 157.

produce had been transformed in a manner which would have astonished those living in earlier centuries. Access to sources of energy
which dwarfed those at the disposal of past generations meant that the
concerns of mid-Victorian society were greatly different from those of
earlier times. Whereas once the assumption that the poor are ever
present was uncontroversial, in Toynbee's day the abolition of poverty
was increasingly regarded as both feasible and morally imperative.

The view, common to all the classical economists, that exponential economic growth was impossible, though apparently unassailable in logic, had proved mistaken.[64] It had appeared unassailable
in logic because land was taken to be as necessary to *all* types of
material production as capital or labour, and because there was
only so much land there could not be indefinite expansion. This
was a physical constraint; it was not a problem associated with a
particular political regime, legal system, or set of social conventions, and it was made the more severe by the relative inefficiency
of plant photosynthesis in capturing energy from sunlight (though
the classical economists were not in a position to appreciate this).
A combination of physical and biological facts, therefore, set limits to material production which it was idle to suppose that mankind could overcome. Advances in productive techniques might
from time to time alleviate the basic problem, but as long as plant
growth underwrote all material output either directly or indirectly
the problem would remain.

There is an important sense in which the problem identified by the
classical economists remains with us today since, as long as fossil fuels
provide the bulk of the energy consumed in advanced economies, difficulties are postponed rather than indefinitely set aside. Fossil fuels
are the result of plant growth accumulated over many millions of
years in long-past geological eras. They make it possible to benefit
from a vast accumulation of plant growth rather than being dependent on a single year's growth, but they are finite and will therefore
become exhausted in the passage of time if they continue to be used
on the current scale.

---

[64] Exponential economic growth means growth which produces the same
percentage growth over any given time interval, as, for example, when output
rises by 2 per cent each year.

W. S. Jevons belonged to the generation that understood clearly that a new era had begun. When he published *The coal question*, in 1865, he showed great alarm at the implications of the exponential growth in coal consumption, given its finite possible supply. He was vividly conscious both of its transforming power and of the dangers of an increasing dependence upon it. He wrote:

Coal in truth stands not beside, but entirely above, all other commodities. It is the material source of the energy of the country – the universal aid – the factor in everything we do. With coal almost any feat is possible or easy; without it we are thrown back into the laborious poverty of early times.

With such facts familiarly before us, it can be no matter of surprise that year by year we make larger draughts upon a material of such myriad qualities – of such miraculous powers. But it is at the same time impossible that men of foresight should not turn to compare with some anxiety the masses yearly drawn with the quantities known or supposed to lie within these islands.[65]

Jevons went on to draw some pessimistic conclusions from this opening statement both for the world in general and more particularly for Britain.

The contrast between Jevons's view of the prospects for the future and that of the classical economists exemplifies the analogy between the events associated with the industrial revolution and those which occurred when Pandora's husband opened her jar. The works published by the classical economists span the period most often depicted as that in which the industrial revolution took place, yet they were unaware of the transformation in train around them and produced what seemed conclusive arguments against the possibility of its occurrence. Pandora had no prior expectation of the irreversible changes which would result from the opening of the jar. For contemporaries the same was true of the industrial revolution. Only the generation of Marx, Toynbee, and Jevons was able to gain an understanding of what had taken place. The new situation brought about by opening Pandora's jar is depicted as filled with dangers and terrors which were novel and fearsome. The character of the new world created by the industrial revolution was far from being uniformly alarming. It

[65] Jevons, *The coal question*, p. 2.

held out the promise of releasing societies from the curse of poverty, but though the industrial revolution brought with it promise of massive benefits, there were also balancing dangers. An enhanced power to produce was matched by a similar increase in the power to destroy. The musket and the sword are puny compared to the long-range rocket and the hydrogen bomb. And all gain remains precarious as long as the source of the cheap energy which underwrites economic growth is a range of fossil fuels. There is a comparative stability in a world based on energy drawn from fungible sources which is lacking when the sources are consumptibles.

Whatever the longer-term implications of moving from an organic economy to one exploiting fossil fuels on a scale which has utterly transformed the quantum of energy per head available for all forms of productive activity, it seems clear that, without making this transition, England and its neighbours would have remained in the state of 'laborious poverty' to which Jevons referred. Before exploring this issue further, however, it is convenient to consider the prior, facilitating transformation taking place in English agriculture and in other aspects of the economy which are the subject of the next four chapters. They led to a progressive improvement in the country's productive capacity, without which it is doubtful whether an industrial revolution would have occurred. The chapters in Part II are designed to throw light on the changes in question.

Favourable developments

As the title of Part II suggests, the next four chapters represent an attempt to review several features of the economy and society which were instrumental in causing England to outstrip its neighbours other than the Netherlands during the early modern period. In each case there was feedback between the features mentioned in the chapter titles which promoted economic growth generally. The four topics considered in these chapters are the following: agricultural change and urbanisation; energy and transport; occupational structure, aggregate income, and migration; and production and reproduction. The purpose of this preliminary note is to stress that, although it is convenient to divide the topics between the four chapters, there were also close links between them. I have therefore included a figure at the end of Part II which tries to define the nature and significance of these links by showing them in a flow diagram which sets out the direction and nature of the links. It may prove helpful to consult this figure before reading Part II, and to refer to it from time to time while doing so. Equally, it provides an opportunity to review the four chapters as a whole before moving on to Part III. For this reason figure 6.7 is included in a section entitled *Retrospect of Part II as a whole* which is placed at the end of chapter 6, the last chapter in this section.

3 | *Agricultural change and urbanisation*

Much of the writing about the industrial revolution is, explicitly or implicitly, about primacy in causation. Was it primarily a demand or a supply side phenomenon; was accelerating population growth a result of economic change or one of its causes; if technological change was the key variable, was it a result of enlightenment science or of opportunity, trial, and error on the part of individuals largely ignorant of the new 'scientific' approach to the understanding of physical and chemical behaviour and problems? The list could be greatly extended. Much of interest has emerged from debates of this type but it is arguable that attempts to establish a hierarchy of causation are less fruitful than examination of the nature of the feedback between the components of change.

The concept has a general relevance. The view of the classical economists was that the dominant character of the growth process was ultimately negative feedback. Adam Smith used the characteristic spread in interest rates among the countries of western Europe to bring home the problem. Since the opportunities for profitable investment, though substantial, were necessarily limited, the return on capital which could be achieved was gradually reduced as the better prospects became exhausted. The more developed an economy, the more prominent the problem. The Netherlands was, in his view, the most advanced economy of the day. As a result rates of interest were very low in Holland, no more than moderate in England, but substantially higher in Scotland and in France, where there remained greater opportunity for profitable investment.[1] England, and at a later date

---

[1] Smith, *Wealth of nations*, I, pp. 101–4. The government of Holland could borrow at 2 per cent and people of good credit at 3 per cent, and the Dutch had invested heavily in French and English funds: 'the great sums which they lend to private people in countries where the rate of interest is higher than in their own, are circumstances which no doubt demonstrate the redundancy of their stock, or that it has increased beyond what they can employ with tolerable profit in the proper business of their own country'. *Ibid.*, p. 103.

other states, might be expected to tread the same path which Holland had taken. Ricardo's exposition of the problem of the fixed supply of land led to the same conclusion. Growth led to an increased demand for food and raw materials. Both were obtained principally from the land. At some point in the growth process this must mean taking inferior land into cultivation or using existing land more intensively. The returns to labour and to capital would both decline as a result, and growth would grind to a halt. The two men were in agreement that the last case, when growth had petered out, might be as uninviting as that found in countries in which no improvements had taken place, even though, for an extended period in between, the speed of growth might bring substantial benefit to all members of society. The classical economists proved to be mistaken in their pessimism, if not in their logic. Negative feedback was indeed inescapable in organic economies and many cycles of growth followed by stagnation had occurred in earlier centuries, a pattern reflected in the relationship between population growth and the real wage shown in figure 1.1.

Viewed in feedback terms, therefore, the key change which defines the industrial revolution was the replacement of negative by positive feedback within the growth process, and in particular the gradual elimination of the fixed supply of land as a constraint which prevented indefinite growth. Negative feedback implied that growth must be at best asymptotic.[2] Positive feedback created the expectation of exponential growth. This suggests that the key issue on which to focus is the identification of the changes which transformed the growth process as a whole from one in which negative feedback must dominate in the long run to one in which positive feedback prevailed.

Positive feedback only became a dominant characteristic within the economy as a whole when the industrial revolution was well in train. Nevertheless, it could, of course, occur also within organic economies and continue in some sectors for long periods. It is instructive to consider an example of this, especially as, by merging with another comparable but novel development, it played a part in overcoming the barriers which had always arrested earlier periods of growth. The example examined in this chapter is the feedback

---

[2] Asymptotic growth describes a situation in which the rate of growth declines progressively as growth itself approaches a ceiling set in this instance by the productivity of the land.

between agricultural development and urban growth. The next chapter describes the feedback between the growing coal industry and several other elements within the economy, examining the development of linkages which were not subject to the Ricardian limitations inherent in an organic economy, and thus marked the escape route from its constraints.

The productivity of those employed in agriculture was the most important single determinant of the possibility of growth and change in all organic economies. Where it was low it was unavoidably necessary for the bulk of the population to live and work on the land if there was to be food for all. Where this was the case it was also inevitable that there was little demand for any but the bare necessities other than food – clothing, shelter, and fuel – and therefore little employment in secondary or tertiary activities. Low productivity might arise for many reasons. High population densities might result in fragmentation of holdings, reducing the amount of land available per head to a level well below the optimum. In some, though not all, types of agriculture a shortage of draught animals for whatever reason might produce a similar result. A list of this kind could be much extended. But frequently, where agricultural productivity was low, the problem lay elsewhere, with weakness of demand rather than inability to increase production. In an archetypal peasant society the first concern of each family is to cover its own needs rather than produce a surplus for sale, and this attitude makes excellent sense where the scale of demand outside the peasant sector is slight. A bad harvest focuses attention exclusively on the needs of the family. A good harvest, while relieving anxiety on this score, does not create much opportunity for profitable sale, since others will also enjoy a surplus and the market price will fall to a level which creates little incentive to make efforts to increase productive capacity.[3]

The feedback between agricultural development and urban growth was central to the advances made in England in the early modern period. Adam Smith summarised the nature of the feedback as follows:

---

[3] More generally, it is often assumed that a bad harvest will boost farmers' incomes because the resulting price rise is proportionately greater than the decline in yield. Similarly it may be assumed that a bumper harvest adversely affects farmers' incomes because prices plunge. But the issue is not straightforward. Wrigley, 'Corn yields and prices'.

The great commerce of every civilized society, is that carried on between the inhabitants of the town and those of the country. It consists in the exchange of rude for manufactured produce ... The country supplies the town with the means of subsistence, and the materials of manufacture. The town repays this supply by sending back a part of the manufactured produce to the inhabitants of the country. The town, in which there neither is nor can be any reproduction of substances, may very properly be said to gain its whole wealth and subsistence from the country. We must not, however, upon this account, imagine that the gain of the town is the loss of the country. The gains of both are mutual and reciprocal, and the division of labour is in this, as in all other cases, advantageous to all the different persons employed in the various occupations in to which it is subdivided.[4]

This may be regarded as a classic description of the most important way in which an organic economy could advance. It captures the central problem of all such economies, that because virtually all raw material supply was animal or vegetable in character, everything hinged on increasing agricultural output. This was intensely difficult to achieve without incurring the penalty of declining marginal returns to labour and capital, but for a time more extensive and effective division of labour, which was facilitated by rural–urban exchange, could allow the basic problem to be side-stepped. In England the difficulty was further eased and eventually overcome by exploiting inorganic sources of raw materials and energy but the process which Adam Smith described played a prominent role throughout the early modern period.

Urban growth

The 'great commerce' to which Smith referred was of recent origin in England, and in many respects the English experience, in both its nature and its timing, differed from the continental norm. It is

---

[4] Smith, *Wealth of nations,* I, p. 401. A similar point was stressed by Overton and Campbell in their introductory chapter to a volume devoted to analysis of European agricultural productivity: 'the foundation of its [England's] industrial revolution of the late eighteenth and early nineteenth centuries was laid by a significant rise in the productivity of land and, more significantly, of labour in agriculture during the immediately preceding centuries'. Overton and Campbell, 'Productivity change', p. 1.

Table 3.1 *Urbanisation in England and the continent: percentage of total population in towns with 10,000 or more inhabitants*

	1500	1600	1650	1700	1750	1800
England	3.2	6.1	10.8	13.4	17.5	24.0
North and west Europe	6.0	8.1	10.7	13.0	13.8	14.7
Europe	6.1	8.0	9.3	9.5	9.9	10.6
North and west Europe minus England		9.2		12.8	12.1	10.0
Europe minus England		8.1		9.2	9.4	9.5

Source. Wrigley, 'Urban growth and agricultural change', tabs. 7.5 and 7.6, pp. 176, 177.

sometimes assumed that urban growth was a widespread phenomenon in early modern Europe. In fact, however, growth was generally modest to a degree. The numbers living in towns increased, but only slightly faster than the European population as a whole. Some countries were already quite heavily urbanised at the beginning of the period. This was notably true of Italy and the Low Countries. But urbanisation did not intensify in these countries in the early modern period, apart from the Netherlands, and even there the period of increasing urbanisation was over by the end of the seventeenth century and thereafter there was decline. In the Mediterranean world the urban percentage was generally lower in 1800 than in 1600. This was true of Italy, Spain, and Portugal.[5] Nor were there marked changes in countries, such as Germany and France, which were not heavily urbanised at the start of the period. Table 3.1 makes clear the extent of English exceptionalism.

The top section of the table shows that north and west Europe outpaced Europe as a whole, with England the most dynamic element within the north and west. The lower section repeats the information but with England subtracted from the totals for Europe and for north and west Europe. This changes the picture significantly. The north and west suffered a decline in the urban percentage in the

[5] De Vries, *European urbanization*, tab. 3.7, p. 39.

eighteenth century, primarily due to the fall in the urban percentage in the Netherlands. Removing English urban totals from those for Europe suggests that in continental Europe as a whole urbanisation was almost at a standstill between 1600 and 1800. The eighteenth century was, if anything, more sluggish than the seventeenth in this regard.

The same information can be recast in a form which makes it possible to express the urban gain in England as a proportion of the urban gain in Europe as a whole. This shows that between 1600 and 1700 England accounted for 33 per cent of the European urban increase; between 1700 and 1750 57 per cent; and between 1750 and 1800 70 per cent.[6] Over the two centuries taken together the comparable figure is 53 per cent. Given that in 1600 the population of England amounted to only 5.8 per cent of the European total, and in 1800 7.7 per cent, this is extraordinary testimony to the exceptional character of the urban growth taking place in England at the time.[7]

The pattern of urban growth in England was far from uniform. Table 3.2 brings out some of its salient characteristics. In the period down to 1700 the scene was dominated by London, which throughout the seventeenth century eclipsed all other towns with 5,000 or more inhabitants. Its increase greatly exceeded the combined growth of all other towns in this category.[8] By the end of the seventeenth century London contained over 11 per cent of the whole population of the country and had twice as many inhabitants as the other towns combined. During the eighteenth century, in contrast, although the capital continued to grow, it did no more than keep pace with the national population as a whole, whereas other towns grew at a furious pace from about 275,000 in 1700 to 1,420,000 by 1800, which represented a tripling of their percentage share of the national total. The towns leading the rush for growth in the eighteenth century included many industrial centres, such as Birmingham, Manchester,

---

[6] The percentages are derived from 'net' gains in population. The 'net' gain at each date represents the difference between the recorded urban population total and the total based on the urban percentage at the base date, 1600. The exercise is described more fully in Wrigley, 'Urban growth and agricultural change', p. 177.

[7] The totals and percentages are taken from *ibid.*, tab. 7.7, p. 179 and p. 177.

[8] London's population increased by 375,000 compared to a total of 140,000 for other towns with 5,000 or more inhabitants.

Table 3.2 *Urban population estimates for England, London, and other towns with 5,000 or more inhabitants*

Population ('000s)

	c.1520	c.1600	c.1670	c.1700	c.1750	c.1800
England	2,400	4,150	5,150	5,200	5,900	8,600
London	55	200	475	575	675	960
Other urban populations (5,000 or more inhabitants)	70	135	205	275	540	1,420
Total urban	125	335	680	850	1,215	2,380
Ten historic regional centres[a]	62	73		107	126	153
Urban populations as percentages of the national total						
London	2.25	4.75	9.25	11.00	11.50	11.25
Other urban	3.00	3.25	4.00	5.25	9.25	16.50
Total urban	5.25	8.00	13.25	16.25	20.75	27.75

Notes. [a] Norwich, York, Salisbury, Chester, Worcester, Exeter, Cambridge, Coventry, Shrewsbury, Gloucester.
The national population totals differ slightly from those in the original table because of revised estimates (Wrigley *et al.*, *English population history*, tab. A9.1, pp. 614–15). The percentages are expressed to the nearest quarter per cent.
Source. Wrigley, 'Urban growth and agricultural change', tabs. 7.2 and 7.3, pp. 162, 166.

Leeds, and Sheffield and flourishing ports such as Liverpool and Hull, but at the other extreme there were also many towns which behaved like their continental equivalents, doing no more than keep pace with the general rise in population. This was true, for example, of the ten historic regional centres shown separately in the middle section of table 3.2. Their growth over the seventeenth and eighteenth centuries closely matched the national trend, a pattern characteristic of most of continental Europe.

Table 3.3 brings out a further feature of urban growth – the rapidly changing urban hierarchy. Here once more England differed from the

Table 3.3 *The urban hierarchy in England 1600–1851 (populations in '000s)*

1600		1700		1750	
London	200	London	575	London	675
Norwich	15	Norwich	30	Bristol	50
York	12	Bristol	21	Norwich	36
Bristol	12	Newcastle	16	Newcastle	29
Newcastle	10	Exeter	14	Birmingham	24
Exeter	9	York	12	Liverpool	22
Plymouth	8	Gt Yarmouth	10	Manchester	18
Salisbury	6	Birmingham	8–9	Leeds	16
King's Lynn	6	Chester	8–9	Exeter	16
Gloucester	6	Colchester	8–9	Plymouth	15
Chester	6	Ipswich	8–9	Chester	13
Coventry	6	Manchester	8–9	Coventry	13
Hull	6	Plymouth	8–9	Nottingham	12
Gt Yarmouth	5	Worcester	8–9	Sheffield	12
Ipswich	5	Bury St Edmunds	5–7	York	11
Cambridge	5	Cambridge	5–7	Chatham	10
Worcester	5	Canterbury	5–7	Gt Yarmouth	10
Canterbury	5	Chatham	5–7	Portsmouth	10
Oxford	5	Coventry	5–7	Sunderland	10
Colchester	5	Gloucester	5–7	Worcester	10
		Hull	5–7		
		King's Lynn	5–7		
		Leeds	5–7		
		Leicester	5–7		
		Liverpool	5–7		
		Nottingham	5–7		
		Oxford	5–7		
		Portsmouth	5–7		
		Salisbury	5–7		
		Shrewsbury	5–7		
		Sunderland	5–7		
		Tiverton	5–7		

Notes. [a] including Salford. [b] including Devonport. [c] including Gateshead.
[d] Stoke and Burslem. [e] The Medway towns: Chatham, Rochester, Gillingham.
Each column lists the twenty largest towns at a given date but where there were other towns of the same size as the twentieth town the list has been extended to include them.

Sources. Wrigley, 'Urban growth and agricultural change', tab. 7.1, pp. 160–1. The 1851 totals are taken from Mitchell, *British historical statistics*, ch. 1, tab. 7, pp. 26–7.

1801		1851	
London	960	London	2,685
Manchester[a]	89	Liverpool	376
Liverpool	83	Manchester[a]	367
Birmingham	74	Birmingham	233
Bristol	60	Leeds	172
Leeds	53	Bristol	137
Sheffield	46	Sheffield	135
Plymouth[b]	43	Newcastle[c]	114
Newcastle[c]	42	Bradford	104
Norwich	36	Plymouth[b]	90
Portsmouth	33	Hull	85
Bath	33	Portsmouth	72
Hull	30	Preston	70
Nottingham	29	Norwich	68
Sunderland	26	Stoke[d]	66
Stoke[d]	23	Brighton	66
Chatham[e]	23	Sunderland	65
Wolverhampton	21	Bolton	61
Bolton	17	Leicester	61
Exeter	17	Nottingham	57
Leicester	17		
Gt Yarmouth	17		
Stockport	17		

continental norm. On the continent the rank ordering of towns rarely changed radically. A given town might slip from being, say, third largest to being sixth largest, but the composition of the top ten or top twenty did not alter greatly and changes in ranking were seldom radical. Table 3.3 shows that this was not the case in England. Throughout the entire quarter millennium 1600–1851 London was by far the largest town in the country but there was striking change elsewhere in the urban hierarchy. For example, already in 1800 of the next six towns after London only Bristol also appeared in the top seven towns in 1600. There are twenty names in all in the 1600 list; of these only seven appear in the top twenty in 1800. A comparable exercise for the Netherlands, a country in which there was also for a time rapid growth in the urban population, reveals a much more stable pattern. Of the twenty largest towns in 1550, at the beginning of the phase of rapid growth in the Dutch economy, nineteen were still among the top twenty in 1800.[9] In Spain, where, in common with much of Mediterranean Europe, the urban percentage was falling between 1600 and 1800, of the twenty largest towns in 1600, fifteen remained in the top twenty in 1800.[10]

That the history of urban growth in England provides such striking evidence of new developments and differs so markedly from events abroad lends powerful support to the view that patterns of expansion and change in England reflect a different dynamic from those in continental Europe, especially after 1700.

As we have seen, in England for a long time the lead role in this process of positive feedback was played by the capital, London. A fully convincing account of the spectacular rise of London among the leading European cities is still lacking, but the bald fact of its surge is striking indeed. In the later sixteenth and seventeenth centuries London grew so markedly that by the end of the period it had become the largest city in Europe.[11] It grew from c.55,000 to c.575,000 between

[9] Using the estimates in de Vries, *European urbanization*, app. 1, p. 271. The only town which dropped out was Enkhuizen, to be replaced by Zwolle.

[10] *Ibid.*, app. 1, pp. 277–8 and tab. 3.7, p. 39. The five towns which disappeared from the top twenty were Segovia, Cuenca, Salamanca, Baeza, and Ubeda whose places were taken by Cadiz, Malaga, Cartagena, Santiago, and Orihuela.

[11] In 1550 London was already one of the larger European cities, within the top ten but not a leader. In de Vries's large table it was sixth at this date. The larger cities in descending order were Naples, Venice, Paris, Lisbon, and Antwerp. De Vries, *European urbanization*, app. 1, pp. 269–87.

1520 and 1700.[12] The size and rapid growth of London provided a massive stimulus to the farming sector. Material production of any given kind takes place only if there is a present or prospective demand for a given product. Those who work the land can count on a local demand for food to satisfy local need but any stimulus to produce beyond this level must come from those living elsewhere in towns and cities. Even in largely rural communities there will, of course, always be a proportion of the population who do not produce the food which they eat but if that fraction is modest and unchanging there will be little or no incentive to change current practice. Population growth in the rural counties of England was generally modest.[13] The local demand for food therefore showed little growth. If, however, there is a substantial and steadily growing urban demand for food the situation is different. A rising trend in the volume of demand creates an incentive to invest and improve. It also stimulates specialisation. Farmers in areas well suited to beef cattle, for example, may find that it pays them to reduce or abandon cereal culture in favour of cattle rearing, with the reverse taking place where the soils favour cereals.[14] This in turn gives rise to inter-regional exchange of foodstuffs between areas with different agricultural specialisms.

The existence of a substantial and growing urban market for food creates a source of demand which does not change significantly between years of good and bad harvest, a situation which provides incentives which are slight or non-existent where urban markets are small or inaccessible because of poor transport facilities. Poor transport facilities reduce the area which can respond to urban food price signals, acting in a fashion similar to the existence of tariff barriers in restricting trade. If transport is slow, uncertain, and expensive the limits to growth will be severe. However, there also exists the possibility that rising urban demand will encourage both rising agricultural productivity and improvement in transport facilities. When any of the three factors change this will encourage sympathetic change in the other two. It is ultimately idle to try to determine primacy among the three since they are so intimately intertwined, but the upshot of

[12] Wrigley, 'Urban growth and agricultural change', tab. 7.2, p. 162.
[13] See tab. 5.2, p.117 below.
[14] On the development of a national market for agricultural products and the changes which this implied, Chartres, 'The marketing of agricultural produce'.

their interaction may in time prove striking. The absence of feedback of this type could have a reverse effect. In Italy in the nineteenth century, for example, population in rural areas reached high densities but lacked productive employment. O'Brien and Toniolo ended a discussion of the situation as follows: 'The poverty of the rural population before 1914 may be more realistically attributed to the fact that Italy's industrial and urban economy (and the international economy as a whole) had not developed rapidly enough to pull under-employed labour from the countryside of Mediterranean Europe.'[15]

The growth of London not only transformed the market prospects for farmers because its inhabitants produced little or no food themselves but disposed of much purchasing power. It also led to a steady increase in the demand for farm produce indirectly. There was a parallel, marked rise in the volume of road transport and therefore in the demand for fodder to 'fuel' the rising number of horses needed to pull carts and wagons.[16] Urban growth, moreover, implies an increased demand for raw materials no less than for food, and, as Adam Smith noted, almost all the raw materials in question were vegetable or animal in nature, and were therefore produced in the countryside. A steadily rising proportion of the labour force no longer worked on the land. Most of them were engaged in secondary activities. Shoemakers, weavers, carpenters, blacksmiths, brewers, framework knitters, printers, and basket makers were all dependent on animal or vegetable raw materials. The great bulk of this demand was met from plants grown on English soil, or from animals fed by those plants.

In the eighteenth century London continued to grow, but no longer more quickly than the country as a whole, rising from 575,000 to 960,000. In 1800 as in 1700 just over a tenth of the national population lived in the metropolis. The urban sector as a whole, however, took over the baton. Whereas in 1700 16.3 per cent of the national population lived in towns with 5,000 or more inhabitants, by 1800 the urban total represented 27.8 per cent of the national total, though London contributed almost nothing to this rising figure. Its percentage share of the national population rose only from 11.0 to 11.3 per cent. In contrast the percentage share of other towns with 5,000 or more inhabitants more than tripled from 5.3 to 16.5 per cent between 1700 and 1800 (table 3.2). This

[15] O'Brien and Toniolo, 'The poverty of Italy', p. 409.
[16] See below pp. 83–4.

was the period in which the major centres in the new industrial areas in the Midlands, the West Riding, and Lancashire rose rapidly up the urban rankings, displacing many of the traditional regional centres and county towns. The combined population of Manchester, Birmingham, Liverpool, and Leeds rose from about 30,000 at the beginning of the century to about 300,000 at its end.[17]

The underlying causes of the astonishingly rapid rise in London's share of the English population between 1520 and 1700 remain imperfectly understood, a phenomenon the more puzzling since its relative growth then ceased for a century, only to resume after 1800 (its share of the national total rose from 11.3 per cent in 1800 to 16.0 per cent in 1851).[18] The massive jump in the relative size of towns and cities other than London in the eighteenth century was principally due to the vigour of growth in industrial towns and ports, and it occurred despite the fact that there were many towns, like the ten historic regional centres mentioned above, which, like London, merely kept pace with the general rise in population in the country as a whole.[19]

One of the effects of the changes taking place in the eighteenth century was to distribute the benefits of rising urban demand much more evenly across the face of the land. The home counties, East Anglia, and the south-east may have benefited disproportionately in the seventeenth century, because of their proximity to London.[20] Thereafter the north and the west Midlands were equally fortunate. With falling transport costs markets became more accessible. Agriculture in these areas could count upon a rising urban demand for food, and was further boosted indirectly by the stimulus associated with the massive increase in transport activity on both roads and canals, which depended upon draught animals for motive power and thus upon fodder supplies. Some forms of mining activity and industrial production which secured mechanical energy from horses reinforced this effect.

The existence of a large and rising demand for food, fodder, and organic raw materials associated with dynamic urban growth

---

[17] Wrigley, 'Urban growth and agricultural change', tabs 7.1 and 7.2, pp. 160–2.

[18] All percentage measures of this sort are subject to significant margins of error since the city's boundary changed from time to time, and both the timing and the basis of the change can mean that like is not compared with like with the passage of time.

[19] See above tab. 3.2, p. 61.

[20] Overton and Campbell, 'Productivity change', pp. 41–2.

brought major changes in the scale and character of the demand for agricultural products and thereby induced matching changes in their supply. And once in train there was feedback between the two. The expectation that such demand would grow made increased investment in agriculture appear prudent rather than hazardous. As a result the growth of the urban sector was not constrained by increasingly tight supplies of food and industrial raw materials. The ability of the agricultural sector to sustain hectic growth in urban populations and the raw material needs of the wide swathes of industry which still depended on home-produced organic products was an essential factor in facilitating the growth which took place.

The national population doubled in size between 1600 and 1800. Almost half the increase took place in towns with 5,000 or more inhabitants.[21] A substantial part of the rest of the increase took place in smaller towns, or resulted from the proliferation of rural occupations other than farming. Indeed, perhaps the most truly remarkable feature of these two centuries was that the number of men working on the land increased only marginally, yet the agricultural workforce continued to meet the food needs of a population which more than doubled. The area under cultivation increased only modestly, which necessarily implies a very marked increase in output per acre, but this is less striking than the fact that labour productivity in agriculture rose in parallel with the demand for food and industrial raw materials occasioned by the population increase. Because of the nature of an organic economy it is normally to be expected that the price paid for securing a large increase in output is an even larger proportional increase in the input of labour for reasons set out so forcefully by the classical economists. That this did not happen in England may be regarded as a necessary condition for the sweeping changes which are conventionally taken to comprise the industrial revolution.

The consumer revolution

The fact that the number of people living in towns with 5,000 or more inhabitants increased from 850,000 to 2,380,000 in the course of the eighteenth century has a major bearing on a question which has attracted much attention in recent years. More than forty years

[21] See tab. 3.2, p. 61 above.

ago David Eversley published an essay on the significance of the home market in sustaining economic growth in the eighteenth century.[22] He noted that it was widely agreed that in the first half of the eighteenth century low food prices had provided 'a large section of the working population' with a margin of income left over after meeting basic needs and that this had sustained demand for consumer goods, 'thus providing the necessary buoyancy of the home market at a time when industry was just beginning to transform itself, in some sectors, by the adoption of power, division of labour, and techniques of mass production and distribution'.[23] After 1750, however, it was also widely agreed, he noted, that home demand faltered and that further expansion depended on a differentially rapid growth in exports. Eversley was intent on challenging this view. He argued that during the three decades after 1750 'exports – were neither at a sufficiently high level nor sufficiently stable to warrant the amount of investment that took place'. Home demand remained the key to continued growth and 'this happened because increased real incomes tended to be spent on consumer goods rather than extra food purchases, thus still further stimulating industrial production and accelerating the movement of existing and new labour in the manufacturing sector'.[24] He added that 'the claim is here put forward that there is one central theme to all industrialization analysis: the emergence, and maintenance of a large domestic market for mass-produced consumer goods'.[25]

Eversley went on to substantiate his claim by referring to Gregory King's famous table to identify the percentage of the population whose incomes enabled them to spend a significant proportion of their incomes in ways which would underwrite the development he described. This 'middling group' increased markedly in size during the eighteenth century both because they were an increasing proportion of the total population and because the population itself rose rapidly. He suggested that the middling group may have tripled in size in the course of the century from 1 to 3 million, or from roughly 20 per cent to 35 per cent of the population.[26] These rough estimates of Eversley are not very different from the urban population totals

---

[22] Eversley, 'The home market and economic growth in England'.
[23] *Ibid.*, p. 208.
[24] *Ibid.*, p. 209.
[25] *Ibid.*, pp. 210–11.
[26] *Ibid.*, p. 214.

quoted in the last paragraph. The experience of urban life, the relatively high incomes of many townspeople, and the degree to which the
market dominated the lives of urban dwellers played a large part in
creating the phenomenon to which Eversley drew attention. Moreover,
an increasing proportion of those who did not live in the larger towns
were engaged in manufacture or in service activities rather than in
agriculture and were much influenced by urban practice.

Eversley was not the first scholar to emphasise the importance of
home demand during the industrial revolution, as he recognised,[27]
but in the decades since his essay was published, the issue of the 'consumer revolution' has attracted much attention. McKendrick inves-
tigated the commercialisation of fashion and offered a persuasive
case that awakening the desire to possess played an important and
very active role in causing a surge in demand in the eighteenth century: 'The fashion doll, the fashion print, the fashion magazine, the
fashion shops, the great manufacturers making fashion goods and
hordes of those selling them were all agents in pursuit of new levels
of consumption from an ever-widening market.'[28] Mokyr, in contrast,
rejects an independent importance for consumer behaviour. He lays
prime emphasis on technological change which by cheapening a wide
range of manufactured goods encouraged larger purchases: 'The role
of demand in the process was largely passive, as consumers responded
to lower prices by buying more or, in the terms of economics, slid
down their demand curves.'[29]

De Vries was sufficiently irritated by the weaknesses, as he saw
them, of the term 'consumer revolution' to remark: 'The term "consumer revolution" should probably be suppressed before frequent
repetition secures for it a place in that used-car lot of explanatory
vehicles reserved for historical concepts that break down directly
after purchase by the passing scholar.'[30] He preferred to attribute
importance to what he termed the 'industrious revolution'. This is not
a simple concept. It focuses on the household as the basic unit of life

[27] *Ibid.*, p. 211. Eversley also stressed the point that the phrase 'home market'
did not always connote the whole country since some areas, like the vale of
Trent which Chambers had studied, were virtually isolated entities.
[28] McKendrick, 'The commercialization of fashion', p. 98.
[29] Mokyr, *The lever of riches*, p. 111.
[30] De Vries, 'Purchasing power and the world of goods', p. 107.

and decision making and examines the way in which time is allocated within the household:

In this framework the industrious revolution, for which evidence can be found from the mid-seventeenth century into the nineteenth, consisted of two transformations: the reduction of leisure time as the marginal utility of money income rose, and the reallocation of labor from goods and services for direct consumption to marketed goods – that is a new strategy for the maximization of household utility.[31]

One element in this description of the concept of the industrious revolution is the reduction of leisure time as households considered that it was to their advantage to work harder or longer hours in order to gain access to goods or services which were supplied through the market. Voth's work lends strong support to the view that there was a marked reduction in leisure time during the second half of the eighteenth century. His analysis of the court records of the Old Bailey suggests that the average number of hours worked per year in London rose by 27 per cent between c.1760 and c.1800.[32]

Both the empirical evidence and the logical problems involved in the concept of a consumer revolution would sustain a lengthy and complex discussion, but Eversley's conviction that there was a major change in the scale of demand for what the classical economists termed 'comforts' and 'luxuries' seems justified. Coleman, in discussing 'the divergence of England', remarked that 'after about 1650 there was gradually building up in England a more substantial and more widely distributed reserve of disposable income than anywhere else in Europe'.[33] One aspect of this complex question seems reasonably clear. Whether the result of a reduction in leisure preference, a shift in occupational structure which gave an increased proportion of the population incomes sufficiently high for them to purchase a wide range of consumer goods, or some other factor or factors, there is little doubt that the range of consumer goods to be found in English households broadened considerably during the decades following the Restoration and throughout the eighteenth century. The evidence for this lies

[31] De Vries, 'The industrial revolution and the industrious revolution', p. 257.
[32] Voth, 'Time and work in eighteenth-century London', tab. 9, p. 51.
[33] Coleman, *The economy of England*, p. 197.

in the probate inventories. The work of Weatherill and of Overton and Whittle demonstrates the increasing frequency with which bed linen, table cloths, curtains, cutlery, grates, fire irons, glass windows, clocks and watches, pottery and chinaware, and similar 'comforts' were numbered among the possessions of the deceased between the middle of the seventeenth and the middle of the eighteenth century.[34] Inventories become in general less informative after the middle decades of the eighteenth century but the fact that the domestic market continued to take a large part of the rapidly rising output of English industries suggests that the trend continued.

Shammas considered a similar range of topics, making use of a wide range of indicators of change in consumer behaviour, such things as the decline in the percentage of the wage of labourers and master carpenters which was spent on food between the late sixteenth and early eighteenth centuries, or the striking rise in the imports of groceries of all types as a percentage of the total value of imports.[35] And she was struck by the willingness of some consumers to make sacrifices in other areas to participate in the new fascination with consumer durables. The final sentence in the main text of her book runs as follows: 'Paradoxically, the individual who drank tea in a teacup, wore a printed cotton gown, and put linen on the bed could be the same person who ingested too few calories to work all day and lived in a one-room house.'[36] This is perhaps a rather highly coloured illustration of the trend in taste and fashion but it brings home the radical nature of the change in attitude towards consumption expenditure which was taking place.

It may be too simple to argue that the spectacular growth of towns in England is a sufficient reason *in ipso* for the changes which are attributed to the consumer revolution, but it is defensible to suggest that it would be surprising if rapid urban growth had not played a major role in invoking the changes which were taking place. Urban life implies dependence on the market to a degree which may not hold in the countryside. Urban growth connotes a change in occupational

---

[34] Weatherill, *Consumer behaviour and material culture*; Overton *et al.*, *Production and consumption in English households*. There was, however, considerable regional variation in the degree of change, as is clear from Overton and Whittle's analysis of the evidence from Cornwall and Kent.

[35] Shammas, *The pre-industrial consumer*, tab. 5.2, p. 128; tab. 4.1, p. 77.

[36] *Ibid.*, p. 299.

structure which is likely to cause average incomes to rise.[37] And with experience of and exposure to urban norms forming part of the lives of a rising proportion of those still living in the countryside, it is not surprising that many of the features of the 'consumer revolution' should become visible countrywide rather than being found only in towns. Much the same changes occurred in the Netherlands a century earlier. Indirectly, and perhaps somewhat paradoxically, a sustained rise in agricultural productivity lay behind these changes.

The agricultural system

In seeking to account for a phenomenon so much at odds with Ricardian expectations, it is convenient first to consider the implications of the fact that English agriculture was not peasant-based. The supposed disadvantages of a peasant agriculture in inhibiting economic growth was an issue much debated among development economists in the decades following the Second World War. It was hypothesised that, at one extreme, and in conformity with the market principles of a cap-italist economy, when the output of the *marginal* worker on a farm fell below the level of the prevailing agricultural wage he would be dismissed from his job since to do otherwise would reduce the prof-itability of the enterprise. At the other extreme, in a peasant society whose guiding principles were very different, a son or daughter on the family holding would only be obliged to leave the household when the *average* product of all family members approached the point where a conventional standard of living could no longer be maintained. The difficulties of engendering rapid economic growth, it was argued, were substantially greater where 'peasant' values were dominant, both because the low real incomes which resulted from their family strategies would adversely affect the structure of aggregate demand and because the size of the pool of labour available to sectors of the economy other than agriculture would be limited by the retention of peasant family members on the land. It should be stressed that the 'peasant' values in question were no less 'rational' than those visible in a market-orientated agricultural system. They were no doubt dif-ferent but were fully consistent with a value system which emphasised

[37] See tab. 5.6, pp. 130–1 below, and associated discussion.

self-sufficiency and family continuity. Equally, as experience in many European countries in the nineteenth century demonstrated, a market-orientated agricultural system with specialisation of function may develop where farm sizes are small no less than where they are large. Peasant farmers have repeatedly shown themselves responsive to market signals. Both in medieval times and more recently market signals were often muffled or minimal because of the effects of distance and poor transport facilities, and also because large urban centres send out much clearer signals over a longer distance than small towns. Urban growth therefore boosted changes in agricultural practice which would otherwise not have occurred.

The subsequent history of countries which were desperately poor in the 1950s contradicts the gloomier prognostications of the time in many cases, but the general contention deserves careful consideration in explaining the changes taking place in early modern England. It is of interest to note that the potential significance of this point was evident to Malthus. When discussing the reasons why a population might never attain the maximum that might in theory be approached, he noted a feature of English agriculture which ensured that population growth would stop well short of this level: 'With a view to the individual interest, either of a landlord or farmer, no labourer can ever be employed on the soil, who does not produce more than the value of his wages; and if these wages be not on an average sufficient to maintain a wife, and rear two children to the age of marriage, it is evident that both population and produce must come to a stand.'[38]

The landlord/tenant-farmer/wage-paid labourer system of agricultural production which became dominant in much of England in this period encourages action of the kind to which Malthus referred. In this system, if the area of farmland remains broadly constant the initial expectation must be that the agricultural labour force will also vary little in size. It is not difficult to imagine circumstances in which this rule might not hold good. A doubling in cereal output, for example, such as occurred in England between the late sixteenth and late eighteenth centuries, implies a commensurate increase in the volume of the crop to be harvested and transported to barns, and this in turn implies a substantial increase in the labour involved. No doubt there was a substantial increase in the expenditure of muscle energy

---

[38] Malthus, *Essay on population*, 6th edn [1826], II, p. 405.

in English agriculture as a direct result of the rising volume of output. Much of this increase, however, may have been secured from animal rather than human muscles. Bigger, better fed, and more numerous farm horses limited the need for greater human energy inputs.[39] Again, one of the reasons for declining labour productivity as population increases in peasant agriculture is the increased subdivision of holdings. In early modern England, however, capitalist farming tended to increase the average size of farm units both by individual purchase and as a by-product of enclosure, and large farms employed fewer men per acre than small farms.

It is of interest to note that Quesnay, a major figure in the development of the physiocratic school of economic analysis in pre-revolutionary France, attached much importance to the distinction between three types of agriculture: that based on human labour alone; that using oxen to draw the plough; and that where horses supplied the necessary muscle energy. He considered that much of the greater productivity of English agriculture was due to the universal dependence on horses as an energy source. Four horses, he noted, could cultivate 100 *arpents*, four men less than 8 *arpents*.[40] He was equally explicit about the superiority of the horse over the ox as a power source, quantifying in some detail the characteristics of each system.[41] The use of horse-drawn ploughs he considered typical of *la grande culture*, where the units were farmed by men of substance who could command the considerable capital needed for large-scale operation.

Quesnay's emphasis upon the significance of using horses rather than oxen to pull the plough or cart is strongly supported by Grantham's discussion of regional differences in labour productivity in northern France c.1800. He estimated that the average labour input per hectolitre of wheat produced was 4.1 man-days on heavy soils and 3.3 man-days on light soils in departments where only horses were used in ploughing, compared with 7.0 and 4.5 man-days in departments using oxen. He concluded that: 'The extension of horse-powered husbandry was one of the important agricultural changes of the nineteenth century.'[42]

---

[39] Wrigley, 'Energy availability and agricultural productivity'.
[40] Eltis, *The classical theory of economic growth*, p. 4.
[41] *Ibid.*, pp. 4–8.
[42] Grantham, 'The *Cinq Grosses Fermes* of France', p. 349.

Towards the end of the eighteenth century, when a capitalist agricultural system, making extensive use of horses as a source of mechanical energy, had achieved marked success in magnifying the productivity of the average agricultural labourer in England, one small group of British men learned from bitter experience the limitations imposed on those largely without draught animals to assist them. When Arthur Phillip, the first governor of the colony, took the first convict fleet out to Australia, the home government assumed that it would become self-sufficient in food within a couple of years. In the event this took decades rather than years. In part this was due to the unfamiliarity of the new environment, which imposed on the new and reluctant colonists a long process of learning by trial and error; in part it occurred because a very high proportion of the convicts were from towns and cities rather than the countryside; but perhaps the greatest single handicap facing the new arrivals was their lack of draught animals. It proved very difficult to keep large animals alive during the very long sea voyage, averaging about six months.[43] Phillip succeeded in keeping a small number of cattle alive, but within six months of landing the convict who was put in charge of six of the cattle which survived the voyage allowed them to escape his care. Many years later their descendants, substantially increased in number to a herd of some sixty beasts, were discovered on the banks of the Nepean river, but for the period of the revolutionary and Napoleonic wars, when contact with England was intermittent, horses and cattle remained few in number and the colony was obliged to revert largely to hoe agriculture, with results which would have come as no surprise to Quesnay. The fact that gangs of convicts were yoked to carts to drag loads of bricks from brick fields to building sites might appear at first glance to reflect a brutal penal regime but in fact merely demonstrated the inescapable reality of an organic economy which lacked draught animals.

In the early years of the colony all its inhabitants, both convicts and their guardians, were at times gravely malnourished. The men were sometimes too weak from hunger to labour in the fields for more than a couple of hours a day. The severity of their situation in times of near famine is well illustrated by a comment made by Collins, the judge advocate and secretary of the colony on its first settlement, which to

---

[43] It proved much easier to keep pigs, sheep, and fowl alive during the long voyage.

later eyes is both illuminating and unconsciously amusing. The government in London was aware of their needs for supplies, but Governor Phillip had also entreated the home government to send out female convicts to improve the sex balance of the infant settlement. The first ship to reach the colony after the arrival of the First Fleet in 1788 was the *Lady Juliana*, which arrived in 1790 after a ten-month voyage. Collins noted: 'It was not a little mortifying to find on board the first ship that arrived, a cargo so unnecessary and unprofitable as two hundred and twenty-two females, instead of a cargo of provisions'[44] – an interesting commentary on the primacy of primitive drives!

The contrast between a 'capitalist' and a 'peasant' agricultural system bears some resemblance to the distinction which is sometimes drawn between 'maximiser' and 'satisficer' mentalities. It is neatly captured in some lines from Goldsmith's well-known exercise in poetic nostalgia, 'The deserted village':

> Ill fares the land, to hastening ills a prey,
> Where wealth accumulates, and men decay:
> Princes and lords may flourish, or may fade;
> A breath can make them, as a breath has made;
> But a bold peasantry, their country's pride,
> When once destroyed, can never be supplied.

> A time there was, ere England's griefs began,
> When every rood of ground maintained its man;
> For him light labour spread her wholesome store,
> Just gave what life required, but gave no more:
> His blest companions, innocence and health;
> And his best riches, ignorance of wealth.

The first of these two verses catches the eye but it is the second which embodies the conviction that happiness and health stem from being content with a modest sufficiency. Avoid the treadmill which accompanies the pursuit of wealth; relax in the contentment which flows from a modest independence. The poem might be termed a satisficer

---

[44] Collins, *Account of the English colony in New South Wales*, I, p. 118. Another vessel, the *Guardian*, had left England shortly after the *Lady Juliana* with a large stock of provisions but had struck 'an island of ice'. In an effort to keep the ship afloat the bulk of the cargo was jettisoned, including not only most of the provisions but also seven horses, sixteen cows, two bulls, two deer, and a number of sheep and goats. *Ibid.*, p. 116.

manifesto. Goldsmith's 'peasantry' were perhaps yeomen rather than peasants of the kind widely found in continental Europe, but his lines express vividly an alternative view of the purpose of life to that which increasingly dominated the lives of those living during the industrial revolution.

The rise in agricultural output

Quantifying the rise in agricultural output which took place between the end of the sixteenth century and the early years of the nineteenth century presents serious difficulties because of the paucity of information concerning the situation at the start of the period.

Agricultural production is conventionally divided between arable and pastoral activities, even though the two in most farms were closely intertwined. Tables 3.4 and 3.5 represent an attempt to identify the main changes in the cereal production taking place between c.1600 and c.1800, a period when the country remained largely self-sufficient in food despite the great rise in population which then took place, from 4.2 to 8.7 millions.

Table 3.4 is designed to make it possible to express net cereal output per acre by a single total for each date. Column 2 shows the gross yield per acre for each of the three main cereal crops. Gross yield, however, is a less useful figure than net yield. After each harvest sufficient grain must be held back to ensure that there is an adequate quantity of seed available for sowing for the next year's crop. Column 4 shows the net yield after making this allowance. Only this quantity is available to be used for food or fodder. Column 5, by showing the calorie equivalent for barley and oats relative to wheat, makes it possible to calculate a single figure for all cereal production by reducing all three grains to the same basis measured in calories. When the net yield is multiplied by its wheat equivalent and then by the share of the cereal acreage devoted to the crop in question, the resulting totals, shown in column 7, when added together provide a single figure for net cereal yield per acre. For example, the net yield of oats per acre in 1600 was 10.5 bushels. This total is then multiplied by 0.75 since a bushel of oats contains only three-quarters as many calories as a bushel of wheat. This figure in turn is multiplied by the share of oats in the acreage under cereals to produce a total representing the contribution of oats to the overall figure for cereal yield per acre (10.5 ×

Table 3.4 *Cereal yields in 1600 and 1800*

(1)	(2)	(3)	(4)	(5)	(6)	(7)
	Gross yield per acre (bushels)	Seed per acre (bushels)	Net yield per acre (bushels)	Wheat equivalent (calories per bushel)	Share of cereal acreage	Weighted wheat equivalent per acre (bushels)
1600						
Wheat	11.5	2.5	9.0	1.00	0.42	3.78
Barley	16.0	3.25	12.75	0.83	0.20	2.12
Oats	15.0	4.5	10.5	0.75	0.38	2.99
Cereal total						8.89
1800						
Wheat	21.5	2.0	19.5	1.00	0.42	8.19
Barley	30.0	2.5	27.5	0.83	0.24	5.48
Oats	35.0	4.0	31.0	0.75	0.34	7.91
Cereal total						21.58

Sources. The 1800 estimates are taken from Wrigley, 'Transition to an advanced organic economy', tab. 2, p. 443, where the sources used are listed and the assumptions made are discussed in the accompanying text.

$0.75 \times 0.38 = 2.99$). When the comparable totals for the other two cereals are added to that for oats the result shows that in 1600 the average acre under cereals produced a net yield of 8.89 wheat equivalent bushels, whereas 200 years later this figure had climbed to 21.58 bushels.[45]

Needless to say, there are substantial margins of error surrounding the estimates shown in table 3.4, especially for the earlier date. The effect of making alternative assumptions can, however, readily be tested by incorporating them into the relevant cells and following through the calculation for the line or lines in question. Experiment suggests that within the range of assumptions that are broadly credible

[45] Rye was not included in the list of cereals in either tab. 3.4 or tab. 3.5. By 1800 it had become a minor crop occupying only a little more than 1 per cent of the cereal acreage. It may be regarded as having been included with wheat in both tables.

the results would not change the conclusion that net cereal yield per acre more than doubled over the period.

Changes in yield per acre, however, need to be supplemented by other estimates to make it possible to arrive at a total of net grain output. This is attempted in table 3.5. As in the previous table, the 1800 estimates are transferred from an earlier exercise while those for 1600 are 'guesstimates' which reflect widely held assumptions, but are subject to wider uncertainties than the later set. The notes to the table list the assumptions which underlie the figures in each column of the 1600 line, where this is necessary, but the figures in column 8 require further comment. The net grain figures in table 3.4 are the result of making a deduction from gross yield of the quantity of grain needed for seed in the following year. This figure, however, still overstates the amount of grain which can be made available for sale off the farm since a significant quantity of oats was consumed on the farm by the horses which ploughed the fields and carted the manure and marl. Overton and Campbell suggest that 50 per cent of the oats harvest was fed to animals in 1600.[46] I have assumed that 85 per cent of the oats fed to animals was fed to farm animals. Since oats provided 2.99 wheat equivalent bushels to the total of such bushels produced per acre, this implies a deduction of 1.27 bushels from the column 7 figure of net grain output $(2.99 \times 0.5 \times 0.85 = 1.27)$. In 1800, oats, the cereal which had achieved the largest increase in output per acre over the two centuries, contributed 7.91 wheat equivalent bushels to total output per acre. Of this figure, 70 per cent was fed to livestock, but because of the massive increase in the number of horses engaged in work off the farm only 60 per cent of the oats fed to horses is estimated to have been fed to horses on the farm, resulting in a farm draught animal deduction of 3.32 bushels $(7.91 \times 0.7 \times 0.6 = 3.32)$.[47]

The final result of the series of calculations is shown in column 9, which suggests that total net cereal output increased almost three-fold between 1600 and 1800. The population rose from 4.16 million to 8.67 million between the two dates, suggesting that the amount of cereal food per head rose by almost 40 per cent. It should not be supposed, however, that the calorie intake per head of the population

---

[46] Overton and Campbell, 'Statistics of production and productivity', tab. 7.11, p. 201.
[47] Wrigley, 'Advanced organic economy', p. 445.

Table 3.5 *The arable sector in 1600 and 1800*

(1)	(2) Arable acreage (millions)	(3) Proportion of arable in crops	(4) Cropped acreage (col.2 × col.3)	(5) Proportion of cropped land in grain	(6) Acreage in grain (millions) (col.4 × col.5)	(7) Net grain output: wheat equivalent yield (bushels per acre)	(8) Draught farm animal deduction (bushels per acre)	(9) Total net grain output (million wheat equivalent bushels) (col.6 × (col.7−col.8))
1600	10.0	0.70	7.00	0.90	6.30	8.89	1.27	48.0
1800	11.5	0.84	9.66	0.79	7.63	21.58	3.32	139.3

Notes. The following assumptions were made in generating the data on the 1600 line. Col. 2: that there was a significant expansion in the arable acreage between the two dates. Col.3: that the practice of fallowing was more widely practised at the earlier date when 30 per cent of the land was fallowed each year. Col.5: that in 1600 far less arable land was devoted to legumes and root crops. Col.7: taken from tab. 3.4.

Sources. The line for 1800 is taken from Wrigley, 'An advanced organic economy', tab. 1, p. 440, where the sources used are listed and the assumptions made are discussed in the accompanying text.

from grain increased by two-fifths. A major reason why the nutritional gain from increased cereal output was quite small lies in the fall in the proportion of the oats harvest which went to human consumption. Combining the estimates of land in arable, proportions cropped, and net yields per acre in tables 3.4 and 3.5, it appears that oats production expanded from 30 to 91 million bushels. However, the proportion of oats eaten by people rather than animals fell from 50 to 30 per cent.[48] Given the very large increase in total output of oats, the total available for human consumption still rose substantially from 15 to 27.5 million bushels, but this is a smaller percentage rise than the comparable increase in population, suggesting a fall in oats consumption of about 12 per cent per head. A large proportion of the barley produced was used in the production of beer, approaching four-fifths of the total in 1800, as against perhaps two-thirds in 1600.[49] Brewing involved a 70 per cent loss of calories. The calorie benefit to the human population therefore increased considerably less than might appear at first sight over the two centuries. A similar calculation to that made for oats suggests that the increase in calorie consumption per head derived from barley rose by about 16 per cent. Wheat output per head increased by about 20 per cent. Given the relative weights of the three cereals, the overall increase in human calorie intake per head over the two centuries is about 12 per cent on the assumptions embodied in the two tables.[50] Since there is a substantial margin of uncertainty surrounding all these estimates and assumptions, it would be hazardous to assert that the increase in human calorie intake derived from grain was other than marginal.

It is a notable feature of table 3.5 that the cropped area increased by 2.7 million acres between 1600 and 1800 even though the arable acreage rose by only 1.5 million acres because of the reduction in the proportion of arable land which was fallowed each year. This was one aspect of the steady increase in the proportion of arable which

---

[48] Overton and Campbell, 'Statistics of production and productivity', tab. 7.11, p. 201.

[49] Wrigley, 'Advanced organic economy', p. 458.

[50] For the sake of simplicity, in making these estimates I have ignored the draught animal deduction (col. 8 of tab. 3.5). Since this rose by a very similar percentage to that for total net grain output, the percentage changes for the individual grains and for the three grains combined just quoted would not change significantly if the draught animal deduction had been included in the calculations.

was devoted to non-cereal crops, such as clover and sainfoin, and later turnips, a trend which began in the mid-seventeenth century and became more and more pronounced over the next two hundred years. Introducing such crops not only led to a steady reduction in the fallowed proportion but also raised nitrogen levels in the soil, and by providing additional animal fodder increased the number of farm animals and thereby the quantity of manure which could be returned to the land. This created what might be termed positive feedback in the annual cycle of agricultural activity. Both arable and pastoral production benefited and innovations begun on a small scale became both more attractive and more readily feasible as the benefit of earlier changes fed through.

Perhaps the most striking single statistic arising from the estimates in table 3.4 and 3.5 is that the quantity of oats available for consumption by animals rose from 15.0 to 63.7 million bushels, an increase of 49 million bushels, or roughly 900,000 tons.[51] This represents, in effect, a massive increase in the quantity of energy available for use on the farm, in transport, in industry, and for leisure. The scale of off-farm demand was very large and growing rapidly. It was estimated, for example, that the transfer of coal from the pits to the coal staithes on Tyneside already employed 20,000 horses at the end of the seventeenth century.[52] The very fact that in a period of rapidly rising population it was possible to devote a large proportion of arable land to animal nutrition is testimony to the ability of English agriculture to meet the food needs of the population relatively easily. Indeed for several decades in the late seventeenth and early eighteenth centuries the problem was rather to find a market for the wheat and barley produced than to match national demand. Deane and Cole, making use of the contemporary estimates of Charles Smith, concluded that exports of corn exceeded imports in each of the first seven decades of the eighteenth century. Net exports reached a peak in the 1750s, when they represented 7 per cent of net grain output.[53] The fact that the net yield per acre of oats rose more strongly than either of the other two grains suggests that whereas in earlier centuries farmers favoured wheat and barley in the rotation of crops, treating oats at times as a

---

[51] Assuming that the average weight of a bushel of oats is 40 lb.
[52] Bagwell, *The transport revolution*, p. 89.
[53] Deane and Cole, *British economic growth*, tab. 17, p. 65.

weed-suppressant as much as a main crop, in the early modern period it became a prized crop in its own right. With a substantial part of the crop being sold off-farm to meet the needs of transport on the new turnpike road system, on the canals, and as a source of mechanical energy in industry and mining, the place of oats in the crop strategy of farmers had changed significantly.

Nor should the value of oats for on-farm consumption be underestimated. Horses had long been used to pull ploughs and farm carts, but the scale of such usage and its distribution over the farming year changed in these centuries. To take a particular example, marling and liming of the land to reduce acidity and improve texture became a major element in the annual round of activities on many farms. In the course of a description of what he saw as the far greater efficiency of English farming compared to practices in France, Arthur Young referred quite casually to the practice of applying marl to farmland at the rate of 100 to 150 tons per acre.[54] Assuming by way of illustration that 50 acres were to be marled in this fashion, and that the marl pit was two miles distant, then treating 50 acres would mean performing between 10,000 and 15,000 ton-miles of transport. Translated into oats to feed horses, this is a vivid illustration of the energy flow at the command of many farmers. The exceptionally informative estate accounts of the Buller family in Cornwall, not a county usually regarded as in the van of agricultural improvement, show clearly what a high proportion of work days was spent on aspects of farm work where constant use was made of draught animals. They also show that labour usage was evenly spread throughout the year. In the late autumn and winter months any slack which would otherwise have occurred was taken up in carting and spreading sand, lime, and manure, an effective way of securing long-term improvement in the land, and feasible only with the employment of many horses.[55] Changes such as this also help to explain a part of the rise in manpower productivity, since the average number of hours spent working on the land by farm labourers presumably increased as a result. The length of the working day was less subject to seasonal variation when

[54] 'Let me demand, of the advocates for small farms, where the little farmer is to be found who will cover his whole farm with marl, at the rate of 100 to 150 tons per acre?' Young, *Travels in France*, ed. Kaplow, p. 314.
[55] Pounds, 'Barton farming'.

winter tasks could occupy the agricultural labour force as fully as those undertaken in summer.[56]

Attempting to quantify changes in arable agriculture involves wide margins of error, but any difficulty under this head pales in comparison with comparable problems in quantifying pastoral activity. Estimates of the totals of horses, cows, sheep, and pigs are insecurely based even at the end of the period and are much more uncertain at its beginning. Even if these numbers were accurately known, moreover, there would still be a major difficulty in interpreting them because the average size of animals increased and because they reached maturity more quickly as a result of being better fed. Selective breeding gradually improved the quality of the livestock. The illustrative calculation shown above shows that these factors could make a major difference to the quantity of meat available.[57] That exercise suggested that a threefold increase in beef production over the period from the end of the sixteenth to the end of the eighteenth century is plausible. Other estimates have suggested comparable increases.[58]

Although also impossible to measure effectively, there can be little doubt that the changes in agricultural practice which occurred between the end of the sixteenth and the beginning of the nineteenth century produced a major expansion in the output of animal fodder, which would translate both into substantial increases in the production of meat, wool, bones, tallow, and hides and also into the availability of greater quantities of mechanical energy provided by animal muscle. The introduction of new fodder crops, notably clover, sainfoin, lucerne, trefoil, vetches, and turnips improved both quantity and variety of fodder available, and reduced the seasonal variation in its quantity and quality. Other innovations were also helpful. For example, the gradual increase in the area converted into water meadows meant an earlier end to the period of fodder shortage traditionally

---

[56] Though the number of hours worked was always dependent on the hours of daylight, of course.

[57] See above p. 30 n.16.

[58] Clark, for example, suggested that between 1300 and 1850 output of meat per cow rose from 168 pounds to 600 pounds, while milk production per cow rose from 100 to 450 gallons per annum, with a comparable rise in the wool clip per sheep. Clark, 'Labour productivity', tab. 8.3, p. 216. And roughly similar increases are suggested by Campbell, *English seigniorial agriculture*, p. 187.

associated with the winter months (flushing the meadows with a few inches of water brought about a burst of growth several weeks earlier than in open grassland).

The uncertainty concerning the numbers of horses, cattle, sheep, and pigs c.1800 is not so severe as to prohibit estimation of the several totals, but for c.1600 the lack of any plausible basis for estimation suggests that a comparable exercise is pointless, even though paradoxically estimates for c.1300 are feasible. Accordingly, I have not included a table for livestock paralleling the two last tables dealing with arable agriculture. In 1800 the approximate totals for each type of animal, expressed in millions, were horses 1.21, cattle 3.5, sheep 20.0, and pigs 2.0.[59] In 1600 the numbers in each category were smaller, but it is difficult to go beyond this. Any differences in number are substantially magnified when increased animal size, better nutrition, and a quicker arrival at maturity are taken into account. Between 1300 and 1800 it is likely that pastoral output rose fourfold or more,[60] and it is certain that the bulk of this increase occurred after 1600. It is probably safe to conclude that the expansion of output in the pastoral sector outstripped that in the arable sector between 1600 and 1800, though the division is somewhat artificial since, for example, the increased energy output from the average horse had much to do with the massive rise in the production of oats. Combining the estimates of increased output in the arable and pastoral sectors suggests that agricultural output as a whole may have risen as much as threefold between the late sixteenth century and the beginning of the nineteenth century.

In addition to contributing growing quantities of meat, milk, butter, and cheese to the food supplies of the country, the pastoral sector underwrote the rapid expansion of several major industries. For example, Deane estimated that the output of the British woollen industry expanded by 8 per cent per decade in the first forty years of the eighteenth century, by 13–14 per cent in each of the next three decades, and by 6 per cent in the final three decades, a cumulative increase of more than 130 per cent.[61] Since the industry remained principally dependent on home-produced wool, it must be assumed

[59] Wrigley, 'Advanced organic economy', tab. 3, p. 448.
[60] *Ibid.*, p. 451.
[61] Deane and Cole, *British economic growth*, p. 52.

that the wool clip increased in much the same ratio. Rough estimates are also possible of the increase in the production of leather. Between 1750–9 and 1800–9 the annual total produced is estimated to have risen from 31.2 million pounds to 43.1 millions.[62] In the first half of the century a more tentative estimate suggests an increase of about a fifth.[63] Over the century as a whole, therefore, leather production probably rose by about two-thirds, and again the hides from which the leather was produced were predominantly British.[64] Both series suggest impressive output gains in the pastoral sector. The production of tallow, bones, and hair is likely to have risen at a similar rate to that of leather. In 1801 the woollen industry was the largest single British industry by value added and leather the fourth largest. Between them they accounted for 34 per cent of the national total of value added in British industry.[65] During the first half of the nineteenth century, local production of the animal and vegetable raw materials used in industry continued to expand but an increasing proportion of the supply used by industry was imported. Until the end of the eighteenth century, however, among the industries dependent on animal or vegetable raw materials only cotton and silk secured all their supplies from overseas. In other industries overseas sources remained marginal before 1800, with one major exception, the import of timber.[66]

Towards the end of the eighteenth century the number of 'ghost acres' located overseas upon which England could draw began to rise with increasing rapidity. For the produce of warmer climes – such crops as cotton, silk, sugar, coffee, and tea – dependence on an overseas source had always been a natural consequence of agricultural geography. For other agricultural produce home soil had long remained the dominant source of supply, but the tide turned when population growth and industrial production accelerated late in the eighteenth century so that during the early nineteenth century overseas

---

[62] Clarkson, 'The manufacture of leather', tab. 5.13, p. 467.

[63] Chartres, 'The marketing of agricultural produce', p. 447.

[64] 'Until the end of the eighteenth century most hides and virtually all bark came from the English countryside, and tanners, therefore, were valuable customers for the by-products of animal husbandry and timber production.' Clarkson, 'The manufacture of leather', p. 466.

[65] Crafts, *British economic growth*, tab. 2.3, p. 22.

[66] The degree of self-sufficiency of England alone as opposed to Britain or to the British Isles was probably less than suggested by this paragraph, but it is difficult to be more precise for lack of firm evidence.

supply gradually increased in importance, in providing both food and organic raw materials. This should not, however, obscure the remarkable nature of earlier achievement in agriculture. In the measurement of its scale, precision is beyond reach, but output probably tripled between 1600 and 1800 and this came from a largely unchanging labour force. Urban growth and the changes which followed in its wake provided much of the incentive to increase output.

The London effect

Urban growth not only played a vital role in stimulating agricultural development, it was also fundamental to a range of other changes which were contributing to the transformation of England. Urban dwelling promoted literacy. A very high proportion of the population of London was able to read, and no doubt numeracy advanced in parallel to literacy.[67] Literacy furthered the interchange of information and ideas, promoting changes in life-styles in ways that were helpful to economic growth. A 'consumer revolution' is much easier to engender among an increasingly literate population than in a society dependent upon word of mouth. London exerted a powerful influence not only on those living in the capital but throughout the whole country. In the eighteenth century, news of the latest London fashions reached all parts of the country metaphorically overnight and immediately affected consumer choice, not only among the more prosperous elements in society but far down the social pyramid.[68]

By the later seventeenth century, when the population of London had risen to the half million mark, about a tenth of the national population was living there, but it is reasonable to suppose that at least a sixth of the population had direct experience of living in London.[69] Many others had made briefer visits. Acquaintance with London life was not confined to those who lived close to it. The notes made by Richard Gough of Myddle, a village close to Shrewsbury, about his fellow parishioners in the later seventeenth century illustrates the frequency and routine nature of contact between his village and London.

[67] See p. 227 below, and Cressy, 'Literacy in context', pp. 315–17.
[68] McKendrick, 'The consumer revolution'; de Vries, 'Between purchasing power and the world of goods'.
[69] Wrigley, 'London's importance', p. 137.

Myddle was about 160 miles distant from London. Hey remarks in his introduction to an edition of Gough that, 'He frequently mentions London in passing as if it were commonplace that his neighbours should have been there. Men and women from all sections of his community went to the capital in search of fortune or excitement or to escape from trouble at home. Most of them kept in contact with their families, and further information about events in London and other parts of the country filtered back to Myddle through "the Gazet" and "our News letters".'[70]

As already noted, the absolute numbers in secondary and tertiary employment increased at least fourfold. A substantial part of this increase took place in towns, where employment was almost exclusively in these two categories. The exact proportion depends upon the definition of settlement size which is taken to denote 'urban' living. If the limit is set at 5,000 inhabitants the proportion is less than half.[71] If set lower at, say, 2,500, it would probably exceed half. But there was also a very large increase in the proportion of the rural population not primarily engaged in working the land. Rural industrial employment increased markedly and increasing numbers made a living in service occupations. Shopkeepers were omnipresent in towns and increasingly in villages by the later eighteenth century; many more places boasted a school master or mistress; and the list of tertiary occupations which were increasing rapidly in small towns and rural areas could be much extended. The immediate cause of rising secondary and tertiary employment in the countryside was the increase in the proportion of local income and expenditure which could be spared for the purchase of 'comforts' and even 'luxuries' rather than being reserved to pay for necessities. Such changes were greatly aided by the improvement in transport facilities which made such purchases available and affordable countrywide. But, at one remove, change of this sort was dependent on the agricultural sector being able to continue to feed a rising population without significantly increasing labour input and without a crippling rise in product prices. The increasing size of the secondary and tertiary sectors of the economy relative to

---

[70] Gough, *The history of Myddle*, p. 19. The scale of movement to London from distant parts of the country in the sixteenth century is vividly clear from the registers of freemen on the rolls of the London livery companies. See also Rappaport, *Worlds within worlds*, esp. pp. 76–86.

[71] Tab. 3.2, p. 61, for the scale of urban growth.

the primary sector was contingent upon the latter avoiding the fate which Ricardian analysis had made to appear inescapable.

Conclusion

There is a saying that 'With each mouth there comes a pair of hands.' It was in the past often taken as a rebuttal of the pessimistic view that further population increase must spell increasing difficulty. It suggests that, although it is true that an additional mouth will cause an increased claim on the available supply of food, the work performed by the new arrival will mean that there is a balancing increase in that supply. In a Malthusian or Ricardian world the pessimists normally had the better of this argument, at least in any country which was long settled and fully peopled. Yet England in the seventeenth and eighteenth centuries represented an important exception to the normal rule. The most important industry of all, agriculture, succeeded in meeting both the increased demand for food and the massive rise in the demand for the industrial raw materials, although relatively little new land was taken into cultivation and despite the fact that the population more than doubled. Moreover, this was achieved without great change in the workforce engaged in agriculture. By the end of the period it was as if with each new mouth on the farm there came not merely one pair of hands but two pairs. There is thus a striking irony in the fact that although the arguments of Malthus and Ricardo hold good generally for organic economies, events in their native land for several preceding generations showed clearly that their analyses were in this instance wide of the mark.

The argument of this chapter has been that there was an intimate connection between urban growth and beneficial change in agriculture. Urban growth and agricultural improvement did not, however, take place in isolation. In the next three chapters other favourable developments or structural features of English economy and society which helped to transform the country during the early modern period are described, beginning with the radical changes taking place in energy supply and its implications for transport facilities.

4 | *Energy and transport*

The central importance of overcoming the energy constraint which haunted all organic economies, and the links between the rise of the coal industry and improvement to transport facilities, have been touched on already. Both the character and the significance of these developments merit further attention. They represent a second area of the economy in which positive feedback brought sustained and increasing benefit.

In organic economies the bulk of the mechanical energy came from human and animal muscle, and wood was the dominant source of heat energy. The production of all types of material goods necessarily involved the expenditure of energy and the same was true of all forms of transport. In early modern Europe there was in general a close similarity between different countries in the scale of energy which could be secured for productive purposes measured per head of population. In northern areas, such as Sweden, the coldness of the winter caused a larger consumption of firewood than further south, but the collection of comparative data on a common basis for an increasing number of countries emphasises the extent of the features common to them all.[1]

The history of energy consumption

The first results are now appearing of a collaborative venture to collect and publish energy consumption information on a common basis, involving scholars from a range of European countries. The first two countries covered have been Italy and England and Wales and for each there is a published volume setting out the results.[2] Italy, having been perhaps the most advanced country in Europe in medieval times, tended

---

[1] The assembly of comparative data is being undertaken by a group of scholars from many European countries as a result of an initiative taken principally by Astrid Kander and Paul Warde.

[2] Malanima, *Energy consumption in Italy*; Warde, *Energy consumption in England and Wales*.

Table 4.1 *Energy consumption in England and Wales (1561–70) compared with Italy (1861–70)*

Annual energy consumption per head of population (megajoules)

	Human	Draught animals	Firewood	Wind	Water	Fossil fuels	Total
England and Wales 1561–70	4,373	6,210	6,324	59	162	2,039	19,167
Italy 1861–70	3,832	3,053	8,894	46	127	1,206	17,158
Percentage distribution							
England and Wales 1561–70	22.8	32.4	33.0	0.3	0.8	10.6	100.0
Italy 1861–70	22.3	17.8	51.8	0.3	0.7	7.0	100.0

Note. Because of the effects of rounding, the constituent percentages do not always sum to 100 exactly.
Sources. Malanima, *Energy consumption in Italy*, app. 1, tabs. 2 and 3, pp. 96–101; Warde, *Energy consumption in England and Wales*, app. 1, tabs 2 and 3, pp. 123–36.

to regress on most measures of economic performance in early modern times and did not recover momentum until late in the nineteenth century.[3] In table 4.1 Italy's pattern of energy consumption in the decade 1861–70 is compared with the English situation three centuries earlier in 1561–70. (For simplicity, reference is made only to England, rather than England and Wales, in this and the following paragraph.)

Both the authors from whose work table 4.1 was constructed would emphasise that exactitude is well beyond reach and that the estimates may well need modification in the light of further research. It is inevitable, moreover, that the error bounds implicitly surrounding the estimates are substantially wider for sixteenth- than for nineteenth-century estimates. Yet the table is nonetheless instructive. Overall energy consumption per head did not differ greatly between the two countries, though separated by three centuries, a reminder that the constraints on productivity imposed by the limited supply of energy provided by photosynthesis were much the same in all European countries before the situation was transformed by gaining access to the vast stores of energy accumulated over geological eras in the form of fossil fuels. There are, however, both instructive similarities and differences in the two series.

Human energy intake was broadly similar in the two countries, though somewhat lower in Italy than in England. Part of the difference may be related to the higher average temperatures in Italy, which would tend to reduce the calorie intake needed to sustain body temperature. The energy consumed by draught animals was more than twice as great in England as in Italy, probably a reflection of the greater suitability of the English climate and soils for grass growth and hence for pastoral production. Heat energy from the use of firewood was more widely employed in Italy (though accurate estimation is especially difficult for this energy source) but even in the 1560s England was deriving more heat energy per head of population from coal than Italy in the 1860s so that the combined total consumption of heat energy was not greatly different between the two. In neither country was wind or water a major energy source and it is notable that the absolute figures for the two countries are remarkably similar. The table makes it clear that human and animal muscle was the dominant source of mechanical energy in the two countries, and that in both countries firewood supplied most of the heat energy. Yet even in the 1560s coal was

---

[3] Malanima, 'Urbanisation and the Italian economy'.

Table 4.2 *Annual energy consumption in England and Wales 1561–70 to 1850–9*

	Human	Draught animals	Firewood	Wind	Water	Coal	Total
Annual energy consumption (terajoules)							
1561–70	14,860	21,100	21,490	200	550	6,930	65,130
1600–9	19,190	21,430	21,810	390	700	14,540	78,060
1650–9	26,080	27,700	22,200	880	900	39,060	116,820
1700–9	27,330	32,780	22,480	1,360	990	84,000	168,940
1750–9	29,730	33,640	22,560	2,810	1,300	140,810	230,850
1800–9	41,810	34,290	18,540	12,660	1,100	408,680	517,080
1850–9	67,800	50,090	2,240	24,360	1,700	1,689,100	1,835,300
Annual energy consumption per head of population (megajoules)							
1561–70	4,373	6,210	6,324	59	162	2,039	19,167
1600–9	4,161	4,647	4,729	85	152	3,153	16,925
1650–9	4,521	4,802	3,849	153	156	6,772	20,253
1700–9	4,789	5,744	3,939	238	173	14,719	29,602
1750–9	4,519	5,113	3,429	427	198	21,403	35,089
1800–9	4,233	3,471	1,877	1,282	111	41,373	52,347
1850–9	3,564	2,633	118	1,280	89	88,779	96,462

Note. The 1850–9 firewood figure refers to 1840–9 rather than the next decade. Warde stopped the series after the 1840–9 decade because firewood usage had by then reached a very low level. Estimated population totals for England and Wales were obtained by multiplying the totals for England alone by 1.07.

Source. Warde, *Energy consumption in England and Wales*, app. 1, tabs 1, 2, and 3, pp. 115–36.

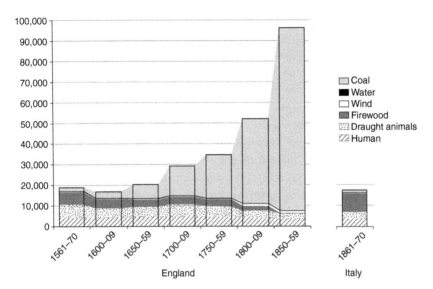

Figure 4.1 *Annual energy consumption per head (megajoules) in England and Wales 1561–70 to 1850–9 and in Italy 1861–70.*
Source. Tables 4.1 and 4.2.

beginning to be a significant source of heat energy in England though its contribution was still dwarfed by that of firewood.

Sufficient is already known about other European countries to leave little room for doubt that with only minor modifications the level and pattern of energy use found in England and Italy would be replicated elsewhere in Europe before the nineteenth century. There are occasional exceptions to this generalisation. In the Netherlands, for example, the abundant and accessible reserves of peat played a role similar to coal in England. As a result, the Netherlands in the seventeenth century was an 'energy-rich' economy when compared to her neighbours, favouring the growth of energy-intensive industries such as brewing, brickmaking, sugar refining, bleaching and dyeing, and the production of salt. Similarities, however, were much more conspicuous than differences. The odd man out, of course, was England, which during the seventeenth and eighteenth centuries drifted slowly but steadily away from the European norm, as will be clear from considering table 4.2. The scale of the change taking place in England and the extent of the contrast between England and Italy which was brought about by this change is visible in figure 4.1, which depicts both the massive rise in energy consumption per head of population and the increasing dominance of coal in the English energy regime between the mid-sixteenth and the mid-nineteenth century and also rehearses the Italian situation at the latter period.

Table 4.2 is divided into two sections. The upper section shows annual total consumption figures for each source of energy, while the lower section shows consumption per head of population. It is instructive to consider consumption per head as well as gross consumption since the population grew more than fivefold between the mid-sixteenth and the mid-nineteenth century.[4] Given the very large increase in population, gross energy consumption was bound to rise markedly, but consumption per head for some types of energy might change little or indeed decline. The lower section of the table illustrates this point. For example, although total human food consumption increased greatly, consumption per head changed very little and was lower at the end of the period than at its beginning. Again, the total of energy derived from firewood did not change greatly until the very end of the period, when it was considered no longer to be a significant element in the energy picture, but even at the beginning of the nineteenth century consumption per head was less than a third as high as in the early years of Elizabeth's reign.

Coal and wind power were the only two energy sources which increased in absolute terms, as a percentage of total energy consumption, and when expressed per head of population. Change over the three centuries covered by the table was dominated by the enormous growth of coal consumption. Its proportionate share in energy consumption rose from a tenth to more than nine-tenths of the total. The increase in wind power reflects the rapid expansion of the merchant fleet, which remained entirely wind-powered until the beginning of the nineteenth century. Coal consumption per head increased by a multiple of about 45 between Tudor and Victorian times, an average annual rate of growth of approximately 1.3 per cent per annum, which implies almost a doubling every half-century. It is a striking fact that the rate of increase varied only modestly from one half-century to the next.

Figure 4.1 conveys effectively both the striking dominance achieved by coal by the early nineteenth century and the fact that its rise was not the product of recent decades but had been taking place constantly

---

[4] Wrigley *et al.*, *English population history*, tab. A9.1, pp. 614–15.

and steadily from Tudor times. It also brings home the scale of the contrast between England and Italy in the mid-nineteenth century whereas there had been no significant difference between the two countries in the mid-sixteenth century. In the mid-sixteenth century mechanical energy was derived almost entirely from human and animal muscle which between them accounted for more than half of the total of energy consumption. Heat energy came mainly from wood, which was roughly three times as important as coal. Energy consumption per head quintupled over the three centuries but if coal is excluded from the picture there is a modest decline rather than striking growth.

In order to construct series covering every energy source over the whole period from the beginning of Elizabeth's reign to the present day, Warde was inevitably obliged to make use of estimates and assumptions which in the earlier centuries involve wide margins of uncertainty. Yet it is unlikely that the 'big picture' would change greatly if more exact data were available. It seems clear that the scale of energy available and its rate of growth set England increasingly apart from other countries.

In considering the several energy sources covered in table 4.2, it is important to bear in mind that the estimates refer to energy 'consumption', which may differ substantially from the totals of useful work performed in the case of mechanical energy or of heat directly captured in the production process in the case of thermal energy. For example, as already noted, a substantial but variable proportion of the food energy consumed by all animals, human or otherwise, is needed to keep the individual person or beast alive. Where food is scarce this may represent a large fraction of the total consumed, leaving little available for productive work.[5] In organic economies, where heavy physical labour on the land was unavoidable for a large fraction of the workforce, the possible implications of prolonged undernourishment were both serious and intermittently real and immediate. Similarly, much of the heat energy released by burning wood or coal on domestic hearths was lost up the flue or chimney, and the same was true of operations in the forge or the glass furnace. This means that the absolute quantities set out in the preceding tables are often

[5] See above p. 15 for an illustration of this point in relation to human food consumption.

misleadingly large when considered in relation to work performed, but trends in energy inputs may still remain a valuable guide to *trends* in energy outputs. It was probably the case that the efficiency with which energy was used improved somewhat over time in most of the energy sources in use, so that the rise in energy consumption per head visible in table 4.2 understates the rate of growth in energy captured in productive processes.

Some series in table 4.2 may need revision in future. For example, the rise in the total of energy consumption by draught animals appears remarkably modest between 1600 and 1800. In this period it rises by only 60 per cent. This may reflect an internal inconsistency in Warde's estimates since the number of draught animals expressed in horse equivalents is recorded as rising by 90 per cent between 1600 and 1800.[6] Other considerations also suggest that the energy output derived from draught animals rose much more substantially than the energy consumption data in table 4.2 suggest. The average size of animals increased and fodder regimes changed in a way which would also have tended to increase energy consumption per animal markedly. For example, during the two centuries in question the production of oats increased more quickly than any other cereal, and the fact that human consumption of oats claimed a steadily falling percentage of the crop suggests a major increase in energy consumption by draught animals.

Despite any minor caveats about particular features of table 4.2, Warde's work represents a contribution of fundamental importance to the appreciation of the changes in the English economy which were taking place in the seventeenth and eighteenth centuries. It brings out perhaps more vividly than any other comparable series the contrast between England and the continent in this period.

Coal already dominated the energy picture in England as early as the end of the seventeenth century, and in the nineteenth century eclipsed all rival sources almost entirely. But this was not true in other European countries until a much later date. Belgium was the first continental country to dig coal on a substantial scale and remained the largest individual continental producer until the 1850s. In 1850–4 the average annual Belgian production was 6.8 million metric tons. In the same period the comparable figures for France and Germany were 5.3 and 6.5 millions respectively. These three countries were the largest continental

[6] Warde, *Energy consumption in England and Wales*, tab. 3, p. 45.

producers. In the same period the average annual output in England and Wales was 61.4 millions.[7] At the beginning of the nineteenth century the disparity was substantially greater. In the early 1850s the combined output of Belgium, France, and Germany was about 30 per cent of the total for England and Wales. Half a century earlier the comparable figure was probably less than 20 per cent.[8] Expressed per head of population the contrast was even starker. In the 1850s the average output per head in the three continental countries combined was c.0.24 tons: the comparable figure for England and Wales was c.3.41 tons.

As already noted, one way of bringing home the degree to which England had moved away from the constraints associated with organic economies by 1800 is to convert coal production into the equivalent acreage of wood which would have been required to produce the same quantity of energy on a sustained-yield basis. Using the production totals for England and Wales given in table 2.1 and on the assumption that, on a sustained-yield basis, an acre of woodland can produce wood providing the same heat energy as a ton of coal,[9] the acreages in question in 1750, 1800, and 1850 are 4.3, 11.2, and 48.1 million respectively. As a proportion of the land surface of the country these figures represent 13, 35, and 150 per cent of the total area. Even the first of the percentages would have represented a significant proportion of the land surface for which there were many other competing uses. The second would have been quite impractical, while the third is self-evidently an impossibility.

It is familiar ground to stress that, although the cheapness and abundance of coal made its use attractive wherever energy was needed on a large scale, the practical difficulties in substituting coal for existing energy sources often presented problems. They were trivial or non-existent in some industries. For example, in heating a dye vat the object to be heated and the heat source were separated by a metal barrier, and coal could be used without altering any other aspect of the operation. But in other cases decades of experiment were

---

[7] For Belgian, French, and German output, Mitchell, *European historical statistics*, tab. E2, pp. 381–91. The total for England and Wales is taken from Church, *British coal industry*, III, tab. 1.1, p. 3.

[8] The output of the continental countries was estimated from the scattered data in Mitchell, *European historical statistics*, tab. E2, pp. 381–91. The total for England and Wales is given in Flinn, *British coal industry*, II, tab. 1.3, p. 26.

[9] Wrigley, *Continuity, chance and change*, pp. 54–5.

needed to find a method of using coal which resulted in a product fully comparable to that produced by traditional methods. The most famous instance of this was the search for a fully satisfactory method of smelting iron with coal, but similar problems were experienced in many other industries. The incentive to overcome any initial difficulties was strong in England in part because coal was so cheap and its advantage over alternative energy sources therefore so clear.

It is also commonplace to regard the gradual supplanting of the 'atmospheric' Newcomen engine, which relied on the creation of a vacuum by the condensation of steam to drive a piston, by an engine which harnessed the expansive power of steam, as the key development of the coal age. It was then possible to provide mechanical energy on an unprecedented scale across almost the entire span of industrial production. Before the steam engine arrived coal had shown that it could transform the thermal energy scene but muscle power remained by far the most important source of mechanical energy. Neither water nor wind power was of more than limited significance, except in the case of sailing ships.[10] The steam engine meant that coal could be exploited to supply mechanical energy as readily as heat energy, thus overcoming the last remaining barrier to the application of fossil fuel energy to all the main productive processes. It was not until the second quarter of the nineteenth century, however, that the steam engine became the dominant source of power in manufacturing processes. A string of inventions and improvements had been needed to overcome the various deficiencies and limitations of the Newcomen engine and to replace it with a machine whose operation was dependable and economical and which could be harnessed to provide rotary motion.[11] Watt's engine represented a decisive advance but it, too, required much development before attaining the levels of efficiency reached in the Victorian period. Nevertheless, the discovery of a way of meeting the energy needs of an economy from a single source, which was not subject to the limitations associated with dependence on the annual round of plant photosynthesis, was the decisive step in ensuring that growth would not be halted by the changes induced by its earlier successes.

[10] Tab. 4.2, p. 94.
[11] See Allen, *The British industrial revolution*, pp. 164–76.

The rapid growth in coal use, to the point where no other source of energy made more than a marginal contribution to the total picture, should not be viewed as demonstrating that coal dominated the landscape of the industrial revolution. All, or virtually all, industries came eventually to depend heavily upon it either for heat or for mechanical energy or for both, but several industries played a prominent part in the transformation for decades before switching to the steam engine as a power source. In the early expansion of the textile industries, for example, mechanical energy came largely from the human arm and the water wheel.

Although prominent in the early expansion of many industries, as in the manufacture of glass or bricks, the strategic significance of coal in the industrial revolution did not consist principally in generating an early momentum, in causing a 'take-off': it lay in the fact that it enabled expansion to continue rather than being brought to a halt by the energy constraints inherent in organic economies which forbade sustained exponential growth over a lengthy period. The quantity of energy needed to underwrite the scale of material production reached in England by the middle decades of the nineteenth century would have been far beyond attainment in an organic economy and, in the absence of coal, this would have prevented growth on a comparable scale. It was not that many of the changes taking place in England in the eighteenth century would have been unthinkable in the absence of coal but that the continued growth of the economy in the following century would have been impossible.

Coal production and transport provision

The importance of coal as an energy source, though sometimes left largely unremarked, has been widely recognised. Its importance in bringing about radical improvements in transport provision has perhaps been less fully acknowledged. It was a basic weakness of organic economies that heavy investment in transport infrastructure was unlikely to produce savings sufficient to justify the expenditure involved. The increasing volume of coal production changed this situation.

Consider first inland transport. Most production in organic economies was areal in nature. To produce the tens of thousands of bushels of wheat needed to feed a large town involved cultivating thousands of acres of arable land. To secure firewood to meet its needs for domestic heating similarly meant cutting and collecting wood from a very large area. Only when the carts and wagons carrying the wheat or wood neared the town did they become concentrated on a few roads bearing a large traffic. Their early miles on the way to the town were inevitably along roads which carried little traffic. Since the bulk of the journey was on poor roads, transport costs per ton-mile were apt to be high. The continued use of pack horses rather than carts into the eighteenth century, and even in some areas into the nineteenth,[12] reflected the existence of many road surfaces so rutted or muddy that wheeled traffic was impractical. Local traffic was also normally light. A large investment in minor roads, whether in new construction or maintenance, was unlikely to produce savings large enough to repay the outlay. Yet roads which were of poor quality and in poor repair discouraged heavier usage, producing a vicious circle of neglect and little traffic.

The state of the roads set limits to much else in early modern England, but inland transport could, of course, be conducted by water as well as by road. Where river navigation was possible it was attractive to send goods by water, especially for bulk cargoes, since costs per ton-mile were much lower on water than by road. And it was probably the case that England was better placed than most countries to benefit from river transport, both because the rainfall regime meant that seasonal fluctuation in the scale of river flows was relatively modest and because river gradients presented severe problems less often than in some continental countries. River improvement schemes were much discussed and occasionally implemented, though the difficulty of reconciling such plans with the interests of those who used river water for other purposes, for example to drive mill wheels or for fishing, often produced conflict. And there remained the problem that although inland water transport could facilitate exchange within a river basin, it could not provide a solution to the problem of improving exchange between different river basins.

Often, in the circumstances prevailing in organic economies, the high cost of transport was instrumental in limiting growth possibilities. It limited severely the possible gains to be achieved by the division of labour, since the size of the accessible market determined how far the division of labour could be carried. However, in relation to

[12] Flinn, *British coal industry*, II, p. 148.

transport provision, as in relation to energy provision, the rising scale of coal production brought solutions to problems which had previously proved intractable.

In contrast to the produce of the land, mineral production was punctiform rather than areal. This meant a more favourable environment for investment in transport facilities since large volumes of goods moved along a single route or a small number of routes. With the passage of time, the weight of coal dug greatly exceeded that of other minerals, and indeed of other goods generally, and so exerted a disproportionate influence in creating new transport facilities. The price of coal to the consumer was powerfully affected by transport cost. It was widely assumed in the eighteenth century that the land carriage of coal doubled its pithead price within ten miles.[13] When the volume of coal output remained modest, traditional methods of transport continued to be widely used. It was, for example, taken by pack horse to the Northwich salt pans from the Staffordshire coalfield and from the Yorkshire pits to the Bradford dyers. But when the volume to be moved was large the incentive to create new facilities increased commensurately. Many individual collieries in the eighteenth century measured their annual output in tens of thousands of tons, occasionally exceeding 50,000 tons.[14] The cost per ton-mile when coal was transported by water was taken to be only one twentieth of the price of land carriage.[15] Where the potential savings from the transport of other goods very seldom appeared to justify constructing a canal to reduce costs, coal, because of the quantity produced, and because its production was punctiform and its consumption also often punctiform (where, for example, the demand came from a single large town), transformed the scale of the prospective gain from the large initial outlay needed to dig a canal.[16]

The reduction in the cost of coal to the consumer which came in the wake of canal construction was notable. A particular instance will illustrate the scale of the reduction which was possible. In Northampton in 1750 coal cost 30d a hundredweight (cwt) even though its price at

---

[13] *Ibid.*, p. 146.

[14] *Ibid.*, tab. 1.1, p. 24.

[15] *Ibid.*, p. 146.

[16] A contemporary calculated that 90 of the 165 canal acts passed between 1758 and 1802 regarded coal as their chief propective traffic. Mathias, *The first industrial nation*, p. 102.

the pithead in Warwickshire which was then the source of its supply was only 4d a cwt. When the river Nene was made navigable a decade later the town was able to obtain Newcastle coal for 21d a cwt. When the Grand Junction Canal was opened some years later it brought canal access to within four miles of Northampton and the price of coal plummeted by half to 11–12d a cwt.[17] Not only did a reduction in cost of this magnitude in many towns undoubtedly mean that average domestic temperatures in the winter months could rise though outlay on domestic heating fell, it also made it possible for a wider range of industries which needed cheap fuel to establish themselves. Later the creation of a railway network carried access to cheap coal a stage further. Advantages which were once confined to coalfield areas and to cities like London which could use coastal shipping to supply their fuel needs were extended to the bulk of the country by the mid-nineteenth century. The canal network took shape only slowly. It took over half a century to produce a national canal network in the later decades of the eighteenth century and early in the following century. Most canals were built to meet a local need and even on trunk canals the length of an average haul was only about twenty miles. Yet the cumulative impact of canal construction both in stimulating growth and in changing the location of industrial activity was marked.[18]

The same considerations also encouraged investment in improving the roads where there was a similar incentive as, for example, from coal pits close to the Tyne to the coal staithes on the river. Roads on Tyneside and elsewhere were converted to wagonways by laying down planks to reduce friction and enable a greater load to be transported with a smaller expenditure of energy. The results could be striking. One horse on a wagonway could pull as much as two horses and two oxen on an unimproved road.[19] Steps were taken to reduce the gradients on wagonways, which added to the gain from reducing friction. Further gains in productivity came in the course of the eighteenth century when cast-iron and later wrought-iron rails and flanged wheels were introduced to reduce friction still further. As a result, with the same expenditure of energy, a horse could produce still more ton-miles. Marrying the railed way to the steam engine to reduce still further the

---

[17] Szostak, *Transportation in the industrial revolution*, p. 118.
[18] These issues are discussed with authority by Turnbull, 'Canals, coal and regional growth'.
[19] Flinn, *British coal industry*, II, p. 149.

cost of transporting coal was obviously an attractive possibility once James Watt had adapted steam power to rotary motion in the 1780s, but it was only in the 1810s that several types of locomotive were developed which performed successfully.[20] Thereafter horses were rapidly replaced by steam power on colliery railways. This in turn proved the preliminary to the construction of a national railway system whose main network was substantially complete by the mid-century.

There was a second aspect of transport provision which was radically improved by the increasing prominence of coal in the national economy, since the movement of goods by sea was also much changed. Adam Smith emphasised the importance of water transport in determining the possible scale and nature of economic growth in an organic economy. He stressed the benefit of access to water transport, especially for heavy and bulky goods:

As by means of water-carriage a more extensive market is opened to every sort of industry than what land-carriage can afford it, so it is upon the sea-coast, and along the banks of navigable rivers, that industry of every kind naturally begins to subdivide and improve itself, and it is frequently not till a long time after that those improvements extend themselves to the inland parts of the country.[21]

He went on to give details of the number of men and animals, wagons and ships, needed to transport goods between Edinburgh and London by the two means of transport, together with the journey times of each type, and summarised his findings as follows:

Upon two hundred tons of goods, therefore, carried by the cheapest land-carriage from London to Edinburgh, there must be charged the maintenance of a hundred men for three weeks, and both the maintenance, and, what is nearly equal to the maintenance, the wear and tear of four hundred horses as well as of fifty great waggons. Whereas, upon the same quantity of goods carried by water, there is to be charged only the maintenance of six or eight men, and the wear and tear of a ship of two hundred tons burthen, together with the value of the superior risk, or the difference of the insurance between land and water-carriage.[22]

---

[20] *Ibid.*, pp. 153–6.
[21] Smith, *Wealth of nations*, I, p. 22.
[22] *Ibid.*, p. 22.

Smith then pointed out that if only land carriage were possible between the two cities only goods with a very high value to weight ratio would be exchanged between them, to the detriment of the prosperity of both.

Smith's example illustrates the general advantage of sea transport over transport by road for bulky cargoes but *improvement* in sea transport sprang disproportionately from the growth of traffic over a single sea route, and once more it was the increasing use of coal which provoked change. It came about, like so much else, from the meteoric growth of London during the sixteenth and seventeenth centuries. Already in Tudor times Newcastle coal was replacing wood as the main fuel used in the capital and London's consumption rose steadily and rapidly thereafter. London was a long way from a coalfield and it would have been impossible to meet her fuel needs with coal supplies if there had not been a major field close to the sea. In Northumberland and Durham there were coal seams close to the surface and close to the Tyne. Geological good fortune therefore made it possible for London to replace wood with coal even though the coalfield from which it was mined was almost 300 miles distant. To satisfy London's demand, however, implied the creation of a large fleet of vessels to satisfy this demand, which reflected the requirements both of domestic heating and of a range of industrial purposes. On the banks of the Thames, for example, glassworks and breweries were built to take advantage of access to a cheap source of heat. London's population grew rapidly and its demand for coal grew roughly in parallel. At the beginning of the seventeenth century the annual import of coal to London was probably in the range 125,000 to 150,000 tons. By the end of the century it was approaching 500,000 tons.[23] Over the same period the population of the capital rose from c.200,000 to c.575,000 people.[24] Consumption per head therefore appears to have risen only very slightly, if at all, during the century. By the end of the eighteenth century London was importing a total of about 1.2 million tons of coal annually, almost exclusively from the same north-east ports.[25] Since London's population had risen to 950,000 by 1800, consumption per head had again changed only modestly, increasing by perhaps a quarter during the century. Yet the capital's growth was so marked that

[23] Hatcher, *British coal industry*, I, tab. 14.6, pp. 501–2.
[24] See tab. 3.2, p. 61.
[25] Flinn, *British coal industry*, II, tab. 7.2. p. 217.

the absolute tonnage of coal imported to London increased roughly tenfold over the seventeenth and eighteenth centuries.

To transport coal on this scale required a very substantial shipping capacity. As with the land carriage of coal, the price of coal carried over water was heavily influenced by the cost of transport to market. At the pithead coal was cheap. Transporting it any distance might make it prohibitively expensive for many purposes, even with the benefit of water carriage. Coal therefore created a stronger incentive than any other commodity carried by sea to increase the ton-miles performed by the average member of a ship's crew in order to reduce shipping costs. Nef estimated that the average size of a cargo of coal imported to London increased from 56 tons in 1592 to 248 tons in 1701 and that during this period the labour requirement per ton-mile performed was reduced by at least half.[26] Already by the time of the Restoration the tonnage of colliers probably exceeded that of all other British merchantmen combined.[27] In addition, the men who sailed on the colliers formed, in effect, a prime reserve of manpower to be pressed into naval service in wartime.

The gains in efficiency in the coal trade which were already substantial during the seventeenth century continued thereafter. There were further efficiency gains during the eighteenth century. Ville estimated that whereas in the mid-seventeenth century the manning ratio on colliers was one man for every 8 tons of coal, this figure had more than doubled to 18 tons by the end of the eighteenth century and lay in the range 25–50 tons by the mid-nineteenth. The vessels employed in the coal trade increased in size and sailed faster, helped by the spread of copper bottoming in the later part of the eighteenth century. The annual average number of voyages per vessel doubled during the century. Quicker turn-round times, improved harbour facilities, and related changes such as lighthouse construction and navigational buoys all supported further improvement, and greater consistency in supply made it possible for merchants to reduce the size of their coal stocks relative to sale volumes.[28] It is probably safe to assume that the productivity both of the capital and of the labour employed in the London coal trade doubled in the seventeenth century and doubled again in the eighteenth, an annual rate of increase of c.0.7 per cent. What was true of the London coal trade may well have been representative of the shipping industry generally.

---

[26] Nef, *The rise of the British coal industry*, I, p. 390.
[27] *Ibid.*, I, pp. 239–40.
[28] Ville, 'The English shipping industry'.

Other improvements in transport facilities

Though many of the developments in transport technology and transport provision were closely linked to large-scale coal production, there were also major improvements in transport facilities which owed little to the coal industry but were associated with other changes taking place in the early modern English economy. The most striking of these changes were the improvements arising from the turnpiking of thousands of miles of roads in the eighteenth and early nineteenth centuries.

The first turnpike trust was created in 1663, but turnpike construction only increased markedly from early in the eighteenth century. By 1770 there were 15,000 miles of turnpiked roads and this figure had risen to 22,000 miles in the mid-1830s, managed by more than 1,100 turnpike trusts in England and Wales.[29] Adopting the principle that the user should pay proved a most effective way of securing better road surfaces. The incentive to do so rose as the volume of current and prospective traffic increased. The results reflect the scale of the benefit. Journey times and costs per ton-mile both fell, while traffic volumes increased sharply. The reduction in journey times was dramatic. Between the 1750s and the 1830s journey times between major centres fell by four-fifths.[30] The result was a marked contrast in journey times between England and continental Europe. For example, in the 1760s French services travelled between 40 and 55 kilometres in a day when the comparable range in England was between 80 and 130 kilometres a day. In both countries services quickened in the following decades but a marked difference in average speed continued.[31] The movement of goods was revolutionised as much or more than the movement of people by the improvements made to the road system. Much larger wagons could be used on turnpike roads. The biggest and most sophisticated road haulage operations centred on London. It has been estimated that the weekly output of the London road haulage industry rose from 13,000 ton-miles in 1715 to 80,000 in 1765, 275,000 in 1816, and 459,000 in 1840.[32] Transport by canal barge was much cheaper per ton-mile than

---

[29] Bagwell, *The transport revolution*, pp. 38–9; Szostak, *Transportation in the industrial revolution*, p. 68.
[30] Bagwell, *The transport revolution*, p. 41.
[31] Szostak, *Transportation in the industrial revolution*, p. 70.
[32] Chartres and Turnbull, 'Road transport', tab. 7, p. 85.

sending goods by turnpike road but the road might still be preferred for some goods. For example, for the long-distance transport of cotton goods turnpike roads were often favoured because they provided a regular and reliable service and were quicker.[33]

High transport costs may be compared to high tariff barriers. Products from other places are denied access to a local market as effectively by the lack of cheap and reliable transport as by an arbitrary charge at an entry gate. Where roads are rutted in summer and muddy in winter movement is difficult, slow, and intermittently dangerous. Their condition may prohibit the use of carts and wagons. In such circumstances a village may have little option other than to satisfy from within its borders the bulk of its material needs. Poor transport facilities and a 'peasant' mentality go hand in hand. Conversely, if transport is relatively easy, cheap, and reliable, economic activity can be organised very differently. Movement along a spectrum of transport provision with difficult, expensive, and unreliable facilities at one extreme and dependable, cheap facilities at the other will produce a host of associated changes. Szostak, for example, suggested that in the early eighteenth century merchants would load their products on pack horses and travel through the country selling their goods directly at fairs and markets, quoting the practice of Abraham Darby as an example. By the end of the century, in contrast, travelling salesmen carrying samples sought orders which were fulfilled by dispatching goods by road carriers. Turnpike roads could accommodate regular wagon traffic and orders taken by the salesmen could be dealt with quickly and reliably. Aikin is quoted by Szostak as noting that the shift from loaded pack horses to travellers with samples took place between 1730 and 1770 in the Lancashire textile industry. Another linked change was the gradual transformation of fairs from a major point of contact between producer and retailer and final purchaser into chiefly social events. The retail shopkeeper assumed the role once played by the fair.[34]

Improvements in road transport were closely linked to rapid urban growth and the transformation in agricultural output, as well as to the continued rise in manufacturing output. They complemented the changes brought about by the problems and opportunities of the massive rise in coal production. The combined result of all the

---

[33] Timmins, *Made in Lancashire*, p. 142.
[34] Szostak, *Transportation in the industrial revolution*, pp. 14–15, 19.

improvements in transport facilities during the seventeenth and eighteenth centuries was a marked fall in the transport costs, much greater speed of movement both of people and goods, and fuller market integration. The improvements were as central to the general transformation of the economy as those taking place in agriculture or in energy provision. All were interconnected to a degree which makes their separate consideration somewhat artificial.

Conclusion

The opening sentence of *The wealth of nations* runs as follows: 'The greatest improvement in the productive powers of labour, and the greater part of the skill, dexterity, and judgement with which it is any where directed or applied, seem to have been the effects of the division of labour.'[35] To drive home the scale of the increase in labour productivity which could be achieved by the division of labour, he then turned to the pin making industry to illustrate the point. He argued that 'a workman not educated to this business' could 'scarce, perhaps, with his utmost industry, make one pin in a day, and certainly could not make twenty'. But pin making could be divided into 'about eighteen distinct operations'. Smith claimed to have visited a 'manufactory' in which ten men could produce 'upwards of forty-eight thousand pins in a day' or 4,800 pins per man.[36] It seems possible that Smith allowed his enthusiasm for the division of labour to influence his arithmetic, since his illustration implies that, assuming a ten-hour working day, each man was producing a pin every 7.5 seconds. Indeed, since each pin was supposed to pass through ten pairs of hands, it implies that each man handled all 48,000 and his individual contribution to the making of each pin lasted less than a second.[37] The principle, however, was sound even if the illustration was rather highly coloured. Division of labour, improved transport facilities, and higher real incomes went hand in hand.

How far the division of labour could be taken was determined principally by the size of the accessible market and this in turn hinged on

[35] Smith, *Wealth of nations*, I, p. 7.

[36] *Ibid.*, pp. 8–9.

[37] It is probable that Smith was also stretching a point in claiming to have visited a pin manufactory personally. He may well have been quoting from French experience: Allen, *The British industrial revolution*, pp. 146–7.

the cost and reliability of transport. The scope for 'Smithian' growth was transformed by the improvements which had taken place during his lifetime and which were to gather pace in the ensuing half-century.[38] The transport improvements culminated in the creation of a national railway network, already substantially complete by the end of the 1840s, but earlier achievements had also been striking. Road transport was vastly improved by the construction of turnpike roads, encouraged above all by London's needs and the multifarious activities of other large and rapidly growing urban centres. Yet the changes brought about in solving the problems and seizing the opportunities resulting from the huge rise in coal production were arguably of still greater long-term significance. They were central to the construction of canals and had a leading role in causing the switch from railed roads to steam railways during the second half of the period. The striking improvement in transport provision which was taking place, therefore, owed much to the fundamental changes in energy supply which increasingly set England apart from the continent in the seventeenth and eighteenth centuries.

All these improvements certainly supported and stimulated 'Smithian' growth. But they also contributed greatly to growth of a different kind since they enabled larger and larger tracts of the country to enjoy the benefits afforded by access to cheap and abundant energy derived from burning coal. Each reduction in the cost of transporting coal from the pithead to a distant centre widened the range of activities which were no longer constrained by the energy limitations of organic economies. When coal could be substituted for other energy sources, expansion could occur without simultaneously creating a matching rise in the pressure on the land. Access to the store of the products of past photosynthesis could relieve pressure on the current supply.

By the increasing exploitation of coal early modern England gradually gained access to energy on a scale which by the end of the eighteenth century dwarfed the comparable figures for continental countries. In so doing, the country opened up opportunities which were largely absent elsewhere. In this chapter, where the focus has been on the part played by coal in facilitating transport improvements, the connection between rising coal output and investment in

[38] Adam Smith was born in 1723 and died in 1790.

transport is plain. In the aspects of change in the English economy which are described in the previous chapter, and again in the next chapter, the links may appear less strong. In many sectors of economic activity energy requirements were limited in the early stages of growth and could be met from traditional sources, but as expansion continued and energy demand rose the dependence on coal increased. Only an ability to meet this demand and to do so without a crippling increase in energy costs enabled growth to continue. The changes which are the subject of the next chapter provide an illustration of the point. The nature of these changes implied an increase in the energy intensity of production growth.

5 | Occupational structure, aggregate income, and migration

At first sight the title of this chapter may appear to bring together an odd group of topics. One pair within the trio of topics, the importance and frequency of migration as urban and industrial growth got into its stride, has already been touched upon, but will support further consideration. Both migration and occupational structure, however, were also very closely connected to changes in the structure of aggregate income, and by considering all three and their interrelation jointly, some of the most important features of the transformation of England in the period between the reigns of Elizabeth and Victoria can be brought into focus.

Occupational structure and migration

Radical occupational change virtually connotes large-scale migration. Primary employment is necessarily spread wide and thin because it is so closely linked to the land. Indeed, controlling for differences in the fertility of the soil, the distribution of agricultural employment, which constituted the great bulk of primary employment as a whole, largely reflected acreage.[1] The bigger the area of farmland, the larger the population. Consider table 5.1. Of the forty-one English counties in 1841 all but eleven had between thirty and fifty males employed in agriculture for every thousand acres of the land surface of the county, a very limited spread. If it were possible to control for land that was of little or no agricultural use, the spread would be even narrower. Counties such as Cumberland, Westmorland, and Northumberland at the bottom end of the distribution would then be indistinguishable

---

[1] This is a large claim to which there will always be many exceptions. The density of the agricultural labour force may differ between pastoral and arable areas, and specialist land use, as in viticulture or market gardening, results in much higher densities than in agriculture generally. As a first approximation, however, it is defensible.

Table 5.1 *Number of males in agriculture per 1,000 acres in English counties in 1841*

	Males in agriculture	Males per 1,000 acres		Males in agriculture	Males per 1,000 acres
Middlesex	15,445	84.8	Norfolk	47,483	36.4
Essex	47,618	48.5	Gloucestershire	28,199	35.3
Bedfordshire	14,193	47.7	Rutland	3,261	33.5
Kent	46,167	46.4	Lincolnshire	56,283	33.5
Hertfordshire	18,718	46.1	Huntingdonshire	7,849	33.1
Suffolk	41,832	44.2	Hampshire	33,460	32.2
Buckinghamshire	20,813	43.9	Leicestershire	16,551	31.7
Worcestershire	20,200	43.5	Shropshire	27,381	31.6
Lancashire	51,499	43.5	Devon	51,587	31.0
Surrey	20,734	42.8	Yorkshire, ER	24,350	30.2
Warwickshire	23,548	40.7	Yorkshire, WR	50,254	29.2
Berkshire	18,721	40.6	Cornwall	25,032	28.9
Staffordshire	30,266	40.1	Herefordshire	15,423	28.5
Oxfordshire	19,054	40.0	Dorset	17,730	28.0
Somerset	41,658	39.9	Derbyshire	17,654	26.6
Cambridgeshire	21,191	38.8	Durham	14,072	19.9
Northamptonshire	24,433	38.1	Yorkshire, NR	25,507	18.9
Cheshire	24,743	37.8	Cumberland	13,889	14.3
Wiltshire	33,051	37.3	Northumberland	15,977	13.0
Nottinghamshire	19,981	37.0	Westmorland	6,201	12.4
Sussex	34,042	36.7	**England**	**1,086,050**	**33.8**

Notes. The totals of males in agriculture are the combined totals of farmers and graziers and agricultural labourers for each county in the 1841 census.

Sources. Males in agriculture: *1841 Census*, Occupation abstract. The acreages used to calculate the figures in the final column were taken from: Wrigley, *The early English censuses*, tab. A1.1.

from the main group. Much of their land surface consisted of hills and moorland. The very high figure for Middlesex reflects the opportunities for intensive land use in close proximity to a very large market (the census did not separately distinguish market gardeners and it may be that some of these were included under agriculture in Middlesex). Because of their size, therefore, big counties normally had large numbers of men engaged in agriculture. The county which heads the list in this respect is Lincolnshire with an agricultural work-force in excess of 56,000, followed by Devon. Third and fourth came Lancashire and the West Riding. These two counties accounted for a tenth of the national total, an aspect of their economies which might easily escape notice, given their fame as hotbeds of industrialisation (the acreages of each of the counties are given in a fuller version of this table in the appendix).

Matters are very different with secondary and tertiary employment, at least in the circumstances which came to prevail as the English economy was slowly transformed between the reigns of Elizabeth and Victoria. Both because of the economies associated with large-scale production concentrated in a few locations and, in the latter half of the period, because of the anchoring effect of proximity to a coal-field, industrial employment became increasingly concentrated in a limited number of favoured regions. Indeed many areas which proved unable to withstand the competitive pressures caused by the new situation lost industries which had once provided a living to a substantial workforce. This was, for example, notably true of the production of woollen and worsted cloth. The woollen industry for centuries had been the most prominent English industry, important domestically and dominant among the export trades. There were major centres of production in many counties in the early modern period: in Devon, Gloucestershire, Somerset, Norfolk, Suffolk, Essex, and the West Riding. By the mid-nineteenth century, however, the West Riding had far outstripped any rivals, causing both relative and absolute decline elsewhere.

In general, concentration was less stark in tertiary employment. Some forms of service employment were closely tied to the overall distribution of population. This was the case, for example, with bar-bers, shopkeepers, and primary schoolteachers. The smallest villages might lack them but they were present wherever the size of the local population provided an adequate demand. There were also, however, many forms of tertiary activity in which employment was concentrated where there were large populations. For example, whereas retail employment was widely distributed, employment in wholesaling was predominantly in the larger towns. It was common for there to be what might be termed graduated concentration. Carpenters, for example, were omnipresent, but cabinetmakers were concentrated in the larger settlements. Much the same was true of several tertiary sectors which employed large numbers. Employment in transport exemplifies the point. The numbers involved grew rapidly during the early modern period and growth was especially vigorous in the early nineteenth century. Transport facilities were needed everywhere but tended to generate proportionately larger gains in employment in major centres.

It was necessarily the case, therefore, that, as the proportion of the workforce engaged in agriculture declined from about 70 per cent to less than 40 per cent between 1600 and 1800 and the proportion engaged in secondary and tertiary activity doubled from 30 to 60 per cent, there was a massive redistribution of population, whether measured by absolute number or as percentages of the total. A simple but very crude way to measure the scale of the transformation which was taking place is to consider population densities on a county basis as shown in table 5.2, and figure 5.1 reproduces some of the information in two graphs. The counties have been placed in four groups: the metropolitan counties; five counties in which industrial growth was especially notable; those counties in which at the time of the 1841 census the proportion of the male labour force engaged in agriculture was over 40 per cent; and other counties. The results are shown as densities per 1,000 acres and are also indexed against the population of the county at the start of the series in 1600. The details provided in the table are for groups of counties. Population totals for each group are also given in the bottom section of the table. Details for each county are set out in the fuller version of the table to be found in the appendix.

The population densities for each group were calculated by relating the overall population totals for the counties in question to their combined acreage. Although the population densities of each group vary, it is striking that in 1600 the densities for the agricultural, industrial, and other counties groups are almost identical. Indirectly this reflects the point made by table 5.1. As long as agriculture was the dominant employer the spread of population densities was constrained by the nature of agricultural employment. The metropolitan group, of course, has a much higher density since London was already a major city by 1600. After 1600, however, the three non-metropolitan groups diverge substantially. The panel containing densities indexed to the 1600 figure shows that the population density in the heavily

Table 5.2 *County population densities (persons per 1,000 acres)*

	Population densities						Densities indexed to 1600 (100)				
	1600	1700	1750	1801	1851		1600	1700	1750	1801	1851
Metropolitan group	552.5	968.3	1,101.4	1,696.1	3,907.1		100.0	175.2	199.3	307.0	707.1
Industrial group	122.2	155.8	212.7	398.4	1,007.0		100.0	127.4	174.0	326.0	823.9
Agricultural group	123.9	140.1	149.8	189.6	298.3		100.0	113.1	120.9	153.1	240.9
Other counties group	118.3	144.8	159.5	221.8	389.3		100.0	122.5	134.9	187.5	329.2
England	129.6	162.2	184.4	270.0	530.2		100.0	125.2	142.3	208.4	409.2

Population totals

	1600	1700	1750	1801	1851
Metropolitan group	369,024	646,668	735,586	1,132,767	2,609,449
Industrial group	602,823	768,190	1,048,822	1,964,973	4,966,482
Agricultural group	1,185,241	1,340,802	1,433,419	1,814,404	2,854,826
Other counties group	2,004,696	2,454,962	2,704,078	3,759,213	6,599,390
England	4,161,784	5,210,623	5,921,905	8,671,357	17,030,147

Note. The counties constituting the metropolitan group were Middlesex and Surrey; the industrial group, Cheshire, Lancashire, Staffordshire, Warwickshire, and the West Riding; the agricultural group, Bedfordshire, Buckinghamshire, Cambridgeshire, Essex, Herefordshire, Hertfordshire, Huntingdonshire, Oxfordshire, Rutland, Suffolk, Wiltshire, and the North Riding; the other counties group, all counties not included in the three previous groups.

Sources. Population totals and acreages: Wrigley, *The early English censuses*, tab. A2.1.

agricultural counties rose by roughly a half during the seventeenth and eighteenth centuries whereas in the industrial counties the density tripled over the same period, with a similar rise in the two metropolitan counties. As might be expected, the other counties group grew slightly faster than the more purely agricultural group but fell well short of the other two groups. In England as a whole the population and therefore its density doubled over the same period.

The seventeenth and eighteenth centuries differed considerably. In the former, the very rapid growth of London set Middlesex and Surrey apart from the other groups which continued to bear a strong resemblance to each other: the metropolitan group grew by 75 per cent. The industrial group grew somewhat faster than either the agricultural or the other counties group but any differences were muted (the percentage increases were 27, 13, and 23 respectively). In the eighteenth century, however, the metropolitan group, which had stood out so notably in the seventeenth century, expanded little faster than the country as a whole (the metropolitan group by 75 per cent; England by 67 per cent). In this century the industrial group was by far the most dynamic. Its population rose by 156 per cent while the equivalent figure for the agricultural group was a mere 35 per cent, and that for other counties 53 per cent. In the final half-century the differences between the group growth rates became less marked. The industrial group remained the fastest growing of the four at 153 per cent, chiefly due to the extraordinary pace of growth of its largest member, Lancashire, which almost tripled in size over the half-century. The metropolitan counties, however, were not far behind, rising by 130 per cent. The agricultural counties remained the slowest growing, at 57 per cent, while the 'others' group grew by 76 per cent. Over the entire 250-year period from 1600 to 1851 the growth percentages were the following: metropolitan 607 per cent; industrial 724 per cent; agricultural 141 per cent; others 229 per cent; England as a whole 309 per cent. The striking changes in the percentage share of each group in the national total over the quarter millennium are shown in the final section of the expanded version of table 5.2 in the appendix. Two groups increased their shares substantially, the metropolitan group from 8.9 to 15.3 per cent, and the industrial group from 14.5 to 29.2 per cent. The former almost doubled its share of the national population; the latter more than doubled its share. Between them the seven counties in these two groups contained less than a quarter of the national

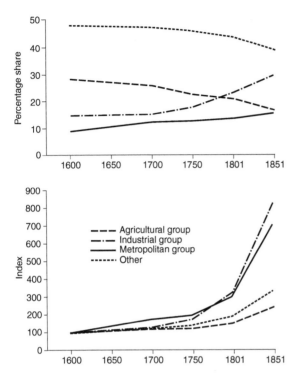

Figure 5.1 *Population growth in four county groups: metropolitan, industrial, agricultural, and other counties.*
Source. Tab. 5.2.

total in 1600, but in 1851 approaching half of the English population lived in one or other of them. At the other extreme, the share of the agricultural group dropped steadily, ending with little more than half the percentage with which it started, while the other counties group, which was at all times the largest single unit, also declined steadily but much less steeply.

Other features of table 5.2 are worthy of note. In 1600 the northern counties were still thinly peopled (see the fuller version of the table in the appendix for details). Cumberland, Westmorland, Northumberland, and the North and East Ridings of Yorkshire all had fewer than 100 people per 1,000 acres. Even the West Riding was still thinly peopled. Elsewhere only Shropshire had a density of less than 100 people per 1,000 acres. But surprisingly, and perhaps significantly, Lancashire was already the sixth most densely populated county in 1600. Apart from the metropolitan counties, only Somerset, Essex, and Devon were more thickly peopled. Lancashire may well already have ceased to be predominantly agricultural. Timmins notes that 'industrial development began to quicken in Lancashire from the mid-Tudor period and that, despite setbacks, it had become well advanced by the early eighteenth century'.[2]

Figure 5.1 converts some of the data in table 5.2 into graphical form. The upper graph shows the changing percentage shares of each of the four groups. The extent of the contrast between the industrial and agricultural groups is the most prominent feature of this graph. One group more than doubles its share of the national population while the share of the other almost halves, and whereas in 1600 the agricultural group is twice as populous as the industrial group, the latter has overtaken the former by the end of the eighteenth century, and by 1851 it is the larger by more than 70 per cent. When presented in this form, however, the similarity in the growth histories of the industrial and metropolitan groups is not readily visible because the latter group has a starting share little more than half as large as that of the former. The lower graph may prove helpful in this regard. For each group the starting population in 1600 is set equal to 100 and later populations are indexed to this figure. Presented in this way there is a broad similarity in the fortunes of the two fast-growing groups over the period as a whole, but the metropolitan group makes the more vigorous start of the two in the seventeenth century, followed in the eighteenth century by a period of modest growth compared with the surge taking place in the industrial group. In the final half-century rates of growth are similar in the two groups. The radical difference between the rates of growth in the two rapidly growing groups and the rates in the other two is striking, especially in the period down to 1800. Thereafter the contrast lessens. The 'other counties' group was the largest of the four in population size throughout, but declined gently in relative size. Its occupational structure was less distinctive than any of the other three groups and its fortunes reflected its mixed economic character, less purely agricultural than the agriculture group and less engaged in manufacture than the industrial group.

These changes are instructive and some are striking but in considering them it should be borne in mind that the county is a clumsy

---

[2] Timmins, *Made in Lancashire*, p. 9.

unit, often containing elements with strongly contrasting economic structures and markedly different demographic histories. Middlesex provides an intriguing example of the lack of uniformity even within a very small county (only Rutland was smaller in area). Estimates of hundred populations at decennial intervals from 1761 onwards have recently been made. Although trends in Middlesex as a whole are completely dominated by London, there remained several hundreds which were little influenced by the capital even in the late eighteenth century. The combined populations of the hundreds of Edmonton, Elthorne, Gore, Isleworth, and Spelthorne grew by only 12.5 per cent between 1761 and 1801, while the population of the rest of the county, essentially London, rose by 60 per cent.[3] Many similar cases could be quoted. There were, for instance, even more striking contrasts in Lancashire in the first half of the nineteenth century. In this period Lancashire was the fastest growing of any English county. The smallest census unit above the level of the parish created when the census system was radically revised in 1851 was the registration subdistrict (RSD), of which there were 142 in Lancashire.[4] So extreme were the varying fortunes of the RSDs that in seven cases population increased more than tenfold in the half-century, while in seventeen cases the increase was less than a quarter.[5] The population of the county as a whole rose roughly threefold from 713,056 to 2,100,081.[6]

The data contained in table 5.2 leave little room for doubt that migration must have played a major role in restraining growth to a very low level in some counties and facilitating rapid growth in others. The net movements involved can only be estimated with some claim to accuracy if the rates of natural increase in each county can

---

[3] Wrigley, *The early English censuses*, tab. A2.7.
[4] To be exact there were 167 RSDs in Lancashire, but in a substantial number of cases it is possible to provide consistent population only by combining data for two or more RSDs since in the early censuses information is available only for larger units than those reported in 1851. This reduces the number from 167 to 142.
[5] The RSDs in question were the following. Growing more than tenfold: Chorlton-on-Medlock, Everton, Hulme, Toxteth Park, Dukinfield, West Derby, and Cheetham. Growing by less than a quarter: Ellel, Sankey, Chipping, Garstang, Edgeworth, Warton, Caton, Wray, Whalley, Mellor, Pendle, Rixton, Arkholme, Billington, Slaidburn, Winwick, and Gisburn. In the case of the last two RSDs the population declined slightly between 1801 and 1851. Wrigley, *The early English censuses*, tab. M2.4.
[6] *Ibid.*, tab. M2.1.

be established. If it were safe to assume that rates of natural increase were uniform throughout the whole of England a simple calculation might suffice. Suppose, for example, that the national population rose by 25 per cent and that the population of a given county at the start of the period was 100,000 and that at the end of the period it had risen to 130,000, it would be reasonable to assume that the county had made a net gain of 5,000 people by in-migration.[7] Direct evidence about rates of natural increase at the county level is lacking but it is of interest to consider the situation in the early years of civil registration when such rates are readily available.

The Preface to the 1841 census contains a table which includes birth and death rates for each county taken from the Annual Report of the Registrar-General for 1843. The data refer to the years 1839–41 in the case of births and 1838–41 in the case of deaths. They suggest relatively modest differences between types of counties with one exception. Using the same county groups as in table 5.2 and taking a weighted average[8] of the crude rates of natural increase for each group produces the following results: the average rate of natural increase in the metropolitan group was 4.9 per 1,000 population; in the industrial group 11.1 per 1,000; in the agricultural group 12.1 per 1,000; and in the remaining counties 10.1 per 1,000. As the notes to the table point out, the absolute rates are probably too low, perhaps from the under-registration of births in the early years of vital registration, but the close similarity between the rates in three of the four groups is unlikely to be misleading.[9] The lower rate in the metropolitan group comes as no surprise. While the pattern in the early nineteenth century is an uncertain guide to earlier periods, there is no strong reason to suppose that it would not have been true previously and it is intriguing to discover what patterns emerge if a uniform rate of natural increase is assumed for three of the four groups while treating the metropolitan group differently. Until late in the eighteenth century, death rates in London were normally higher than birth rates but matters improved substantially thereafter, as indeed the metropolitan rate listed in the last paragraph makes clear. Although it is at best only

---

[7] This is to ignore the possibility of international migration but might hold as a first approximation.
[8] Weighted by the population of each county in the group in 1841.
[9] *1841 Census*, Occupation abstract, Preface, pp. 10–11.

a rough approximation, I have assumed that there was no natural increase in the metropolitan group in the period down to 1801 but that thereafter the surplus of births over deaths accounted for half of the total increase which occurred. It should be noted in relation to the seventeenth and eighteenth centuries that the adverse situation in London itself was somewhat offset by the healthier situation in the rural areas of Middlesex and Surrey which would influence rates in the metropolitan counties as a group.

Rates of natural increase in the counties in the other three groups were assumed to be the same. Jointly they were taken to account for the whole rise in population in England between 1600 and 1801. In the final half-century when local natural increase in the metropolitan group supplied half the increase taking place in the group, the natural increase in the other three groups was adjusted accordingly. As an illustration of the calculations involved, consider the first period. Between 1600 and 1700 the national population rose from 4,161,787 to 5,210,623, an increase of 1,048,836. The increase is assumed to have occurred exclusively in the industrial, agricultural, and other counties groups. The combined population of these three groups in 1600 was 3,792,760. Since the rate of natural increase is assumed to have been the same in each of the three groups, in the absence of migration the population of each group would have risen in the ratio 1,048,836/3,792,760, or by 27.65 per cent. The population of Bedfordshire, for example, in 1600 was 43,550 and in the absence of migration it would have risen by 27.65 per cent to 55,593 in 1700, but at that date its population was 50,163 and therefore the net out-migration from the county during the century was 5,430 persons. The summary results of the exercise are given in table 5.3 which shows the net migration totals for each of the four groups. A more detailed version of the table in the appendix provides estimated net migration totals for each county.

It is scarcely necessary to say that this is a highly artificial exercise. It makes use of assumptions which are at best rough approximations. The empirical base for the calculations is fragile and the probable margins of error are uncertain. It ignores completely some factors which would modify the picture which it presents, for instance by assuming implicitly that England was a closed population without external migration flows whereas at times there was substantial migration both into and out of the country. Further, assumptions which may hold broadly true for large units are certain to be wildly inaccurate in relation to

Table 5.3 *Estimated county net migration totals 1600–1851*

	Net migration				
	1600–1700	*1700–50*	*1750–1801*	*1801–51*	*1600–1851*
Metropolitan group	277,644	88,918	397,181	665,031	1,428,774
Industrial group	−1,337	160,913	360,133	1,034,307	1,554,017
Agricultural group	−172,202	−116,345	−378,921	−776,488	−1,443,955
Other counties group	−104,107	−133,486	−378,392	−922,850	−1,538,834

Notes. For an account of the method of calculation see accompanying text. Positive figures represent net in-migration; negative figures net out-migration. Owing to rounding of the county totals to produce whole numbers, the cumulative totals for the county groups do not exactly sum to zero.

Sources. The individual county totals underlying the results set out in the table were taken from Wrigley, *The early English censuses*, tab. A2.6.

some of their constituent parts. There were considerable tracts of rural England where the mortality regime was as severe as in the metropolis, as for example in low-lying, marshy areas such as Romney Marsh, where malaria remained a major killer until well into the eighteenth century.[10] Nor should it be overlooked that the table lists totals of *net* internal migration. This means that it understates the scale of migration flows generally, since the net figures are arrived at after deducting movement in one direction from movement in the other. Gross flows were sometimes considerably larger than the net figures. Despite these reservations, however, tables 5.3 and 5.4 contain much that is illuminating and the broad patterns which they suggest are unlikely to be misleading. And it should be noted that, using the method just described, it is a simple matter to consider the effect of making different assumptions about rates of natural increase in the four groups and in so doing to establish a range of plausible possibilities.

[10] Dobson, *Contours of death*, pp. 350–67.

Table 5.3 makes certain features of the history of internal migration in England immediately clear. In the seventeenth century, for example, the five counties forming the industrial group grew exclusively by local natural increase. The net migration total was virtually zero, in marked contrast with the three later periods when net in-migration rose sharply, culminating in the first half of the nineteenth century when the total into the counties of Cheshire, Lancashire, Staffordshire, Warwickshire, and the West Riding exceeded one million, of which almost two-thirds was into Lancashire alone (see the larger version of table 5.3 in the appendix). The agricultural group experienced continuous out-migration on a steadily increasing scale. The other counties group, which had a population roughly twice as large as the agricultural group (table 5.2), also experienced continuous net emigration but relative to population on a more modest scale. Finally, the metropolitan counties were the only group to have experienced continuous net immigration on a substantial scale, though the scale was much lower in the first half of the eighteenth century than at other times. The early eighteenth century was a period in which London's population grew only slightly, but this is one instance of the fallibility of an exercise of this kind since death rates reached a very high level in London in this period and the true figure for net immigration may well have been substantially higher than the total in the table, even allowing for the fact that the inclusion of the populations living in the rural parts of Surrey and Middlesex within the metropolitan group muted the impact of London somewhat.

It is, however, much easier to appreciate the patterns of net migration if the information is expressed in the form of annual rates in relation to the population of each group, as in table 5.4. In this table the net migration is shown as a rate per 1,000 population in the group at the beginning of each period. The rate for the first period is then directly comparable with those for the later periods, despite the fact that it is twice as long as the later periods.

When net migration is recast in the form shown in table 5.4 it emphasises the steady rise in the scale of net in-migration into the industrial group: in the first period, local natural increase accounted for the whole of the rise in population, whereas in the early nineteenth century the rate of net in-migration in the industrial group rivalled that in the metropolitan group. The agricultural group experienced a steadily rising rate of net out-migration, very roughly providing a

Table 5.4 *Net migration rates expressed as a rate per 1,000 population in the first year of each period*

| | Net migration rates per 1,000 per annum | | | |
	1600–1700	1700–50	1750–1801	1801–51
Metropolitan group	7.52	2.76	10.59	11.74
Industrial group	–0.02	4.19	6.73	10.53
Agricultural group	–1.45	–1.74	–5.18	–8.56
Other counties group	–0.52	–1.09	–2.74	–4.91

Sources. Migration totals from table 5.3. Population totals from Wrigley, *The early English censuses*, tab. A2.6.

mirror image to the pattern in the industrial group. There are four-teen counties in the agricultural group and net migration was meas-ured for each of them for each of the four periods shown in table 5.4. Of the fifty-six individual readings which result, in only five instances was the net movement inward rather than outward (see the more detailed version of table 5.3 in the appendix). The other counties group paralleled the agricultural group in experiencing net out-migration in each period at roughly half the rate of the latter, a pattern which conforms to expectation given its more mixed occu-pational structure. Given the crude and arbitrary assumptions which formed the basis for the construction of the net migration estimates shown in tables 5.3 and 5.4 no reliance should be placed on their exact accuracy, but it is at least highly probable that they capture the broad trends in net migratory movement over the 250 years in ques-tion. In the seventeenth century only London was a magnet for the ambitious or uprooted. In the other groups, levels of net migration were modest, indeed negligible except for the agricultural group. By the end of the period migration was a major feature of life through-out the whole country. In the metropolitan, industrial, and agricul-tural groups the final column of table 5.4 suggests that in each year about one person in every hundred was a recent immigrant or emi-grant. But this substantially understates the prominence of migra-tion in everyday life since *gross* migration substantially exceeded *net* migration.

The two tables leave no room for doubt that migration was an important and growing feature of English life in the early modern period, matching the lopsided character of growth as the economy changed. The prominence of short-distance migration has often been demonstrated. Inter-county movement is not easy to measure effectively but, if severe suffering was to be avoided as population growth accelerated, it was essential and deserves close attention. Even given the crudity of the present exercise, its principal features seem clear. They show that the existence of employment opportunities in London and the northern and midland industrial areas was the feature which made it possible to avoid a piling up of population in rural agricultural districts where additional employment opportunities were very limited and immiseration a constant threat.

Markedly different population growth rates and the large volume of migration which these imply reflect equally striking structural change in the economy. One of the features of the period which helps to explain what was in train was the intimate connection between occupational change and the structure of aggregate demand which is the subject of the next section.

Occupational change and aggregate income

The significance of the relationship between occupational change and aggregate income has attracted relatively little notice but may be helpful in resolving one of the logical conundrums in reconciling estimates of the various components of growth during the industrial revolution. Real wage series tend to support the relatively pessimistic view that average incomes were not rising significantly whereas evidence about the possession of an increasingly wide range of durable consumer goods suggests the opposite.[11] Taking into account changes in occupational structure may serve to reduce the apparent inconsistency of the two types of data.

Since individuals in different occupations were very differently rewarded, it is clearly possible that, to take a limiting case, even without any change in the average income received by individuals in each branch of employment, there may be a substantial change in the *average* income of the workforce as a whole. A simple hypothetical exercise may serve to illustrate what is at issue. Suppose that during the

[11] See pp. 71–2 above.

'long' eighteenth century the proportion of the workforce which made a living from agriculture declined from 55 to 40 per cent of the total but that nothing else changed, what would be the result for average incomes and for the structure of aggregate demand (the proportion of demand spent on primary, secondary, and tertiary products)? An estimate of the scale of the change is feasible and proves instructive.

The relative incomes of those in the farming sector on the one hand and those in other sectors of the economy were calculated using the tables constructed by Gregory King, Massie, and Colquhoun, all of whom were greatly interested in the subject. Between them they cover the 'long' eighteenth century (King's data relate to 1688, Massie's to 1760, and Colquhoun's to 1803). The following exercise is based on an article on the social structure of England and Wales in the eighteenth century published by Peter Mathias almost half a century ago in which he compared the estimates of the three men.[12] To make the comparison possible, he was obliged to combine their more detailed social categories into seven broad groups, and in the case of Massie to recalculate his original table to enable direct comparison with the other two.[13] The results were consolidated in a single table which shows the number of families in each category, the total annual income of that category, and the percentage of the total income of the country as a whole enjoyed by the category in question.[14] It is therefore a simple matter to calculate the average income of a family in each category. In the case of Massie, Mathias provided two estimates, but only one is reproduced here. Table 5.5 repeats the relevant elements from Mathias's table.

The average incomes shown in table 5.5 make it possible to explore the impact of a change in the occupational structure on overall average incomes and hence on the trend of aggregate demand, on the supposition that during the 'long' eighteenth century the proportion of the workforce which made a living from agriculture declined from 55 to 40 per cent of the total but that nothing else changed. There must be, of course, a matching rise in the percentage of the workforce outside agriculture but each occupational group is assumed to keep the same *relative* size within an increased overall non-agricultural sector and to receive the

[12] Mathias, 'The social structure in the eighteenth century'.
[13] *Ibid.*, p. 36. The make-up of the seven larger groupings from the original finer divisions is set out in *ibid.*, tab. II, p. 44.
[14] *Ibid.*, tab. III, p. 45.

Table 5.5. *Estimates of average annual family income for different social groups by King, Massie, and Colquhoun*

	King (1688)			Massie (1760)			Colquhoun (1803)		
	Families ('000s)	Total income (£'000s)	Average income (£s)	Families ('000s)	Total income (£'000s)	Average income (£s)	Families ('000s)	Total income (£'000s)	Average income (£s)
Nobility and gentry	16.6	6,286	378.7	18.0	8,720	484.4	27.2	32,800	1205.9
Professions, office holders	90.0	5,770	64.1	83.0	4,822	58.1	172.5	31,300	181.4
Freeholders, farmers	330.0	16,936	51.3	365.0	16,950	46.4	660.0	48,540	73.5
Labourers, cottagers	764.0	8,060	10.5	648.0	10,870	16.8	290.7	2,910	10.0
Artisans, handicraft	60.0	2,400	40.0	80.0	4,200	52.5	541.0	51,080	94.4
Merchants, shopkeepers, seamen	100.0	5,200	52.0	277.5	15,400	55.5	242.9	48,725	200.6
Vagrants, etc.	30.0	60	2.0				123.5	2,385	19.3
Total	1,390.6	44,712	32.2	1471.5	60,962	41.4	2,057.8	217,740	105.8
Total less vagrants	1,360.6	44,652	32.8				1,934.3	215,355	111.3

Notes. The estimates refer to England and Wales. Public receipts by the poor were excluded in King and Colquhoun. They are not mentioned by Massie. The names for each of the seven categories seen in this table are not the same as those used by Mathias in the source table, though the statistics are exactly the same. The renaming reflects the differing aims of the two exercises.

Source. Mathias, 'The social structure in the eighteenth century', tab. III, p. 45.

Table 5.6. The impact of a declining proportion of families in agriculture on aggregate incomes

	King				Massie				Colquhoun			
	Average income (£s)	Weighting			Average income (£s)	Weighting			Average income (£s)	Weighting		
Farmers	51.3	1			46.4	1			73.5	1		
Farm labourers	10.5	3			16.8	3			10.0	3		
Average agricultural income	20.7				24.2				25.9			
	Families ('000s)	Total income (£'000s)			Families ('000s)	Total income (£'000s)			Families ('000s)	Total income (£'000s)		
Nobility and gentry	16.6	6,286			18.0	8,720			27.2	32,800		
Professions, office holders	90.0	5,770			83.0	4,822			172.5	31,300		
Artisans, handicraft	60.0	2,400			80.0	4,200			541.0	51,080		
Merchants, shopkeepers, seamen	100.0	5,200			277.5	15,400			242.9	48,725		
Vagrants, etc.	30.0	60							123.5	2,385		
Total	296.6	19,716			458.5	33,142			1,107.1	166,290		
Average income (non-agricultural)	66.5				72.3				150.2			

	Part shares	Total income (£'000s)	Part shares	Total income (£'000s)	Part shares	Total income (£'000s)
Agriculture	55	1,140.8	55	1,330.5	55	1,424.2
Other than agriculture	45	2,991.3	45	3,252.8	45	6,759.1
Total (A)	**100**	**4,132.1**	**100**	**4,583.2**	**100**	**8,183.3**
Agriculture	40	829.7	40	967.6	40	1,035.8
Other than agriculture	60	3,988.4	60	4,337.0	60	9,012.2
Total (B)	**100**	**4,818.1**	**100**	**5,304.6**	**100**	**10,048.0**
Ratio total B/ total A		116.6		115.7		122.8

Note. I have included vagrants in the calculations for King and Colquhoun (Massie provides no comparable data). To do so is debatable since they are individuals rather than families and, furthermore, it is not clear that they should be regarded as 'belonging' outside agriculture. The last jobs of many vagrants may well have been agricultural. But their inclusion must reduce the contrast between the average income of the agricultural and non-agricultural sectors, helping to ensure that the ratios shown on the bottom line of the table can be regarded as minimal estimates of the impact of the posited change in occupational structure.

Source. Tab. 5.5.

same average income throughout. This is the simplest possible model in which there is agriculture on the one hand and 'non-agriculture' on the other hand. In agriculture there are only farmers and farm labourers, with the latter outnumbering the former by three to one. The average income in agriculture is calculated using these weights. Outside agriculture the average income is calculated by weighting the average incomes for the non-agricultural categories by their relative size. In other words, the exercise is intended to assess the extent to which, with every other variable held constant, a reduction in the relative importance of agriculture in the economy might alter overall average incomes and thus change the structure of aggregate demand.

The results of the exercise are set out in table 5.6. The top section of the table contains the calculation which provides an average income for families in agriculture derived from the tables of King, Massie, and Colquhoun. For example, King's table suggests an average annual income of £51.3 for a farmer and £10.5 for an agricultural labourer, and therefore, on the assumption of three labourers for each farmer, an overall average of £20.7 for all families engaged in agriculture. The second section repeats the information in table 5.5 for all the other categories in the table. The totals of families and of their incomes are cumulated and an average for all 'non-agricultural' families is shown. In the final section two alternative scenarios are given. In the first, 55 per cent of families are in agriculture; in the second, 40 per cent. The total incomes of the agricultural and non-agricultural sectors are shown in each case, assuming a representative population consisting of 100 families. Thus, on Gregory King's estimates fifty-five agricultural families will enjoy an aggregate income of £1,140.8 (55 × 20.7).[15] The corresponding figure for forty-five non-agricultural families is £2,991.3 (45 × £66.5). Summing the two totals produces a figure of £4,132.1. Parallel calculations when the relative size of the two elements is 40/60 rather than 55/45 produce a total of £4,818.1. This is turn shows that a shift in the occupational structure on this scale and on the assumption that the relative size of the constituent elements of both the agricultural and non-agricultural sectors remained constant

[15] The slight discrepancy between the total and the product of the multiplicand and the multiplier here and throughout the table arises because the quantities involved have been rounded down to a single place of decimals whereas the calculation was made without rounding.

would cause the average income of the population as a whole to rise by 16.6 per cent (the figure shown on the final line of the table).[16]

The estimates of the relative size of the different groups within the population and of their total incomes made by Massie and Colquhoun produce similar results to that derived from King. Colquhoun's estimates produce the highest percentage increase. This is not surprising on the widely held assumption of an increase in the Gini coefficient as a result of the economic changes in train during the eighteenth century but the difference is not pronounced.[17] All three sets of estimates suggest that, on the assumptions set out above, the level of average income per family, and in consequence the scale of its expenditure, would have risen substantially during the 'long' eighteenth century as a result of the decline in the relative importance of agriculture in the overall occupational structure of the country.

The point of this exercise is to suggest that there is good reason to think that, even on the assumption that real wage studies are correct in concluding that the purchasing power of particular types of employment did not change materially, changes in the relative size of different occupational groups were sufficient to have raised average real incomes significantly, and that as a result the structure of aggregate demand changed in sympathy.[18] In some respects this exercise runs in parallel with the arguments made by Eversley described above.[19]

The wider implications of the assumed change in occupational structure are substantial. Given the income elasticities of demand for different types of goods and services, the effect of the change would be to promote a disproportionately rapid growth in the demand for the products of the secondary and tertiary sectors of the economy. Several studies of real wage trends have suggested little improvement in purchasing power in the course of the 'long' eighteenth century and have thus made it difficult to reconcile this

---

[16] $(4818.1/4,132.1) \times 100 = 116.6$.

[17] The Gini coefficient measures the degree of inequality of income or wealth in a population. It varies beween 0 and 1. A low coefficient indicates a relatively equal distribution of income or wealth; a high coefficient the opposite. It is widely assumed that the nature of the changes taking place in the classic period of the industrial revolution increased the Gini coefficient.

[18] There is a fuller discussion of the difficulties involved in attempting to measure real wage change below pp. 142–3.

[19] See pp. 69–70 above.

sobering apparent fact with evidence of a growing acquisition of
a wide range of consumer products throughout a broad swathe
of the population. For example, Feinstein concluded an extended
and sophisticated review of the evidence as follows: 'Wage earners'
average real incomes were broadly stagnant for 50 years until the
early 1830s.'[20] If average incomes were rising because of composi-
tional change, however, the apparent anomaly between the two
types of evidence is reduced. It also suggests caution in accepting other conclusions derived from an assumption of stagnant or
declining average incomes, for example the inference that the per
caput demand for human food products declined over the latter
part of the century.[21]

The assumptions embodied in this exercise are, however, too
restrictive to capture the overall impact of occupational change on
average incomes and therefore in turn on the structure of aggregate demand. It was assumed that the proportional share of each
non-farming occupational group identified in their tables by King,
Massie, and Colquhoun did not change. Each such sector grew in
size, but only because of the decline in the proportion of the workforce in farming. To identify the 'pure' effect of shrinkage in agriculture's share of the workforce this was an appropriate assumption
to make, but it is entirely possible that the better-paid occupations
outside farming grew more rapidly than those which were less
well remunerated. If this were the case, it would, of course, further increase the average gain in income, while if the better-paid

---

[20] Feinstein, 'Pessimism perpetuated', p. 649. Allen's recent work supports the
same conclusion both for masons and builders' labourers in London and for
farm labourers in the southern countryside. Allen, 'Real wages in Europe and
Asia', figs 5.2, 5.3, and 5.4, pp. 116–17.

[21] Food consumption patterns and levels are difficult to measure directly for
lack of reliable data. Indirect methods, taking into account such issues as
the rise in the price of agricultural products relative to industrial goods,
often lead to pessimistic conclusions. Crafts, for example, remarked that
'national income estimates tend to confirm Hobsbawm's argument that
food consumption deteriorated during the early industrial revolution
period': Crafts, *British economic growth*, p. 98. The changing occupational
structure itself has a bearing on the interpretation of the average individual
intake of food. Because the energy needs of, say, a tailor are much less than
those of an agricultural labourer, a rise in the proportion of the workforce
engaged in tertiary sector occupations will reduce average calorie intake,
other things being equal.

occupations were growing less quickly than the poorly paid there would be a reverse effect.

Work in train at the Cambridge Group for the History of Population and Social Structure should shortly make it possible to specify the extent of change in the occupational structure of England during the eighteenth century, and thus to provide an empirical base for calculations of its impact on the structure of aggregate demand. The work is likely to show that the scale of the change is at least as great as that suggested by table 5.6.

Aggregate income trends and migration

The existence of a link between aggregate income trends and migration is implied by the other two pairs of links. There is a sense in which the very possibility of an industrial revolution is contingent upon the existence of substantially different income elasticities of demand for the products of primary, secondary, and tertiary industries. In particular the elasticity of demand for the first must be less than unity, so that as incomes rise the proportion of total income spent on food will decline.[22] We may be grateful for the fact that the marginal satisfaction derived from eating more food declines quite rapidly as the quantity of food put on the plate rises, though the fact that better-quality food will replace plainer types of nourishment reduces the impact of this effect. It is an implication of the differing income elasticity of demand for the products of the primary, secondary, and tertiary sectors that when incomes rise there is a disproportionately rapid rise in the demand for industrial goods and a consequent boost to the branch of the economy which is generally most closely associated with the industrial revolution. The proportionate change may be particularly marked when average incomes are relatively low. In the illustrative case used earlier,[23] a poor household had an income of 100 units, of which 75 units went on necessities, leaving only 25 units for 'comforts'. The income of the household then rose to 150 units. Their spending on necessities increased to 100 units, leaving a further 50 units to be

---

[22] If the elasticity of demand for a given product is less than unity, then if incomes rise by, say, 20 per cent, the demand for the product in question will rise by less than 20 per cent, and, conversely, that if the elasticity is greater than unity, the demand for the product will rise by more than 20 per cent.

[23] See above p. 20.

spent on, say, a clock, curtains, pottery tableware, chairs, window glass, etc.[24] Spending on necessities rises by a third; spending on other items doubles.

This example is far too simple to mirror historical reality but it does identify an issue of importance. The scale of demand for the products of secondary industry is highly sensitive to relatively small changes in the level of average incomes when the income level is modest. To make this numerical example more realistic, it would be important to include demand for tertiary services in attempting to capture the effect of income change. The proportion of the workforce in the tertiary sector was rising faster than that in the secondary sector throughout the 'classic' period of the industrial revolution. The *absolute increase* in tertiary employment was probably smaller than in secondary employment, but in considering trends in the structure of aggregate demand it is important not to neglect the fact that *the rate of growth* of the tertiary sector exceeded that in the secondary. A major element in the tertiary sector was transport. Employment in transport grew rapidly in the later eighteenth and early nineteenth centuries. Much of the increased employment in transport was closely linked to industrial growth, especially in the movement of heavy and bulky goods, and was therefore 'downstream' from the expansion of the secondary sector. But it is also true that many other elements within the tertiary sector were also growing very rapidly: the retail trade and a wide range of professions, for example, expanded vigorously. The relative growth rates in primary, secondary, and tertiary occupations which characterised the industrial revolution period have continued subsequently. They are the reason for the fact that, whereas in organic economies four-fifths of the workforce may be engaged in agriculture, nowadays in advanced economies four-fifths are commonly employed in the tertiary sector. This change is foreshadowed in the differing income elasticities of demand for primary, secondary, and tertiary products and the steady rise in average real incomes.

Given the significance of the structure of aggregate demand in determining the rates of growth in employment in the secondary and tertiary sectors, it will be clear that the structure of aggregate demand, albeit at one remove, exercises a powerful influence on

[24] See above pp. 71–2.

migration. A decrease in the percentage of the workforce engaged in agriculture is normally a sign that average real incomes are rising and causing a change in the structure of aggregate demand. Similarly, industrial expansion implies a rising demand for industrial products which in turn is likely to spring from a matching change in the structure of aggregate demand and therefore in occupational structure. And further, only if the proportion of aggregate income which is devoted to the purchase of tertiary services rises will there be an increase in the proportion of the labour force in the tertiary sector. Growth of the sort which took place during the industrial revolution, in other words, must be lopsided. It will be differentially rapid in industrial, commercial, and service activities, which must have implications for the changing distribution of population and the migration flows which allow this to happen. It is true that these generalisations are less applicable if there is extensive foreign trade providing alternative sources of supply and alternative markets for home-produced goods. In a relatively small country which flourished by trading contact, such as the Netherlands, this point has weight. The relative importance of foreign trade was much smaller in the case of England, and the link between the structure of aggregate domestic demand and change in the domestic economy correspondingly closer.[25]

A change in the structure of aggregate demand implied migration, since the types of industry in which employment was boosted were distributed in a very different fashion from agricultural employment. Population growth was geographically lopsided. The lack of growth in agricultural employment combined with the opportunities afforded by the growth of secondary and tertiary employment induced migratory flows, principally of young people seeking a job and aware that this frequently meant leaving their native area and settling elsewhere in places in which the change in demand structure was providing new employment prospects.

[25] The relationship between international trade and the growth of the economy generally has been much debated and disputed. I incline to the view expressed by Deane and Cole towards the end of a long discussion of the evidence when they remarked of the growth of the economy in the eighteenth century: 'More generally, however, it seems that the explanation of the higher average rate of growth in the second half of the century should be sought at home rather than abroad.' Deane and Cole, *British economic growth*, p. 85.

In his pioneering study of migration during the industrial revolution period, Redford laid stress upon the evidence that agricultural wages were highest near the new concentrations of industry and declined steadily with distance from these centres. In rural areas close to manufacturing, mining, or commercial centres people moved to the town from the country to better their lot. The increase in the prevailing wage level in agriculture which resulted in turn attracted agricultural labourers to move from more distant parishes to replace them. He insisted that 'the motive force controlling the migration was the positive attraction of industry rather than the negative repulsion of agriculture'.[26] As Chaloner remarked in his preface to the third edition of *Labour migration*, Redford insisted that 'The rural population was attracted into the towns by the prospect of higher wages and better opportunities for employment, rather than expelled from the countryside by the enclosure movement.'[27]

Conclusion

The thrust of the argument in this chapter has been to suggest that it is important not to treat changes in occupational structure, the structure of aggregate income, and migration as if they were distinct entities. They were intimately related. As with many other aspects of the industrial revolution, the links between them were so complex and close that they are best regarded as different elements within an ongoing process between which there was constant feedback, rather than as distinct entities. Treated collectively they formed a central feature of the industrial revolution process. For reasons discussed in earlier chapters their interplay could not in itself have produced indefinite advance, but they formed one of the formative, dynamic processes by which some of the central features most closely associated with the industrial revolution came into being.

The first three chapters in Part II have been devoted to the consideration of the feedback between different elements within the economy which fostered growth in the early modern period. The next and

[26] Redford, *Labour migration*, p. 70.
[27] *Ibid.*, p. v.

final chapter in Part II extends the analysis to the interplay between economic and demographic change over the same centuries, between production and reproduction. The demography of England in this period was in some respects as distinctive as its economy and played a major part in creating the context in which an industrial revolution became possible.

6 | Production and reproduction

Because it was not possible to break out from the constraints of an organic economy without gaining access to fossil fuels, it is reasonable to view the gradual transfer to a new source of energy as a *necessary* condition for the 'industrial revolution' to take place. The logical status of the relationship between production and reproduction in this context is less clear, but if it was not a necessary condition for the gradual transformation which took place, a relatively benign interaction between the two was clearly a most important facilitating factor. A 'high-pressure' demographic system could rule out any possibility of change by keeping real incomes low and causing the resulting structure of aggregate demand to be such as to prohibit the kind of change which constitutes an industrial revolution.[1] The nature of the relationship between production and reproduction and its functioning in early modern England is the subject of this chapter.

Figure 1.1 illustrated the way in which differing demographic regimes may influence the prevailing level of average real incomes. Where fertility is high and invariant the population is driven to a high level until eventually mortality increases to match fertility leaving the bulk of the population living miserably. Where fertility is both lower and responsive to population pressure, declining in the face of deteriorating economic circumstances, population stabilises at a lower level, with benefit to living standards. Another aspect of the same tension between production and reproduction is captured in figure 6.1.

Whereas the graph in figure 1.1 portrayed three situations which represent the end product of three different demographic regimes, the graph in figure 6.1 deals with change over time in England between the mid-sixteenth and the mid-nineteenth centuries. It plots the rate at which real wages rose or fell in relation to the rate at which

---

[1] See pp. 17–19 above for a discussion of high- and low-pressure demographic systems.

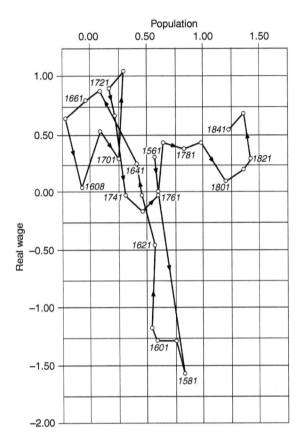

Figure 6.1 *Real wage change and population growth rates in England.*
Note. The points on the graph are ten years apart and each point represents change over a thirty-year period centring on the date shown. Thus,
for example, the population in 1546 was 2,908,465, in 1576 3,447,944,
an increase of 18.55 per cent, which equates to a rate of annual increase of
0.57 per cent. The midpoint of this period is 1561, the earliest date shown
on the graph. The real wage change was taken as the rate of increase or
decrease between two readings thirty years apart, each of which represents the average real wage over a ten-year period. Thus the first reading
is the rate of change between 1541–50 and 1571–80. The location of the
point on the graph representing 1561 is determined by these two readings.
Source. Wrigley, 'Coping with rapid population growth'.

population was increasing or decreasing. Until the last quarter of the eighteenth century the predominant orientation of the broad belt of points is north-west/south-east across the figure. It suggests that the early modern English economy was growing at a little less than 0.5 per cent per annum (because population growth at this level did not cause real wages to fall). This in turn suggests that it was a relatively successful economy. In many organic economies a similar plot might be expected to show that zero population growth and stationary real wages coincided. However, when population growth exceeded 0.5 per cent annually, real wages plummeted. This happened during the later sixteenth century and appeared to be starting again during the middle of the eighteenth century. In contrast, when population growth was slow, real wages improved, though the symmetry of the relationship is spoiled towards the end of the seventeenth century when the real wage rose less than might have been expected. However, against all previous experience, when the rate of population growth rose to an unprecedented level at the end of the eighteenth century and into the first half of the nineteenth century, real wages also rose, if somewhat hesitantly, instead of falling precipitately as 'should' have happened. The relationship between population growth and real income which was inescapable in an organic economy had vanished.

The limitations of real wage calculations are both serious and well known. They are predominantly based on male wages whereas it was the earnings of the whole family which mattered. The earnings of wives and children were often a substantial part of family income and varied greatly as a fraction of the family total.[2] Further, depending on a real wage series in effect embodies an assumption of continuous employment. Periods of unemployment or underemployment varied in length and severity and could make the reported real wage at times unrealistic. Seasonal variation in employment produced similar problems. And the composition of the 'basket of consumables' by which the nominal wage was deflated introduces additional difficulties, especially in a long-run series moving between periods in which, say, the types of food and drink placed on the dinner table changed significantly, as when the potato became a major basic food. Using wholesale rather than retail prices is sometimes unavoidable,

---

[2] For a discussion of this and a range of related issues, de Vries, *The industrious revolution*, ch. 4 generally, and especially pp. 107–10.

but the scale of rises or falls in a wholesale series may differ substantially from its retail equivalent. For example, because Phelps Brown and Hopkins used information about the wholesale cost of food in the sixteenth century in constructing their cost of living index, there appeared to be a dramatic decline in living standards during the century. When a retail price series became available as a result of Rappaport's work on the London livery companies, the resulting scale of the fall was roughly halved.[3] Despite these weaknesses it is probably safe to assume that the radical change in the relationship between the rate of population growth and change in real wage trends visible in figure 6.1 would also be present if an incontestably reliable real income series were available which overcame all the problems just listed.[4]

Figure 6.1 in a sense rescues the traditional chronology of the industrial revolution by demonstrating that a radical break from previous experience occurred in the later decades of the eighteenth century and the early decades of the nineteenth. In particular it suggests that one of the measures which is sometimes used to judge the impact of the industrial revolution on living standards should be recalibrated. It is true that the rate of improvement in real wages was modest during the early decades of the classic period of the industrial revolution, if judged against the zero growth rate. But it is more realistic to judge success not by the absolute rate (that is how far it was above or below zero) but against what was to be expected based on earlier experience. An annual rate of population growth well above 1 per cent in any earlier period would have resulted in a fall in real wages by at least the same percentage. Indeed, given the nature of the relationship between the two variables, it would probably have produced a disproportionately larger fall in the real wage. Viewed in this way, the decades in question appear as a period of dramatic achievement rather than one of marginal and uncertain gain, the impression given by much of the literature on real wage trends.

---

[3] He summarised his findings as follows: 'From the 1490s through the first decade of the seventeenth century the daily wages of skilled and semi-skilled construction craftsmen in London lost approximately 29 per cent of their real value. That is a substantial loss, but it is only *one-half* the decline in real wages estimated by Phelps Brown and Hopkins across the same twelve decades.' Rappaport, *Worlds within worlds*, p. 150.

[4] The problems associated with real wage series are further discussed on pp. 128–35.

The components of population change

To understand what underlay the population behaviour which is summarised in a graph like that in figure 6.1 it may be helpful to review briefly the individual components which in combination determined population trends. Changes in population totals themselves reflect the combined effect of changes in fertility, nuptiality, and mortality: births, marriages, and deaths.[5] This also provides the background to a discussion of ways in which demographic behaviour was influenced by economic and social factors and structures and in turn influenced them. As in so many other contexts, the examination of the feedback between related factors has at least as much to offer as the attempt to determine primacy of causation.

1. Marriage

Consider first nuptiality. In all societies the process leading to the contraction of a marriage is strongly influenced by social convention and institutional constraints. These differ substantially from one culture to the next and are themselves bound up with other features of the society: its social structure, legislative enactments, local custom, and religious teaching. At the risk of oversimplifying a complex reality, it may be helpful to focus initially on one salient feature of the marriage system in early modern England. On marriage a couple were expected to establish an independent household. The presence of more than one married couple in the same household was rare, usually reflecting exceptional circumstances such as a sudden influx of population into a community with a limited stock of housing. As Laslett remarked, 'Every child had to leave the parental household at marriage, usually though not absolutely necessarily at once. One of the conditions permitting marriage was to be able to found and maintain your own household, but a little leeway was occasionally allowed before a married child was expected to depart.'[6]

The need to set up a new household represented an economic barrier to marriage. Couples would commonly need either savings of

---

[5] Strictly speaking, this statement only holds good for a closed population. In all other populations net migration may play an important role in determining population trends, but to simplify an initial discussion of the topic this component is ignored.

[6] Laslett, 'Family, kinship and collectivity', p. 155.

their own or a transfer of resources from the older generation in order to marry. This in turn meant that marriage seldom took place close to the attainment of sexual maturity and for a proportion of each rising generation it debarred them from marrying at all. In societies in which marriage meant entering an existing household rather than creating a new, independent household, this barrier was absent. Its presence in much of western Europe meant that the timing and incidence of marriage was influenced by economic circumstances in a fashion largely absent in most of the rest of the world.

Much of the period between adolescence and marriage in early modern England was characteristically spent away from the parental hearth in service with another family. A high proportion of both sexes between the ages of 15 and 25 were in service in the households of others. Being in service normally meant remaining single. In his analysis of sixty-three listings of the inhabitants of English communities in the early modern period Laslett found that servants formed 13.4 per cent of the total population. In this period the proportion of the total population in the age range 15–24 was typically about 17 per cent, suggesting that roughly three-quarters of the age group were in service. Some servants were, of course, younger than 15 or over 25, but the calculation leaves little doubt that a majority of young men and women spent long periods in service.[7]

It was normal for each individual period of service to last a year. Annual hiring fairs enabled a new period of service to begin as the old one ended. A young man or woman in service had very few current expenses since food and accommodation were provided by the servant's master. The successive lump sums received at the end of each year's service could be saved by abstemious young men and women to bring nearer the day when the joint savings of a couple would enable them to enter upon marriage.[8] It is no coincidence that

---

[7] Laslett, 'Mean household size', tab. 4.13, p. 152.

[8] Kussmaul's data suggest that a young man and young woman in service might reasonably expect to have saved enough to set up on a small farm of their own from their savings after ten years of service. The annual wage of a male servant commonly fell in the range £6–8. Wages for female servants were always lower, at roughly three-fifths of the male level. A prudent servant might save between a half and two-thirds of his or her annual wage. For those who were willing to settle for a cottage, a cow or two, and a garden, a much shorter period in service would suffice. Kussmaul, *Servants in husbandry*, pp. 35–9, 81–3.

in many parishes as many as a half of all the marriages contracted during a year took place within a few weeks of the local hiring fair as those who had decided not to seek work in the household of a new master began the next phase of their lives as married couples (hiring fairs were normally held at Michaelmas in arable districts in the south and east, while in the north Martinmas was common;[9] in pastoral areas spring hirings were commoner).[10] Apprenticeship was a more formal type of service in another household, commonly lasting for a seven-year period; apprentices, like servants, remained single.

It has long been known that *short-term* fluctuations in marriage totals were strongly influenced by the fortunes of harvest. A good harvest caused a significant reduction in the cost of living since in most families food was by far the largest element in the family budget. A good harvest therefore encouraged those hesitating on the brink of marriage to be bold. A bad harvest had the opposite effect. More recently it has also become clear that *long-term* fluctuations in marriage frequencies also reflected economic circumstances. The strength of the link between the two is visible in figure 6.2 which plots trends in real wages, in the crude first marriage rate (CFMR), and in female age at first marriage. The CFMR is more strongly influenced by changes in the proportion never marrying than by changes in age at marriage (if the same proportion of each generation married, a change in the average age at marriage age would only alter the CFMR in that fewer would reach that age if age at marriage rose, with the opposite effect if age at marriage fell). Therefore, to clarify the impact of secular changes in the real wage upon marriage age as distinct from the proportions marrying, a plot of changing marriage age for women is also shown in figure 6.2. The plot of marriage age is inverted because a rise in the real wage is expected to be associated with a fall in marriage age and vice versa. Female age at marriage is shown, since it was this variable which directly influenced fertility levels, but it is worth noting that male age at marriage and male proportions never marrying closely paralleled female trends.

In the long term no less than in the short, marriage trends moved in sympathy with changing economic circumstances. This sensitivity

[9] Michaelmas, 29 September; Martinmas, 11 November.
[10] Settlement examinations suggest that on leaving service more than 40 per cent of servants married immediately. *Ibid.*, tab. 5.4, p. 84.

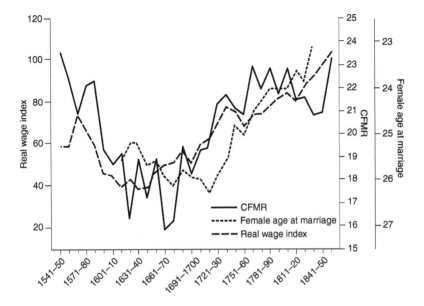

Figure 6.2 *Crude first marriage rates, female age at marriage, and real wage trends in England from the mid-sixteenth to the mid-nineteenth century.*

Note. The CFMR was calculated by relating first marriages to a weighted average of the population in the four five-year age groups 15–34 in which most marriages took place. Further details may be found in the source quoted below. The female age at marriage was calculated from bachelor/ spinster marriages.

Sources. CFMR and real wage index: Wrigley, 'British population during the "long" eighteenth century', fig. 3.7, p. 78. Age at marriage: Wrigley *et al.*, *English population history*, tab. 5.3, p. 134.

followed from the conventions governing decisions to marry. Between the mid-seventeenth century when it was at its nadir and the end of the following century the CFMR increased by about a fifth, a considerable change. Female age at first marriage reached a peak in the four decades 1690–9 to 1720–9 when it averaged 26.0 years, but had fallen to an average of 23.6 years over the first four decades of the nineteenth century. In figure 6.2 the broad similarity in the trends of these two measures of nuptiality is notable, as is also the closeness of their relationship to the real wage index.

The inherent potential flexibility of marriage behaviour in England will be clear from the foregoing. In this, England and some other areas of western Europe differed markedly from most other cultures. Where, for example, it was the prevailing rule that a girl ought to be married on attaining sexual maturity (or indeed before that time in some cases) the extent to which marriage could be influenced by changing economic circumstances was limited. In such communities, marriage for women was virtually universal. Only those conspicuously handicapped physically or mentally were likely to stay single.[11] In one system marriage was triggered by economic opportunity; in the other by physiological maturation.

2. Fertility

The graph shown in figure 6.2 suggests that long-term trends in nuptiality were strongly linked to trends in the real wage. The preventive check thus appears to have been present and effective in early modern England.[12] Indeed, if it were true that almost all children were born in wedlock and that age-specific fertility within marriage could be treated as a constant because there was little or no conscious attempt to limit births within marriage, the scale of impact of the preventive check could be inferred from figure 6.2. Things, however, were not so simple. Trends in fertility were inevitably heavily influenced by trends in nuptiality but the proportionate changes in the two variables could differ significantly. This is especially clear and important in the 'long' eighteenth century. The crude first marriage rate rose by about a fifth from trough to peak but the gross reproduction rate (GRR) rose much more steeply. The GRR is a 'pure' measure of fertility. It represents the number of female children that an average woman would bear in passing through the child-bearing age groups at the prevailing rates of age-specific fertility, assuming that all women survived to the end of

[11] Hajnal collected data which illustrate the extent of the contrast produced by differing marriage customs. The percentages of women aged 45–9 who were single in the interwar period (1920s and 1930s) in Japan, Korea, and India, for example, were 2, 0, and 1 (his table covered many other countries with similarly low figures). Much the same was true of countries in eastern Europe c.1900. For example, the comparable percentages in Greece, Hungary, Romania, and Bulgaria were 4, 4, 3, and 1. In western Europe the percentages at the same period were very different. Again a few examples must suffice: in Austria, Belgium, Portugal and Sweden the percentages were 13, 17, 20, and 19. Hajnal, 'European marriage patterns', tabs. 2, 3, and 4, pp. 102–4.

[12] For definitions of the preventive and positive checks, see above p. 34.

the child-bearing period (that is, to age 50).[13] Between 1671–90 and 1801–20 the GRR rose by 37 per cent, from 1.99 to 2.72.[14]

The reasons for the difference in the two percentages are illuminating. Mean age at first marriage for women in bachelor/spinster marriages fell from 26.0 to 23.9 years between the two twenty-year periods in question.[15] At the levels of age-specific marital fertility prevailing during the early modern period in England, a fall of 2.1 years would increase the number of children born to a woman who survived to age 50 from 5.02 to 5.84 on average, an increase of 16 per cent.[16] Direct information about the proportion of each generation of women who never married remains sparse, and indirect methods of estimating this statistic are subject to wide margins of error, but it is probable that the proportion never marrying fell over the 'long' eighteenth century perhaps sufficiently to raise the ever married proportion by between 5 and 10 per cent, implying a proportionate change in the GRR, *ceteris paribus*.[17]

Two other changes also contributed to the rise in overall fertility. There was a fall in the mean interval between births of about 5 per cent between the late seventeenth and early nineteenth centuries and a commensurate rise in marital fertility rates.[18] This was principally due to a steep decline in the stillbirth rate which was probably between 100 and 125 per 1,000 total births at the start of the period but had fallen to 40–50 per 1,000 by its end: a striking change. The estimate of its scale is confirmed by parallel movements in two closely related phenomena. The maternal mortality rate fell from 16.3 to 5.8 per 1,000 birth events between 1650–99 and 1800–37, and between the same two periods infant mortality within the first month of life halved from 107 to 54 per 1,000 legitimate live births.[19] Maternal mortality and

---

[13] It therefore takes into account the experience of each successive age group, reflecting the proportion of women in the age group who are single and therefore less likely to bear a child, and measuring illegitimate as well as legitimate fertility.

[14] Wrigley *et al.*, *English population history*, tab. A9.1, pp. 614–15.

[15] *Ibid.*, tab. 5.3, p. 134.

[16] The age-specific marital fertility rates were taken from *ibid.*, tab. 7.1, p. 355. The rates relate to the period 1600–1824.

[17] The complexity of the issue is evident in the exchange between Weir, 'Rather never than late' and Schofield, 'English marriage patterns revisited'.

[18] Wrigley, 'British population during the "long" eighteenth century', p. 71.

[19] *Ibid.*, tab. 3.8, p. 83 and tab. 3.6, p. 81.

infant death rates immediately before and after birth were influenced by similar factors and usually moved in close sympathy with each other in the past.[20] The fact that all three fell so substantially over the same period is the more notable in that infant mortality rates excluding the first month of life did not alter significantly between the two periods and childhood rates up to the age of 15 declined only modestly.[21]

The final major change which boosted fertility during the 'long' eighteenth century was fertility outside marriage. In the last quarter of the seventeenth century about 1.8 per cent of all births were illegitimate but by the first quarter of the nineteenth century this figure had almost quadrupled to 6.2 per cent, which implies a rise in overall fertility measured by the GRR of almost 5 per cent.[22] Other things being equal, it might seem natural to expect that when a large proportion of young people were marrying late and some never married at all there would be more illegitimate births than when marriage was early and almost universal, but in early modern England the reverse was the case. The proportion of all births which took place outside wedlock was much *lower* c.1700 than it was a century later, even though marriage was late and far from universal.[23] And the illegitimacy percentage is a measure which understates the true scale of the change, since the average number of years which women who were of child-bearing age spent unmarried was much higher at the beginning than at the end of the period, so that the illegitimacy *rate* rose much more sharply than the illegitimacy *percentage*. It is especially intriguing that the pattern of change that might be expected in the abstract *was* found in France in the same period. A rise in marriage age was there accompanied by an increase in illegitimacy.[24]

Between them, earlier and more universal marriage, a shorter average birth interval, and a rise in illegitimacy adequately account for the rise in fertility over the 'long' eighteenth century. The change in

[20] This issue is discussed at length in Wrigley, 'The rise in marital fertility'.
[21] Wrigley, 'British population during the "long" eighteenth century', tabs. 3.6 and 3.7, pp. 81–2.
[22] Wrigley *et al.*, *English population history*, tab. 6.2, p. 219. (100/93.8)/(100/98.2) = 1.047.
[23] See above pp. 146–7.
[24] Wrigley, 'Marriage, fertility and population growth', pp. 174–82. There were other contrasts between the two countries. In France the older a woman was at marriage the more likely she was to be pregnant. In England the opposite was the case.

marriage age taken in isolation would have produced a rise of 16 per cent; the fall in the proportion never marrying 5–10 per cent; the reduced birth interval 5 per cent; and increased illegitimacy 5 per cent. Combined, these changes roughly match the rise in the GRR of 37 per cent. But there was another change which indirectly boosted fertility still further, causing the acceleration in population growth rates to be even more striking. This was the improvement taking place in the proportion of female children surviving to maturity and therefore able to raise further the ratio between successive generations.

3. Mortality

The relative size of successive generations is affected by mortality as well as fertility. A fall in mortality can increase the ratio of one generation to its predecessor as effectively as a rise in fertility. The impact of falling mortality on this ratio is captured by the contrast in the percentage changes in the GRR and the NRR, the net reproduction rate. Between 1671–90 and 1801–20 the former rose by 37 per cent but the latter by 64 per cent, from 0.99 to 1.62.[25] Whereas the GRR is a pure measure of fertility, the NRR also takes mortality into account. It is obtained by multiplying the GRR by the proportion of women who reach the mean age at maternity and provides a measure of the relative size of successive generations. Whereas the GRR measures the number of female children an average woman would bear if no woman died before the age of 50, the NRR measures the average number of female children a woman will bear given that a proportion of each cohort of women will die before reaching the end of the child-bearing period. One measures potential, the other performance. A significant fall in mortality, by ensuring that a higher proportion of each generation of girl babies survives to bear children in turn, will increase the NRR even if the GRR remains the same.

Expectation of life at birth (e_0) declined substantially during the seventeenth century, reaching a nadir in the period 1661–90 when, for the sexes combined, it averaged only 33.8 years. By the beginning of the nineteenth century there had been a major change. In 1801–30 e_0 averaged 40.8 years.[26] The mean age at maternity fell by almost two

---

[25] Wrigley *et al.*, *English population history*, tab. A9.1, pp. 614–15.
[26] *Ibid.*, tab. A9.1, pp. 614–15.

years during the eighteenth century, from 33.0 to 31.3 years.[27] This fall combined with the increase in the proportion of women surviving to these mean ages would serve to increase fertility by about a fifth, which in turn accounts for the difference between the 37 per cent rise in the GRR and the 64 per cent rise in the NRR.

It is worth noting that although overall levels of mortality improved markedly, the improvement was not evenly spread among the different age groups. In the seventeenth century adult mortality had been very severe; infant and child mortality, in contrast, though crippling by the standards of the twenty-first century, had been relatively mild. During the ensuing century adult mortality improved sharply. Expectation of life at age 25 (e_{25}) for the sexes combined rose by five years from 30 to 35 years between the end of the seventeenth and the end of the eighteenth century.[28] In contrast, at younger ages any improvement was very limited, with one exception. Mortality within the first month of life, often termed endogenous mortality, fell dramatically. As already noted, it tends to move in close sympathy with maternal mortality and the rate of stillbirths.[29] Exogenous infant mortality (deaths later in the first year of life), caused above all by infectious disease, in contrast, was as high in the early nineteenth century as it had been a century earlier.[30] Death rates later in childhood tended to decline during the eighteenth century but the trend was not marked and remained inconsistent.[31]

England in a wider setting: the concomitants of faster population growth

The changes in nuptiality, fertility, and mortality which occurred in England between the later decades of the seventeenth century and the early decades of the nineteenth century resulted in a surge in population growth without previous or later parallel. England moved from a situation in which births and deaths were in balance and the population roughly stationary to one in which the population was rising faster than in any other country in western Europe. The absence of

---

[27] *Ibid.*, p. 534.
[28] *Ibid.*, fig. 6.20, p. 305.
[29] See above pp. 149–50.
[30] Wrigley *et al.*, *English population history*, tab. 6.4, p. 226.
[31] *Ibid.*, tab. 6.10, pp. 250–1.

growth in the earlier period was brought about on the one hand by a combination of low fertility due to late marriage and the frequency with which both men and women, though surviving into adult years, did not marry, and on the other hand by a relatively severe mortality regime. The subsequent changes which have just been described transformed the situation. The scale of the change was without precedent, given the nature of the constraints which plagued organic economies. In the late seventeenth century fertility and mortality were such that the intrinsic growth rate stood at zero.[32] Little more than a century later the intrinsic growth rate at its peak was such that the population would have doubled approximately every forty years.[33] In an organic economy a rate of growth as high as this was normally only possible in a land of new settlement, and unsustainable once the land had been fully settled.

Rapid growth without the severe consequences for living standards was an indication of exceptional success all the more remarkable because the rapid growth was primarily the result of a major rise in fertility. This necessarily caused a sharp increase in the economic burden to be borne by the average family because the age structure of a population is largely determined by its fertility level. A high level of fertility results in a youthful population. Organic societies normally experienced little or no growth and therefore birth and death rates were close to each other. But a balance between births and deaths might occur either when both rates were high or when both rates were low. There were clearly considerable advantages in an equilibrium being maintained with both rates at a low rather than a high level. The advantages of low fertility in the circumstances of organic economies was well summarised by Roger Schofield in an illuminating discussion of the relationship between demographic structure and the social and economic environment in such economies. In his examination of the significance of the age structure of a population, he wrote as follows:

---

[32] The intrinsic growth rate measures the long-term growth rate which would supervene if current levels of fertility and mortality were to be maintained indefinitely. It is therefore not affected by the current age structure of the population, which may make the current rate of increase misleading as an indication of the future course of events.

[33] In the period 1811–26 the intrinsic growth rate averaged 1.71: Wrigley *et al.*, *English population history*, tab. A9.1, pp. 614–15.

In particular the proportion of a population under, say, age 15 is heavily dependent on the level of fertility. Thus late marrying populations with low fertility, such as can be observed in pre-industrial western Europe, had a much more advantageous 'dependency ratio' of children to the working population than was the case in other populations, for example in eastern Europe, where marriage was early and fertility relatively high. Populations with large numbers of very young persons also need to devote a higher proportion of their time and goods to child-rearing. In terms of family budgets this may lead to greater expenditure on food, with a reduced demand for non-agricultural goods, and fewer opportunities for saving.[34]

The sharp increase in fertility in England during the eighteenth century entailed changes in age structure of the type which increased the problems of poorer families substantially. The proportion of the population aged 0–14 averaged 29.5 per cent in the forty-year period from 1661 to 1701. The proportion of the population aged 15–59, the age range which included the bulk of the productive workforce, was 61.1 per cent. The ratio of producers to dependants was therefore 2.07. In the first thirty years of the nineteenth century, when the pace of population growth was at its maximum the comparable figures were 0–14, 37.8 per cent; 15–59, 54.8 percent; and the ratio of producers to dependants was 1.45.[35] The ratio therefore decreased by 30 per cent, enough to represent a major increase in the dependency burden upon adult members of the community. In the period when the industrial revolution was gathering momentum the young posed an economic burden not dissimilar to that posed by the elderly in the early decades of the twenty-first century. Using Schofield's terminology, England moved from a 'western' almost to an 'eastern' pattern in the course of the eighteenth century and was obliged to suffer the attendant consequences.

To bring home the extent of the divergence between English demographic history and that of neighbouring countries, it is instructive to compare England with continental countries over the period from the beginning of the seventeenth century until 1850, since this demonstrates both the general similarity between them in the first half of the period and an increasing contrast thereafter. Table 6.1 provides information about total populations, growth rates, and the relative

[34] Schofield, 'Demographic structure and environment', p. 148.
[35] Wrigley *et al.*, *English population history*, tab. A9.1, pp. 614–15.

Table 6.1 *Population totals of selected European countries 1600–2000 and related growth rates*

	England	The Nether-lands	France	Germany	Sweden	Italy	Spain
1600	4.2	1.5	19.6			13.5	6.7
1650	5.3	1.9	20.3			11.7	7.0
1700	5.2	1.9	22.6	16.0	1.4	13.6	7.4
1750	5.9	1.9	24.6	17.0	1.8	15.8	8.6
1800	8.7	2.1	29.3	24.5	2.4	18.3	10.6
1850	16.7	3.1	36.3	35.4	3.5	24.7	14.8
2000	49.0	15.9	58.9	82.2	8.9	57.8	39.5
Percentage annual growth rates							
1600–50	0.49	0.47	0.07			−0.29	0.08
1650–1700	−0.04	0.00	0.21			0.30	0.11
1700–50	0.25	0.00	0.17	0.12	0.55	0.30	0.30
1750–1800	0.77	0.20	0.35	0.73	0.56	0.29	0.42
1800–50	1.32	0.78	0.43	0.76	0.79	0.60	0.67
1850–2000	0.72	1.10	0.32	0.56	0.62	0.56	0.66
Relative size of national populations England = 100							
1600	100	37	471			325	161
1650	100	36	382			220	132
1700	100	36	434	307	26	261	142
1750	100	32	416	287	30	267	145
1800	100	24	338	283	27	211	122
1850	100	19	217	212	21	148	88
2000	100	32	120	168	18	118	81

Sources. England 1600 to 1850: Wrigley *et al.*, *Population history of England*, tab. A9.1, pp. 614–15. Other countries 1600 to 1850: Livi-Bacci, *The population of Europe*, tab. 1.1, pp. 8–9. All countries 2000: *Population trends*, Office of National Statistics, no. 113 (2003), tab. 1.1, pp. 41–2 and tab. 1.4, pp. 45–7.

size of the several countries. Figure 6.3 displays the changes taking place in slightly different form.

In the seventeenth and early eighteenth centuries population growth in England was marginally quicker than in the other countries for which estimates are provided in the table but the differences were slight. The bottom panel of the table shows that, relative to the populations of other European countries, the population of England remained much the same between 1600 and 1750. Relative to the

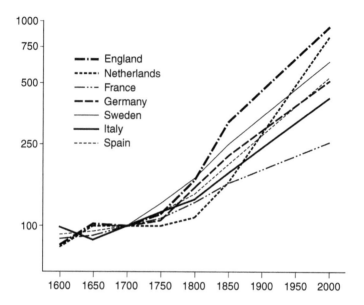

*Figure 6.3 Population growth in seven European countries 1600–2000.
Source.* See source note to table 6.1.

combined population of the four countries for which there are estimates both for 1600 and 1750 (the Netherlands, France, Italy, and
Spain), if England is taken as 100 the other four stood at 992 in 1600
and 860 in 1750. England had gained slightly but the change was
minor. Thereafter it became striking. The index figure for the same
four countries fell to 696 in 1800 and 472 in 1850.

From 1700 onwards there is also information for Germany and
Sweden. If the same comparison is made between England and the
larger group of six other European countries the same pattern is
found. In 1750 the population of England was 5.9 million compared
with a combined total of 69.7 million for the other six countries. The
English total was therefore only 8.5 per cent of their combined total.
A century later the English total had risen to 16.73 million, or 14.2
per cent of that of her neighbours whose combined population had
increased to 117.8 millions. The English total had risen by 183 per
cent; the total of the other six by 69 per cent.

I have added data for the year 2000 in table 6.1. It emphasises the
unusual nature of the century 1750–1850. Both before 1750 and after
1850 population trends in England were not far out of line with a

European norm. England continued to grow marginally faster than the other countries taken as a group after 1850 but the difference was slight. As a result the ratios in the bottom section of the table, which were markedly different in 1850 when compared to 1700, changed far less rapidly in the 150 years after 1850. France continued to grow more slowly than other countries. Elsewhere small falls in the ratios continued, with the notable exception of the Netherlands, whose ratio increased sharply. As the growth rates shown in the middle section of the table make clear, the Dutch population was growing much more rapidly than that of any of the other countries in the later nineteenth and twentieth centuries. The Netherlands is the only country in the table whose population relative to that of England was much the same in 2000 as in 1600.

In figure 6.3 the population of each of the seven countries represented in table 6.1 is indexed to 100 in 1700, the date from which all seven are in observation. The vertical scale is logarithmic so that the eye can appreciate more readily contrasts in the growth rate of the countries in different time periods. Prior to 1700, growth was slow and uncertain in the five countries for which estimates are available and England did not stand out from the others, and this remained true of the following half-century, when all seven countries figure in the graph. Between 1750 and 1850, however, the exceptional character of English growth is apparent. The English line breaks clear from those of the other six. The exceptional nature of English population growth in the classic era of the industrial revolution stands out. After 1850, as already noted, the pattern in general reverted to what had been true before 1750. England grew marginally faster than four of the other six countries, and the growth rate in France remained below that of other countries. The Netherlands, however, provided an eye-catching exception to earlier growth patterns. In the eighteenth century the Dutch population rose much less fast than that of the other six countries, but from 1850 onwards its growth rate outstripped them by a wide margin.

The demographic history of many European countries in the period before regular census taking is known only in outline, but that of France and of Sweden has been reconstructed in sufficient detail to allow comparison with the English experience over the period from 1750 to 1850. Figure 6.4 shows how diverse their several histories were.

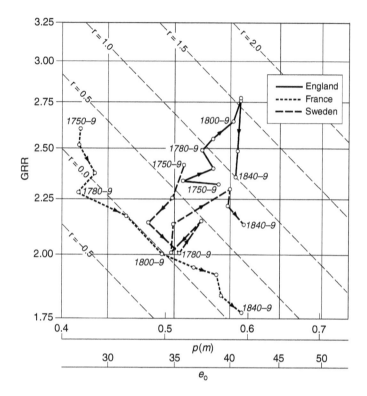

Figure 6.4 *England, France, and Sweden compared.*
Note. This figure is a slightly modified version of a graph published as shown in the source note. The principal changes are that all the data refer to decennial periods and that the English data are now taken from Wrigley *et al.*, *English population history*, tab. A9.1, pp. 614–15. The data for France and Sweden are taken from the figure listed in the source note. *Source.* Wrigley and Schofield, *The population history of England*, fig. 7.13, p. 246.

The broken diagonal lines running north-west/south-east across the graph represent rates of population growth, *r*. Thus the line $r = 0.5$ represents a growth rate of 0.5 per cent per annum. This line captures all the combinations of fertility and mortality which produce this growth rate. The vertical axis measures fertility by the gross reproduction rate (GRR) while the horizontal axis measures mortality expressed as expectation of life at birth (e_0), which in turn determines the proportion surviving to the mean age at maternity $p(m)$.

The line $r = 0.5$ shows, for example, that when $e_0 = 35$ years a GRR of just over 2.25 will produce this rate of growth. If $e_0 = 45$ years, a GRR of about 1.80 will produce the same growth rate.[36]

Although the graph in figure 6.4 may appear unfamiliar at first sight, the use of this method of describing the population histories of the three countries between 1750 and 1850 allows the contrasts between them to be brought out simply and clearly. The population of France during this period was increasing at much the same sedate pace throughout, tracing a path running parallel to, though normally slightly above, the diagonal representing a zero growth rate, but her situation at the end of the period was very different from that at its beginning. In the mid-eighteenth century, expectation of life at birth was 28 years but fertility was high with a GRR of about 2.6. A hundred years later mortality had improved dramatically, with expectation of life at birth having risen to more than 40 years, but fertility had fallen substantially, with the GRR at about 1.75. In Sweden the growth rate rose substantially if unsteadily over the century owing to a significant but irregular decline in mortality which became pronounced and consistent only after 1810, increasing by six or seven years over the next three decades. Fertility showed no clear trend. The trend line of French change was diagonal, that of Swedish change roughly horizontal, if considered over the century as a whole. In the English case most of the movement was vertical.[37] There was a marked rise in fertility over the first half of the period followed by a broadly similar fall in the last three decades. Mortality was lower than in the other two countries in 1750 but improved only modestly, changing less than in either of the other two countries in the ensuing

[36] This is a simplified account of this method of representing the growth rate, which results from different combinations of fertility and mortality. For example, r should be referred to as the intrinsic growth rate and represents the situation which is reached if given levels of fertility and mortality are maintained long enough for temporary sources of distortion such as the initial age structure to disappear and the *stable* characteristics of the population to emerge. For a fuller discussion of the intrinsic growth rate, with some illustrative applications, see Wrigley and Schofield, *The population history of England*, pp. 236–48.

[37] It may be of interest to note that the assumption that the 'normal' reason for an acceleration in population growth rates in the later eighteenth century was a fall in mortality is partly due to the fact that the history of change in Sweden was clear before there were comparable data for other countries in Europe.

century. French demographic history during this century was *sui generis* because the employment of practices to reduce fertility within marriage became widespread in some French provinces far earlier than in western Europe generally. And a period of exceptionally high fertility set England apart from both France and Sweden.

It should be noted that in one respect the pattern of change depicted in figure 6.3 may be misleading. Mortality improved less rapidly in England than in France or Sweden. At the beginning of the period expectation of life at birth was marginally higher in England than in Sweden and much higher than in France, but by its end it was slightly below the level in the other two countries. The period from the mid-eighteenth to the mid-nineteenth century was, however, a period of very rapid urbanisation in England, while Sweden remained principally a rural country, and this was largely true also of France. This raises the possibility that, controlling for settlement type, mortality trends in England may have improved more than appears at first sight. Woods has shown how during the later nineteenth century the absence of any significant improvement in mortality at the national level in England is consonant with improvement in every type of settlement from the village to the metropolis because mortality was positively correlated with settlement size. The bigger the town the less healthy it was.[38] An increasing proportion of each successive generation living in the least salubrious environments might counterbalance an improving trend in each settlement type taken separately.[39] William Farr suggested that mortality rose as the 8th root of population density and during his period at the Registrar-General's office he collected a mass of data to substantiate the claim. As the percentage of the population living in densely crowded conditions rose it may have offset a gradual improvement in each type of settlement.[40]

---

[38] Woods, 'The effects of population redistribution'.
[39] The same may have been true earlier. Mortality in London, for example, improved greatly during the eighteenth century, to the point where a high level of natural decrease was replaced by modest levels of natural increase. A small surplus of births over deaths replaced a very heavy surplus of deaths over births, but the metropolis remained unhealthy when compared with country districts. Any rise in the proportion of the population living in the metropolis, therefore, would worsen the national position, even though London itself was becoming a healthier place to live in.
[40] Farr, *Vital statistics*, pp. 165, 174–5.

In one sense, the proximate causes of the population surge which took place in England between the later eighteenth and mid-nineteenth centuries can be enumerated with confidence. They were described in earlier sections of this chapter. Nuptiality rose significantly, roughly tracking, as in earlier times, real wage change (figure 6.2), but the nuptiality change alone would have increased fertility only by a quarter, which represents less than half of the increase in the NRR which took place. Combined with the change in nuptiality (a lower age at marriage and less celibacy), there was a higher level of marital fertility, a sharp increase in illegitimacy, and a moderate fall in mortality. These in combination brought about a much increased and ultimately exceptionally high rate of population growth.

At one remove, however, a fully convincing explanation of the acceleration is still lacking. The tendency for the average real wage to rise, or at worst to avoid any general decline, suggests that the demand for labour was firm, keeping pace with the accelerating supply of labour, which resulted from the speed of population growth. This point was emphasised by Goldstone in a thoughtful and rounded discussion of fertility behaviour in England in the later eighteenth century. He referred to a 'structural transformation of the conditions of labour which changed the timing of marriage within the life-cycle'.[41] He defined his view in the following terms:

The industrial revolution appears to have played a critical role, not because it created proletarians, but because it provided employment opportunities for a labour force, in both agriculture and manufacture, that was already becoming proletarianized as a result of population growth and changes in agriculture.[42]

He contrasted the industrial revolution period when rapid population growth did not severely depress living standards with events two centuries earlier when the economy failed to cope with the problem of population growth, even though the rate of population increase was much lower in the late Tudor and early Stuart period than during the industrial revolution. Goldstone emphasised the preliminary status of his thesis, but it remains a landmark contribution to discussion of the issue with which he dealt.

[41] Goldstone, 'The demographic revolution in England', p. 30.
[42] *Ibid.*, p. 30.

One aspect of the changes taking place appears somewhat differently now from its characterisation in Goldstone's summary. He considered that employment opportunities in agriculture were rising. This seems unlikely. Population growth in wide tracts of rural England was remarkably muted. Any rise in agricultural employment can have played only a very minor role in coping with the employment needs of successively larger generations entering the labour force.[43] The scale of *local* employment opportunities for each rising rural generation was little different from that available to their parents. It continued to be possible to find work, but for a substantial proportion of each rising generation in rural areas this meant finding employment *elsewhere*, often at some distance from their place of birth. It meant leaving their native community, reduced contact with family members, and meeting the challenges of adjustment to life in an urban setting or in 'industrial' or mining villages.

Migration, a change in occupation, and marriage had long been closely linked in English life.[44] All these characteristics were encouraged, even enforced, by the strength of the convention that marriage involved setting up a new household, but where earlier migration for this reason was predominantly between communities with similar characteristics, during the industrial revolution it increasingly meant movement to a very different environment. The scale of net migration from rural to urban and industrial areas rose to new heights. Gross migration flows were, of course, substantially larger. Perhaps in part because of the patterns of contact which resulted, changes in demographic variables were notably similar across the whole country. Female age at first marriage declined in all types of parish.[45] Trends were similar in all types of community, not just in places which were drawing in many migrants. Other demographic variables also showed common trends in parishes of all types. The percentage rise in illegitimacy, for example, was much the same in rural and urban areas. But, because gross movements were larger than net movements, the existence of common patterns in all types of parish is less surprising than might appear at first sight. Although more people left than entered areas of out-migration, experience of life in other settings was widespread even in places which

---

[43] See tab. 6.2, p. 165.
[44] Kitson, 'Family formation, male occupation'.
[45] Wrigley *et al.*, *English population history*, pp. 182–94.

were experiencing a considerable net loss of population, making it less surprising that urban and rural practice changed broadly in parallel.

The surge in the population growth rate in England which broadly coincided with the 'classic' period of the industrial revolution contained several unusual and instructive features. The dynamics of the surge were greatly at variance with past experience, and not only because the rate of growth far surpassed anything which had happened previously. In the past such a surge would have caused real wages to fall sharply which would have increased both average age at marriage and the proportion of each generation who did not marry, which in turn would have reduced the population growth rate. In a dominantly rural society chiefly dependent upon agriculture the increased pressure on the land made this reaction predictable, given the existence of a requirement that each newly married couple should establish their own household. In the later eighteenth century, however, there was a new safety-valve which dissipated the build-up in pressure which would otherwise have occurred. The rise in numbers which took place nationally was not mirrored in the countryside. The rise was concentrated chiefly in urban areas, industrial villages, and mining communities. In the countryside local rates of *natural increase* were high but this did not mean that rural *population increase* was rapid. Migration removed the natural surplus. It was as if the changing occupational structure of England provided opportunities which in past ages might have been offered by lands of new settlement. For several decades the national rate of population growth was too high to enable real wages to rise other than marginally, but since real wages were not falling, marriage patterns did not change greatly. Internal migration linked to occupational change provided an escape route which had not existed in the past and gave rise to a changed relationship between population growth and real wage trends.

Regional diversity

This review of population change in England and her neighbours leaves no doubt that during the classic period of the industrial revolution what happened in England set her apart from other countries in western Europe. Her population rose much faster than elsewhere principally because of the sharp rise in fertility which took place. If, for example, fertility had remained at its level in the mid-eighteenth century, growth rates in England would not have differed greatly from those in Sweden. The rapid growth which took place, however, was anything but uniform when viewed geographically. This feature was clearly apparent in the discussion of internal migration in the last chapter but may bear further emphasis. The discussion in the last chapter was based on county-level data. Table 5.2 and the associated discussion made clear the wide difference in population growth rates between, for example, industrial and agricultural counties, and illustrations were given of the clumsiness of the county as a measurement unit. The internal diversity within counties was emphasised.[46] The extraordinary contrasts in local growth rates deserve further examination. This can be achieved effectively because recent work has enabled the populations of each of 610 English hundreds to be estimated for forty years before the inception of census taking, yielding totals at ten-year intervals from 1761 onwards.[47] Table 6.2 summarises the results, making it abundantly clear that growth was strikingly uneven.

The table is in two sections. In the upper section the 610 hundreds have been divided into five groups, four containing equal numbers of hundreds ranked according to their rate of growth over the period 1761–1851 (the four quarters), and one containing the sixty-one hundreds which formed the top 10 per cent of hundreds in which the percentage increase was highest.[48] The lower section of the table lists the same five groups, but this time divided not by their rate of growth but by their absolute growth over the period. Thus the first line in the top section presents information about the top 10 per cent of hundreds in which growth was fastest over the period. These hundreds had a population of 1,299,810 in 1761. Ninety years later in 1851 this total had risen to 7,314,073, an increase of 463 per cent (column 6). Equally, the comparable line in the second section shows that in the sixty-one hundreds in which the absolute scale of growth was greatest population rose from 2,043,341 to 9,080,630. By definition this is a larger absolute increase than in the same line in the top section (7,037,289 compared to 6,014,263) but, again by

---

[46] See above pp. 116–22.

[47] The method by which hundred totals were estimated is described in Wrigley, 'English county populations'.

[48] Since a quarter of 610 is not a whole number, the number of hundreds in each quarter is not exactly equal. Quarters 1 and 3 consist of 152 hundreds; quarters 2 and 4 have 153 hundreds.

Table 6.2 *Population growth in English hundreds 1761–1851*

	(1)	(2)	(3)	(4)	(5)	(6)	(7)
	Population 1761	Increase 1761–1851	Population 1851	Percentage of national population total 1761	Percentage of national population total 1851	Percentage increase 1761–1851	Percentage of total national increase 1761–1851
			Hundreds grouped by percentage increase				
Top 10 per cent	1,299,810	6,014,263	7,314,073	20.6	43.0	462.7	56.1
1st quarter	2,304,593	7,884,595	10,189,188	36.5	59.8	342.1	73.6
2nd quarter	1,432,202	1,608,926	3,041,128	22.7	17.9	112.3	15.0
3rd quarter	1,278,485	836,081	2,114,566	20.3	12.4	65.4	7.8
4th quarter	1,295,060	387,538	1,682,598	20.5	9.9	29.9	3.6
England	6,310,340	10,717,140	17,027,480	100.0	100.0	169.8	100.0
			Hundreds grouped by absolute increase				
Top 10 per cent	2,043,341	7,037,289	9,080,630	32.4	53.3	344.4	65.7
1st quarter	3,308,293	8,739,568	12,047,861	52.4	70.8	264.2	81.5
2nd quarter	1,340,344	1,179,730	2,520,074	21.2	14.8	88.0	11.0
3rd quarter	954,630	569,492	1,524,122	15.1	9.0	59.7	5.3
4th quarter	707,073	228,350	935,423	11.2	5.5	32.3	2.1
England	6,310,340	10,717,140	17,027,480	100.0	100.0	169.8	100.0

Sources. The method used to estimate hundred populations before the first census is described in Wrigley, 'English county populations'. Individual hundred totals are set out in Wrigley, *The early English censuses*, tab. A.2.7.

definition, a smaller percentage increase (344 per cent compared to 463 per cent). It is of interest to note that only just over half of hundreds in the first line of the top section of the table were also among the hundreds in the first line of the lower section (thirty-four out of sixty-one).

There are several features of the table which call for comment. The starting populations of the four groups in the top section of table 6.2 are not greatly different. The population of quarter 1 is less than twice as large as that of quarter 4 (for convenience the quarters will be referred to in future as quarter 1, the top quarter, through to quarter 4, the bottom quarter). Yet quarter 4, though it contained more than 20 per cent of the national population in 1761, accounted for only 3.6 per cent of the increase in the national population (column 7). Quarters 3 and 4 combined accounted for only 11.4 per cent of the increase, while in quarter 1 alone little short of three-quarters of the total growth took place. The population in quarter 1 hundreds was growing by almost 1.5 per cent annually; in quarter 4 hundreds, by only 0.26 per cent. Because the grouping in the lower section of the table is by absolute increase the concentration of the total national increase taking place in quarter 1 is even more marked (81.5 per cent), while quarter 4 in this section accounts for only 2.1 per cent of the total and the combined figure for quarters 3 and 4 is a remarkably modest 7.4 per cent, though 26.3 per cent of the national population was living in these hundreds in 1761. The degree to which growth was concentrated in a small fraction of the English hundreds is further emphasised by considering only the top 10 per cent of hundreds. Of the overall growth in the national population taking place over the ninety-year period, the top 10 per cent of hundreds grouped by percentage growth accounted for 56.1 per cent of the national increase, while if the grouping is made on the basis of absolute growth the comparable figure is almost two-thirds of the total, or 65.7 per cent.

Table 6.2 provides no direct information about migration but indirectly the most important message that it conveys relates to migration. Rates of natural increase in the rural areas in which population increase was slight were probably little different from areas in which population growth was fastest.[49]

---

[49] See above p. 122.

Figure 6.5 provides a different insight into the pattern of change visible in table 6.2. It shows percentage population growth rates between 1761 and 1851 by individual hundred, the same criterion used in grouping the hundreds in the top half of the table. It is not feasible to detect regional patterns directly from the table, but a map allows some important aspects of change during the formative decades of the industrial revolution to be picked up almost effortlessly. For example, it is intriguing to note that there is a relatively small compact block of hundreds in east Lancashire, the West Riding, and Cheshire, which were all in the fastest-growing group. The impact of explosive growth caused by dramatic changes in textile production technology was not general to whole counties but restricted to limited areas within them. It was as evident, for example, in the hundred of Macclesfield in Cheshire or the hundred of Morley in the West Riding as it was in the hundreds of Salford and Blackburn in Lancashire. Or again, there were large areas of England in which growth was notably sluggish. Whereas the national population grew by 170 per cent over the ninety-year period, there were many hundreds in which growth was less than 50 per cent. There was, for example, an arc of land in Northumberland, Westmorland, and the North Riding enclosing the areas of rapid growth in Durham and south Northumberland which fell into this category. And the same held true of much land along the Welsh border and in Wiltshire and Somerset. Rapid growth was not confined to industrial hundreds. Fen drainage in northern Cambridgeshire and south Lincolnshire led to substantial percentage increases; and growth in parts of Cornwall was boosted by the expansion of tin and copper mining. The map would support a much lengthier discussion in a different context, but it is worth stressing once again the point that trends in population growth as divergent as England was experiencing in this period must imply large-scale migratory movement.

In organic economies it was normal for agriculture to provide employment for roughly three-quarters of the workforce. Primary employment was by its nature geographically dispersed to match the spread of productive farmland.[50] As long as agriculture provided work for the great bulk of the labour force, in periods of population growth it was to be expected that the differences in regional growth rates

---

[50] See tab. 5.1, p. 114 and associated text.

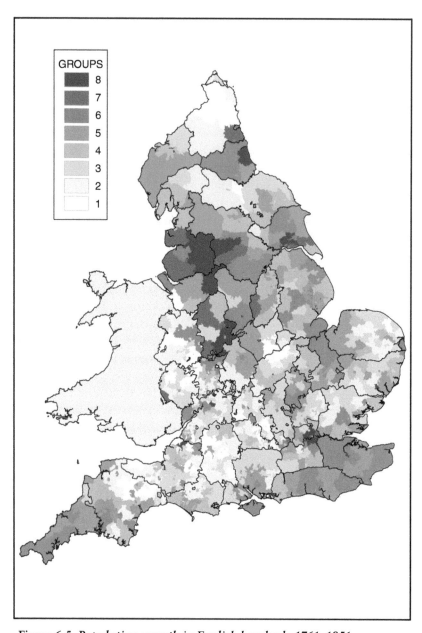

Figure 6.5 *Population growth in English hundreds 1761–1851.*
Notes. The eight groups between which the hundreds are divided are the following, according to their rate of growth over the period 1761–1851: Group 1: less than 25 per cent; Group 2: 25–49 per cent; Group 3: 50–74 per cent; Group 4: 75–99 per cent; Group 5: 100–149 per cent; Group 6: 150–299 per cent; Group 7: 300–399 per cent; Group 8: 400 per cent and over.
Source. A table containing the hundred totals may be found in Wrigley, *The early English censuses*, tab. A2.7.

would be minor, unless there was opportunity to take up new land. There were, of course, exceptions to this rule: the growth of London in seventeenth-century England or population change in the Dutch republic in its golden age illustrate the point. But regional contrasts on the scale visible in table 6.2 and figure 6.5 were without previous parallel. There was little change in primary employment in agriculture but massive expansion in secondary employment in industry, and an even more rapid rise in tertiary employment in service industries and transport (if measured by percentage growth rather than by absolute numbers). In contrast to the geography of agricultural employment, secondary and tertiary employment was spatially concentrated in areas like the Salford hundred in south-east Lancashire, the heartland of the cotton industry; in the metropolis, which had spearheaded the change throughout the seventeenth century; or in towns like Birmingham, Manchester, Glasgow, and Liverpool which changed from being minor centres to leading cities during the eighteenth century.[51]

One effect of the markedly different rates of regional population growth is captured in figure 6.6. The rather clumsy term 'weighted mean centre' is more simply understood as the point which would minimise the total distance travelled by every person in England if all were to assemble at a single place. It is based on new estimates of county totals for the seventeenth and eighteenth centuries and census data from 1801 onwards. In order to construct the map the crude assumption was made that the population of each county was located at the centre point of that county. A more refined estimation, however, would probably only result in very minor changes to the location of the successive points on the map.

The first two points on the map, for 1600 and 1700, are virtually identically placed; they are only half a mile apart. At first blush this is very surprising, since during this century London grew rapidly. Middlesex was the fastest growing of any county; at the beginning of the century it contained 6.8 per cent of national population, rising to 9.9 per cent at its end. However, the second and third fastest-growing counties in the seventeenth century were Northumberland and Durham, and because they were more than twice as far as London

---

[51] See above tab. 3.3, pp. 62–3. Some of these issues are explored further in Wrigley, 'Country and town'.

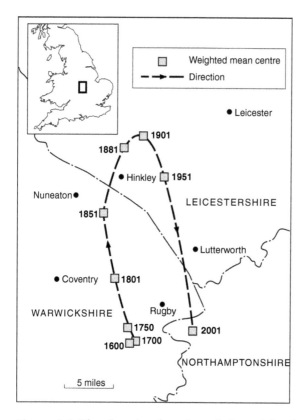

Figure 6.6 *The changing location of the weighted mean centre of the population of England over four centuries.*
Source. Wrigley, 'Rickman revisited', fig. 2.

from the weighted mean centre, their influence upon its location was greater than their population totals might suggest. There were also above-average growth rates in Staffordshire, Worcestershire, and Derbyshire in this period. Indeed, considered in a broader context, the absence of marked change during the seventeenth century is no surprise. If the south and the north are treated as two simple blocks, the percentage growth rate of the south over the seventeenth century still falls marginally short of the comparable figure for the north (24.3 per cent compared to 26.9 per cent).[52]

---

[52] The county population estimates which underlie this analysis may be found in Wrigley, *The early English censuses*, tab. A2.7, app. 4. Rather than list all the counties in the north and south blocks, it will suffice to define them

In the following half-century there was the first slight move north-wards, though the distance involved was no more than 1½ miles. Lancashire, Cheshire, Warwickshire, and the West Riding were growing rapidly but their absolute size was not such as to move the mean centre significantly. The next two half-centuries, 1750–1801 and 1801–51, saw far greater change, with roughly equal movements of 5 and 6½ miles in the two periods, moving almost directly north-wards, though with a slight tilt towards the west. It is remarkable that the movement was almost as great in 1750–1801 as in the next half-century, since the populations of the industrial counties were much smaller relative to the rest of the country in the earlier half-century. *Ceteris paribus*, this would have produced less movement in the earl-ier period.

In the second half of the nineteenth century the county boundary between Warwickshire and Leicestershire was crossed and the mean centre moved further than in any earlier half-century (in total 8½ miles as the crow flies), though the bulk of the change had already taken place by 1881. Again the greatest gain was to the north but now with an eastward rather than a westward bias, a bias which became more pronounced after 1881. In the course of about three centuries, therefore, the impact of the 'industrial revolution' was sufficient to move the centre of gravity of the population of England about 20 miles north from its initial position. This might seem a modest change but it should be judged against the size of the north–south spread of the country. As an illustration of its relative magnitude, consider the following. Berwick-on-Tweed and Bournemouth are virtually on the same line of longitude. As the crow lies they are about 350 miles apart. The midpoint between them is therefore 175 miles from each of them; 20 miles constitutes a substantial movement from this midpoint.

Adding 1951 and 2001 makes it possible to consider further aspects of the long-term impact of the industrial revolution and its aftermath on population distribution in England. Despite the travails of the north during the interwar depression and the much greater relative prosperity of the south-east, the mean centre moved only 4½ miles

by noting that the southern border of the northern group consisted of the counties of the East and West Ridings of Yorkshire, Nottinghamshire, Leicestershire, Warwickshire, Worcestershire, and Shropshire, while the northern border of the southern group consisted of Lincolnshire, Northamptonshire, Oxfordshire, Gloucestershire, and Herefordshire.

to the south and east in the first half of the twentieth century. In the ensuing half-century, however, change was more dramatic, moving the mean centre more than 15 miles to the south with a further slight eastward tendency. Over the four centuries the centre travelled just over 42 miles in all and moved through three counties but it finished only 6½ miles from where it had started, its latest position being almost due east from the starting point.

Conclusion

Indirectly the novel features of population growth revealed by table 6.2 also suggest an answer to an initially puzzling aspect of the acceleration in population growth rates in the later eighteenth and early nineteenth centuries. With the characteristics of an organic economy in mind, Malthus had discussed the features associated with the operation of the preventive and the positive checks. His model, which was common to the other classical economists, was one in which rising numbers caused pressure on resources and tended to depress living standards, which in turn either created an incentive to behave 'prudently' by delaying or avoiding marriage (the preventive check), or led to higher mortality associated with poorer nutrition (the positive check), or both. In an organic economy with the bulk of the population working on the land the pressure was felt locally, either because the number of 'niches' available did not rise in line with the increase in young couples wishing to marry (what might be termed the peasant economy situation) or because employment opportunities were limited and unemployment or underemployment were on the rise (the problem where tenant farmers and wage-paid labourers predominated).

The nature of an organic economy implied limited opportunity to find alternative employment elsewhere, especially as the overall situation was likely to have depressed demand for industrial products, thereby resulting in fewer opportunities to secure alternative employment. In these circumstances, those working outside agriculture were often more exposed than those on the land when conditions grew harsh. Goubert provided a vivid illustration of the last point in his work on the Beauvaisis. The harvest failure there in 1693–4 caused very heavy mortality. Of the communities which he studied in detail, the small town of Mouy suffered especially severely. Prior to the crisis the quarterly total of deaths averaged about twenty. When the crisis was at its worst in the first quarter of 1694, the death toll exceeded 100. Mouy was dependent primarily on woollen manufacture for its income. The price of food had soared. Mouy suffered a double disadvantage, since its inhabitants produced little food themselves and saw their incomes shrivel because their potential customers were obliged to spend what little money they had exclusively on food.[53]

The situation in eighteenth-century England was significantly different from what had previously been normal. In agricultural districts population was rising only slightly, even though in the country as a whole it was rising fast, and in spite of the fact that there were many more births than deaths in rural parishes. Young men and women could have confidence that by moving from their parishes of birth to the centres of industry and commerce they would find employment, make a living, and in due course be able to marry. The pressures which would have arisen in a more purely organic economy were not absent but were not felt as severely as would previously have been the case, and it proved unnecessary to delay or avoid marriage. Indeed the absence of the pressures which would have arisen in similar circumstances in earlier generations meant that marriage age remained lower than in the past, and relatively few men and women passed through the child-bearing years unmarried. Circumstances which would have led to a sharp fall in real incomes in earlier times ceased to have the dire consequences which would once have been inevitable. Rapid population growth no longer necessarily spelled increasing misery for the mass of the population. The demand for labour elsewhere in the economy rescued those who might otherwise have suffered most from a combination of a high level of local natural increase and the absence of any significant rise in the local demand for labour.

The model which Malthus framed, and which seemed to embody relationships which *must* hold true indefinitely since based ultimately on an unalterable physical constraint, the fixed supply of land, was steadily losing its relevance as the English economy became less and less organic in nature. Growth today no longer necessarily implied grief tomorrow, nor did a rising population necessarily carry with it an acute danger of falling real wages.

In the middle of the sixteenth century the English economy was no less 'organic' than the economies of her neighbours. There was little

[53] Goubert, *Beauvais et le Beauvaisis*, I, pp. 52–3 and II, p. 57.

to suggest that, if any country was to break free from the constraints of an organic economy, it was more likely to happen in England than elsewhere. Countries such as Italy, France, and the Low Countries employed more advanced techniques in agriculture, industry, and commerce. Each had a larger fraction of its population living in towns and cities than England.[54] Because the economies of all these countries remained organic, however, none could expect to escape from the Ricardian curse, apart from the Netherlands where for a time the availability of peat as a source of energy mirrored what was to happen later and on a much larger scale in England. Yet from the mid-sixteenth century onwards England's chance of escaping the Ricardian curse gradually improved as its dependence on the land as the prime source of energy was reduced by the steadily increasing use of coal. This in itself, however, was no guarantee of ultimate success. Put simply, coal use could overcome a barrier which had long appeared insuperable on the supply side, but without a matching change in demand a breakthrough might have proved elusive. Coal was mined and consumed on a substantial scale in parts of China from the fourth century onwards and may have reached a peak in the eleventh century, but it did not lead to a transformation of the economy.[55] It is in this context that the demographic characteristics of a country assume importance.

Production only takes place in response to the existence of demand, immediate or potential. And it is less the absolute scale of demand than its structure which is important. Where poverty is widespread and severe the demand for products other than food, clothing, fuel, and housing will be slight. Rising real incomes rapidly alter the structure of aggregate demand because, although the absolute amount spent on the four basics will rise, the proportion spent on them falls.[56]

Where the positive check is the principal means of curbing population growth, living standards are at risk to be forced down to the point where the demand for products other than necessities is minimal. The demand for luxuries from elites is met by specialist craftsmen producing on a very small scale. Where the preventive check is the chief arrester mechanism, the demand situation may be substantially different. As long as organic regimes continue, the difference between

---

[54] De Vries, *European urbanization*, tab. 3.7, p. 39.
[55] Golas, '*Mining*', esp. pp. 195–6.
[56] See above p. 20 for a simple example.

the two will be limited to contrasts in prevailing living standards arising from the structural difference between them illustrated in figure 1.1, but whereas the positive check situation leaves little expectation of escaping from the problems of an organic economy, the preventive check raises other possibilities. In itself it was not capable of leading to fundamental change, for the reasons which the classical economists explained very clearly, but, in conjunction with other factors, it could facilitate change which might not otherwise have occurred.

In England the conjunction of a favourable demographic regime with the progressive escape from sole dependence on the annual cycle of plant growth as the ultimate source of useful energy provided the possibility of achieving exponential growth in productive capacity, and led to differentially rapid growth in secondary and tertiary production. This in turn meant that whole populations might in due course be well fed, well clothed, and well housed, and indeed might secure a far wider range of material benefits, while also enjoying greatly improved health and universal access to education. In organic economies, where growth was characteristically asymptotic rather than exponential, only a small minority at best could hope to be equally fortunate. This contrast is what exemplifies the meaning of an industrial revolution.

Retrospect of Part II as a whole

The last four chapters were all concerned with 'favourable developments', changes taking place over the quarter-millennium following the end of the Tudor period which resulted in the industrial revolution. Though divided between four chapters, the developments and structural features were all intertwined. There was constant feedback between them. Figure 6.7 represents an attempt to capture the chief inter-relationships involved.

The main part of the figure sets out the functioning of an advanced organic economy, that of England in the early modern period. The boxes represent important features of the system. A line between two boxes indicates the existence of connection between them. Each line has an arrow on it together with a plus or minus sign in a small circle. This shows the direction and character of the connection between the two. For example, real income per head and nuptiality are linked and the connection between them is positive. A rise in real income induces

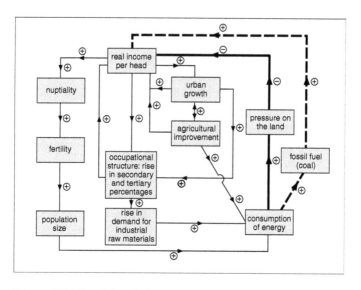

Figure 6.7 *The old and the new*

a rise in nuptiality (and equally, of course, a decline in real income will induce a fall in nuptiality). Sometimes a line may have two arrows on it, pointing in opposite directions, as, for example, between urban growth and agricultural improvement. This symbolises direct positive feedback between the two boxes. Urban growth fosters agricultural improvement and vice versa. Frequently the feedback may be indirect. For example, urban growth also leads to changes in occupational structure, which in turn tends to increase real income per head and thus facilitates further urban growth.

Two of the lines are thicker than the rest to emphasise their importance. The first is solid. It links the consumption of energy first to pressure on the land and then to real income per head. The arrow forming the second of these two links is the only case in the whole complex where the nature of the link is indicated by a minus sign. This was the key to the functioning of the system as a whole in the view of the classical economists, symbolising the Ricardian curse. There were several pathways by which a period of prosperity giving rise to rising real incomes per head caused the consumption of energy to rise. More mouths to feed means a greater consumption of energy in the form of food. Other changes linked to rising prosperity have the same effect. A change in the occupational structure as a result of the change in the structure of aggregate demand meant major increases in employment in secondary occupations and therefore a sharp rise in the demand for industrial raw materials and the means to process them. Both these developments meant an increase in the consumption of energy, either in the form of fodder to sustain increased sheep flocks to meet an increased demand for wool (and its equivalents to support growth in industries using leather, horn, hair, etc.) or in the form of wood to provide heat energy to smelt metals. Within agriculture the need for more and better-fed draught animals paralleled industrial developments in increasing energy consumption. A major expansion in transport facilities had the same effect.

Up to the box representing energy consumption, the feedback within the system is positive. A rise in real income per head stimulated urban growth and agricultural improvement, and increased secondary and tertiary employment, and these changes in turn increased real income per head, a process which ultimately increased the pressure on energy supply. And there were several other feedback loops which produced comparable effects. However, every organic economy had an Achilles heel. A rising demand for energy could only be met from the products of plant photosynthesis. It therefore necessarily meant increased pressure on the land. And this spelt trouble in the long run. Hence the minus sign on the line linking pressure on the land to real income per head. The more rapidly energy consumption increased, the quicker pressure on the land would rise, and as a result the sooner real incomes would start to fall rather than continuing to rise, thus putting the whole process into reverse and ensuring that in the system as a whole negative feedback predominated.

There is, however, a second thick line in the diagram, but broken rather than solid. It runs round the right-hand side of the figure and represents an escape route from the negative feedback which limited growth possibilities in an organic economy. If the rising level of energy consumption can be met not from the products of current plant photosynthesis but from the accumulated store of energy represented by past plant photosynthesis present in coal seams, the constraints present in all organic economies can be first eased, and then largely by-passed. In the course of the seventeenth and eighteenth centuries, the increasing resort to this alternative energy source gradually changed the growth prospects of the country. For a long time it was only a partial escape from the traditional constraints. As long as coal was only a source of heat energy the issue was doubtful. Once, however, the energy released by burning coal could also be converted into mechanical energy, future growth was no longer put at risk by the limitations on energy use imposed by dependence on the annual cycle of plant growth.

Figure 6.7 does not contain boxes representing all the factors discussed in the past four chapters. The part played by the increasing output of coal in transforming transport provision, for example, is not represented. It would have been possible to include it and and to show its links in turn to several boxes which are shown in the figure, but only at the risk of overcrowding the diagram and making it difficult to read. Again, mortality was discussed earlier in this chapter but is not included in the figure. In this case the reason for exclusion was different. Although changes in mortality must influence population size and therefore play a part in the functioning of the system as a whole, the causes of mortality change in England in the early modern period remain obscure. The prevalence and virulence of infectious diseases greatly influenced the level of mortality but changes in these variables took place unpredictably; they were largely exogenous to the socio-economic system shown in the figure. Inasmuch as mortality was affected by socio-economic conditions, their overall impact was also difficult to predict. Periods of improving real income led to better nutrition and so tended to lower mortality, but they also raised the urban percentage, which had the opposite effect. Once again, it seemed preferable to exclude mortality rather than to overload the figure by attempting to do justice to the complexity of its links to other factors. For the sake of clarity, the picture has been kept artificially simple. The figure is not intended to do other than to illustrate the character of organic economies and the effect of the gradual development of a new element in the situation which ultimately proved capable of overturning the dominance of negative feedback within the system as a whole, creating a much more favourable state of affairs in which positive feedback could take over.

In Part III some of the topics treated in Part II are re-examined by considering the chronology and character of change in England in the early modern period and by comparing the course of change in England to that taking place in the Netherlands which for two centuries was a pacesetter in economic achievement for the rest of Europe.

What set England apart from her neighbours

7 | *The timing and nature of change in the industrial revolution*

Preliminary considerations

As a background to the discussion of the issues involved, consider first the prevailing orthodoxy half a century ago. The leading figure in the first post-war decade was T. S. Ashton. He summarised his thinking in a short book entitled *The industrial revolution* which was published in 1948. The first two sentences convey well the flavour of the prevailing orthodoxy.

In the short span of years between the accession of George III and that of his son, William IV, the face of England changed. Areas that for centuries had been cultivated as open fields, or had lain untended as common pasture, were hedged or fenced; hamlets grew into populous towns; and chimney stacks rose to dwarf the ancient spires.[1]

He extended his list of the prime characteristics of the new age considerably, but then expressed doubt about the appropriateness of the term 'industrial revolution' as an inclusive term to cover all the changes which were taking place, many of which, he noted, were social or intellectual. He drew attention to the fact that: 'The system of human relationships that is sometimes called capitalism had its origins long before 1760, and attained its full development long after 1830: there is a danger in overlooking the essential fact of continuity.'[2] He concluded, however, by noting that the term 'industrial revolution' had become so firmly embedded in common speech that it would be pedantic to offer a substitute. Nevertheless, he made very sparing use of the term elsewhere in the book or more generally in his writing, and 'industrial revolution' does not appear in the index of the book.[3]

---

[1] Ashton, *The industrial revolution*, p. 1.
[2] *Ibid.*, p. 2.
[3] Ashton was not the only economic historian to display a notable wariness in using the term 'industrial revolution'. Clapham, perhaps the dominant figure

Ashton, in short, broadly accepted the orthodox chronology of the industrial revolution but had major reservations about the term.[4] It is striking that in this book he also largely avoided quantitative measures to bring home the scale of the changes taking place; the book contains no tables. In part this was no doubt because it was aimed at a very wide audience. In other publications Ashton did include tabular material and developed his argument round statistical evidence. However, the lack of a satisfactory basis for integrating quantitative material within a convincing analytic scheme caused the discussion of the industrial revolution to take a very different form in the first half of the twentieth century from what became conventional later.

Fourteen years after Ashton's book was published there appeared the book which has a strong claim to have begun a new era in the description and analysis of the industrial revolution. The book, by Deane and Cole, was entitled *British economic growth 1688–1951*. The authors made use of the technique of national income accounting to test the orthodoxy of the day about the timing and scale of the acceleration of growth which was believed to have started in the later decades of the eighteenth century and to have transformed the economy within the next half-century. Since their measurement of growth and change began with the Glorious Revolution, well before the 'classic' period of the industrial revolution, they were in a position to decide whether their new quantitative estimates supported the conclusion that a sharp acceleration in economic growth did indeed take place in the period c.1780–c.1840.

Deane and Cole's work provided powerful support for the received wisdom by quantifying both overall growth rates and the relative importance of different industries or sectors of the economy in producing growth. The series which they created suggested a sharp break from past trends just at the time that earlier work had identified as

in economic history in the interwar years, eschewed its use almost entirely in his great three-volume *An economic history of modern Britain*. The term does not appear at all in the index of volumes I and III and although it occurs in the index of volume II, it does so only because Clapham was quoting a passage from another author in which the term was used.

[4] It may be overstating the case to say that he accepted the orthodox chronology of the industrial revolution. In his inaugural lecture he remarked: 'We know that the essential changes began long before the year of the accession of George III', and added, 'Every first-year student is now aware, moreover, that 1830 was in no sense a terminal date.' Ashton, 'The relation of economic history to economic theory', p. 167.

representing the start of the new era. The economy displayed a range of novel characteristics which underwrote a marked upturn in growth rates, especially visible in the sectors in which technological advance was most pronounced, textiles and iron manufacture in particular. It was not long, however, before their conclusions were challenged and a different view came to predominate. Crafts's rejection of the key conclusions of Deane and Cole did not result from the assembly of new data sets which suggested a different picture, nor because he made use of a different method of analysis. His rejection turned on the relative weight to be allotted to several of the series upon which the measurement of aggregate growth rates depended.[5] His revision suggested much slower growth during the 'classic' period of the industrial revolution.

Crafts's revised interpretation of the series which Deane and Cole had assembled has become widely accepted. Accepting his view has a most important implication. There is little disagreement about the size of the economy in the middle of the nineteenth century. It may therefore be taken as a fixed point. If the rate of growth for the century preceding this point was much slower than had earlier been supposed, then it must follow that the economy in the middle of the eighteenth century was substantially larger than implied by the earlier work. Crafts provided a table showing estimated rates of annual growth in national product and national product per head for four periods, 1700–60, 1760–80, 1780–1801, and 1801–31. Concatenating the rates for the period 1760–1831 to produce an estimate covering the whole period, which corresponds roughly to the classic period of the industrial revolution, his estimate for the whole period can be derived. His estimates suggest that if 1760 is taken as 100 the national product in 1831 had risen to 272 and that the corresponding figures for national product per head rose from 100 to 126.[6] It is possible to produce corresponding figures using Deane and Cole's estimates. They suggest that if the national product is taken to equal 100 in 1760 it had risen to 403 by 1831 and that the corresponding figures for national product per head rose from 100 to 199.[7] The same sets of figures can be inverted, with

---

[5] The reasons for the differences between the two sets of estimates are discussed at length in Jackson, 'What was the rate of economic growth during the industrial revolution?'

[6] Crafts, *British economic growth*, tab. 2.11, p. 45.

[7] Deane and Cole, *British economic growth*, p. 280 and tab. 73, p. 283. Crafts himself also made estimates of growth rates over the same period using Deane

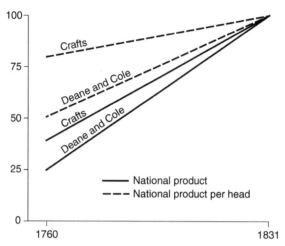

Figure 7.1 *Deane and Cole or Crafts: the path of growth between 1760 and 1831.*

Source. Deane and Cole, *British economic growth*, p. 280 and tab. 73, p. 283; Crafts, *British economic growth*, tab. 2.11, p. 45.

the position in 1831 being taken as equalling 100. Viewed in this way, Deane and Cole's work suggests that national product in 1760 stood at 25 and national product per head at 50, whereas on Crafts's estimates the corresponding figures are 37 and 79. The massive difference between the two sets of estimates is perhaps most easily grasped when displayed in the form of a graph as in figure 7.1. It brings out in particular a fact of fundamental importance: national product per head according to Deane and Cole grew massively between 1760 and 1831, whereas according to Crafts the change was comparatively modest.

It would be common ground between Deane and Cole on the one hand and Crafts on the other that their estimates are subject to very wide margins of error, especially for the earlier years of the period covered. Where there is empirical information at the base of the calculation for a given sector of the economy, it is often fragmentary, and it is necessary to make heroic assumptions to obtain any estimate at all for some large and important sectors. For example, both series embody the assumption that growth in the service sector simply paralleled population growth,

and Cole's data. They are broadly similar to mine but suggest slightly greater expansion over the period 1760–1831. If the total is taken to be 100 in 1760 his reworking of Deane and Cole's estimates suggest a figure of 431 in 1831 rather than 403.

which is deeply improbable. There is, however, good reason to suppose that Crafts's estimates are closer to the truth than the earlier series, and most subsequent work has tended to reinforce this view.[8]

Much turns on this issue. On Deane and Cole's reckoning, between 1760 and 1831 product per head doubled; on that of Crafts it rose by barely a quarter, an enormous difference. If Deane and Cole were right the living standards of the bulk of the population must have been barely above subsistence level in the mid-eighteenth century. On the alternative calculation, it remains reasonable to entertain the possibility that the English economy was already achieving substantial progress in the period between Tudor times and the accession of George III, a view which accords with the argument and evidence presented in earlier chapters. For example, when Henry VIII was sitting on the English throne his country was among the least urbanised in western Europe. When George III succeeded to the throne it was more urbanised than any other country apart from the Netherlands, and the urban proportion was rising far faster than elsewhere.[9] In Henry's day it is probable that about three-quarters of the workforce was labouring on the land, whereas in the mid-eighteenth century at least half the workforce had ceased working on the land: it was employed instead in manufacture, transport, and services. The list of similar contrasts could be greatly extended. It might seem tempting to argue, in view of this, that, while it has become clear that it is no longer possible to argue convincingly for the industrial revolution as a change which occurred abruptly and was complete within a couple of generations, all that is necessary is to change the time frame but retain the view that it was a continuous, unitary process; that two centuries should be substituted for two generations. It is right to acknowledge that the time frame should be greatly widened but, in my view, a mistake to see what happened as a unitary process, for reasons discussed in the next three sections of this chapter.

The implications of the differing conclusions of Deane and Cole on the one hand and of Crafts on the other run wide. For example, if Crafts's view is correct, the rate of growth in output per head over the

---

[8] The assumptions made in both exercises, their weaknesses, and the possible scale of the inaccuracies that are involved are reviewed cogently in Jackson, 'What was the rate of economic growth during the industrial revolution?'

[9] De Vries, *European urbanization*, tab. 3.7, p. 39.

period 1760–1831 was a modest 0.3 per cent annually where Deane and Cole's estimates result in a figure of 1.0 per cent. In Crafts's model the large rise in national product was primarily related to the very rapid population growth (output came close to tripling but output per head rose only by a quarter), whereas in that of Deane and Cole output per head played a much larger role (output more than quadrupled but output per head doubled).[10]

If Crafts's estimates are preferred there is no compelling reason to think that the rate of growth of national product per head was any greater in the classic period of the industrial revolution than over the preceding century. Figure 6.1 suggests, for example, that the early modern English economy was growing fast enough for the real wage to fall only when population growth exceeded about 0.5 per cent annually. During the hundred years from the mid-seventeenth to the mid-eighteenth century population growth was well below this level and the real wage rose significantly.[11] That the real wage was consistently in positive territory during this century and for much of the time rising between 0.5 and 1.0 per cent annually suggests that output per head was rising at least as fast as between 1760 and 1831. Rates of growth in the real wage in this range are well within the compass of an organic economy as it marshals its resources more effectively by creating the kinds of feedback which have been the subject matter of earlier chapters, notably that between urban growth and agricultural change, provided that the rate of growth of population remains low.

The probability that the rate of growth in output per head was much the same in the century before the conventional period of the industrial revolution as during its 'classic' period does *not* mean, however, that the achievement of the economy during the industrial revolution period was other than remarkable. The misery that was to be expected if a population doubled in half a century did not happen.[12] Both output per head and the real wage tended to rise rather than fall abruptly, as had happened in the last period of rapid population growth in the

---

[10] See above pp. 183–4.

[11] Between 1651 and 1751 the population rose from 5.308 million to 5.922 million, or by only 11.6 per cent: Wrigley *et al.*, *English population history*, tab. A9.1, pp. 614–15.

[12] The English population did not quite double in any half century but between 1801 and 1851 it rose by 93 per cent from 8.67 million to 16.73 million. *Ibid.*, tab. A9.1, pp. 614–15.

second half of the sixteenth century, even though the rate of population growth then, though high for an organic economy, was notably slower than during the industrial revolution period. Between 1561 and 1601, the forty-year period of fastest growth in Tudor times, the population grew by 37 per cent; in the period 1791–1831, the comparable period of maximum growth rate in the later population surge, the population grew by 69 per cent, almost twice the earlier figure.[13] Elizabethan England paid the traditional penalty for over-rapid population growth. The real wage plunged. Elizabethan England was a country without an urban/industrial safety valve. The urban proportion had risen slightly from earlier in the century but only from 5 to 8 per cent.[14] The problem of the 'sturdy beggar' (of men fit to work but who could find no employment) did not have a direct parallel in England at the time of the Napoleonic wars, partly because of the provisions of the poor law, but chiefly because population growth rates in rural areas remained modest. The great bulk of the overall rise in population was absorbed by a small number of urban, industrial, and commercial centres where new jobs were being created at a rate which roughly matched the expansion of the labour force, which in turn prevented a fall in real wages.

Relative growth rates

Before discussing the central question further, it may be helpful to deal with two related matters. The first is a simple, statistical point to which attention has often been drawn in the past but which will bear repeating, though my purpose in describing it is to raise a doubt about its applicability to the English industrial revolution, at least in the context in which it is usually introduced. Suppose that an economy is growing rather slowly by, say, 0.5 per cent per annum,[15] and that a transformation occurs in a limited segment of the economy in which the rate of growth is far higher, say 3 per cent per annum. Two possibilities are considered to illustrate the point at issue, that where the 'modern sector' is initially 4 per cent of the economy as a whole and

---

[13] *Ibid.*, tab. A9.1, pp. 614–15.

[14] Wrigley, 'Urban growth and agricultural change', tab. 7.2, p. 162.

[15] See fig. 6.1, p. 141 and associated text, which suggest that this is broadly true of early modern England.

that where it is initially 8 per cent. They are compared with the growth outcome if the economy lacked a dynamic sector and simply grew at 0.5 per cent a year. How long will it be in either case before the higher rate of growth in the dynamic sector makes a significant difference to the overall size of the economy? The answer is set out in table 7.1.

It need not be said this exercise is ludicrously oversimplified. It is intended only to illustrate the point that if a small sector within the economy begins to grow rapidly while the rest of the economy main-tains its traditional and much more sluggish pace of advance, it takes quite a long time for the economy as a whole to become galvanised into rapid growth. Even after half a century, on the '4 per cent initially modern' assumption, the difference is less than 10 per cent, though twice as large, of course, if the 'modern' sector is initially twice as big. The difference becomes very much more pronounced over a century, and after 150 years the economy is dominated by the faster growth of the 'modern' sector.

Where only general measures of the growth of the economy are possible and they are subject to significant margins of error, if a small element within the economy begins to grow at an unprecedented pace while the rest of the economy remains in a long-established pattern of modest change, it may be a considerable time before the impact of the new, dynamic element can be detected with confidence in measures relating to the economy as a whole. In the latter part of the eighteenth century cotton and iron were the two most clearly 'modern' sectors, undergoing rapid change in production technology and increasing their output very rapidly, but initially they were dwarfed by long-es-tablished and much less dynamic industries. It is not surprising, there-fore, that initially the overall growth rate did not reflect the speed of change in the more dynamic sectors of the economy, nor that differing views about the 'weights' to be attached to the most dynamic sectors of the economy make a substantial difference to conclusions about the overall growth rate, as exemplified in the two cases considered in table 7.1 and in the differences between the growth estimates of Deane and Cole and those of Crafts.

The statistical point illustrated in table 7.1 is instructive and its potential relevance to the interpretation of the history of the English economy in the industrial revolution period may seem evident. Its implications have figured prominently, whether explicitly or implicitly,

Table 7.1 *An illustrative exercise in differential growth rates*

	Year 0	Year 25	Year 50	Year 75	Year 100	Year 150
	Size of economy on three different assumptions about its initial split between 'traditional' and 'modern' sectors					
100 per cent 'traditional'	100.0	113.3	128.3	145.4	164.7	211.3
96 per cent 'traditional', 4 per cent 'modern'	100.0	117.1	140.7	176.3	235.0	539.9
92 per cent 'traditional', 8 per cent 'modern'	100.0	121.0	153.1	207.1	305.3	868.5
	Size relative to the 'traditional' total					
100 per cent 'traditional'	100.0	100.0	100.0	100.0	100.0	100.0
96 per cent 'traditional', 4 per cent 'modern'	100.0	103.4	109.7	121.3	142.7	255.5
92 per cent 'traditional', 8 per cent 'modern'	100.0	106.8	119.3	142.4	185.4	411.0

Note. In the 'traditional' sector the economy is growing at 0.5 per cent per annum; in the 'modern' sector at 3 per cent per annum.

in many treatments of the English economy in the later eighteenth and early nineteenth centuries. But it is worth wondering whether focusing on industries where rates of growth suddenly accelerated to a level far higher than in industry generally, and tracing the way in which their lead was followed by other industries, may not obscure a matter of equal or greater importance, for as long as an economy is essentially organic in nature whatever encourages swifter growth also increases the imminence of a marked deceleration because of the operation of the law of diminishing returns. Growth in organic economies implies an increasing demand for raw materials and, though capital and labour may be capable of responding with a matching acceleration, land cannot do so beyond a point which will be reached sooner when the growth rate rises sharply than when it remains modest. From this perspective what mattered most were the changes which caused a gradual loosening of the constraints which limited growth in all organic economies, without which any period when an increasing proportion of the economy is experiencing rapid growth is likely to be brief.

For many decades the gradual loosening is easy to overlook. The raw materials of industry changed little but it was feasible to increase their supply without creating increasing competition for land because the steady growth in coal use in most contexts where heat was needed in the production process limited any increase in the demand for wood. It also lowered production costs across an increasing range of industries. If it had been necessary to continue to burn wood rather than coal to provide heat in manufacturing processes the cost both of wood and of other organic raw materials would have risen as pressure on the land increased. The change became more readily visible as mineral raw materials began to be substituted for organic raw materials not just as a heat source but as a prime raw material. Bricks made from clay and baked with coal increasingly replaced wood as a constructional material in the building industry. The houses built from brick could also have glass windows. The massive increase in the use of iron was an even more dramatic change, though beginning at a later date. And, in the course of time, there were comparable changes involving a range of other inorganic raw materials. Mass-produced pottery pipes, for example, made possible both effective field drainage in the countryside and ultimately a revolution in sanitary provision in towns.

Thus there was a change analogous to that illustrated in table 7.1, but different in nature, which for long was little remarked. At the time when it became clear that it would free societies from the Ricardian curse it had been in train in England for two centuries. Both the scale and the phasing of this change were summarised in table 4.2, which records the increasing scale of coal production in England. The change was comparable to the process which slowly transformed the growth rate in table 7.1, though taking an even longer time to bring about a transformation. But it was nonetheless a very different process. Coal was simply a substitute for wood in most of the industries in which it came to be widely used, as it was also on the domestic hearth. It did not revolutionise manpower productivity as the key inventions did in the cotton or iron industries. It was only late in the day that technological advance came into play, making it possible to transform manpower productivity with the new source. This occurred with the development of an effective steam engine to provide motive power driven by the energy released by the combustion of coal. But long before the appearance of the steam engine the increasingly widespread use of coal as a source of cheap heat was of benefit to a wide range of energy-intensive industries. And there was a double benefit from its use. It lowered costs directly because coal heat was cheaper than wood heat, but in addition it economised in land use. The latter point involved knock-on benefits elsewhere in the economy. For example, the massive rise in the size of the oats crop which facilitated a big expansion in the deployment of mechanical energy from horses both on the farm and in transport would have been much more difficult to achieve if larger and larger areas were being devoted to woodland to ensure an adequate source of heat energy. The energy bottleneck which set limits to growth in organic economies was widened progressively as fossil fuel replaced organic fuels. Drawing upon stores of energy which had accumulated in past geological ages gradually overcame the problems which had beset all previous periods of rapid economic growth.

The second preliminary point is also simple and has been alluded to several times previously. It is closely connected to the first point. Kipling once wrote: 'And what should they know of England who only England know?'[16] Much the same might be said of any economic history which relies exclusively on economic factors or theories to explain economic change in the past. To find adequate explanations for change or lack of change in the economic fortunes of a community is always likely to involve considering factors which are not economic.[17] It has become commonplace to take into account social, political, cultural, and institutional factors, but it is often also important to consider physical and biological circumstances. This is especially the case in relation to organic economies, a fact

[16] Rudyard Kipling, *The English flag*.
[17] North, for example, stressed the fundamental importance of institutional forms and especially clear and enforceable property rights. 'The technological change associated with the industrial revolution required the *prior* development of property rights, which raised the private rate of return on invention and innovation.' North, *Structure and change*, p. 147.

widely acknowledged, indeed, in considering short-term change; for example, the recognition that the weather largely determined the quantity and quality of the harvest. The prospects for each year were profoundly affected by the fortunes of the previous harvest and the prospects for the next one. For contemporaries this was a truism so obvious that it scarcely needed to be made explicit, and it is universally recognised by economic historians. When food was cheap the demand for other goods and for services could expand without detriment to standards of nutrition; when food was dear the prospects for producers of other goods darkened. A couple who can scarcely afford to put sufficient food on the table to feed themselves and their children will not spend money even on clothing and certainly not on crockery or benches.

Physical and biological circumstances, however, were important not only in relation to short-term change. They were also deeply important in relation to long-term developments. Malthus's pessimism about the future prospects for mankind was ultimately based on his appreciation of the nature of the physical and biological constraints which all societies faced. What gave a special force to his argument in the first *Essay on population* was superficially a statistical point, that the nature of a geometrical progression when compared with an arithmetic progression must mean that population growth could readily match and might well exceed any expansion of output secured from the land. His knowledge of mathematics no doubt suggested to him this immensely effective method of making his point, but underlying it was a combination of biological and physical considerations. He was explicit that:

Among plants and animals the view of the subject is simple. They are all impelled by a powerful instinct to the increase of their species; and this instinct is interrupted by no reasoning, or doubts about providing for their offspring. Wherever there is liberty, the power of increase is exerted; and the superabundant effects are repressed afterwards by want of room and nourishment, which is common to animals and plants; and among animals, by becoming the prey of others.[18]

It was, of course, reading the *Essay on population* that, forty years later, was to provide Darwin with an engine to drive the process of

[18] Malthus, *Essay on population* [1798], pp. 13–14.

natural selection and thus to explain the origin of species. Malthus recognised that in human populations matters were more complicated than in animal populations but, in his view, the basic biological point about the nature of the drive to reproduce applied to men and women no less than animals. The tension which this produced sprang equally from a physical consideration, the same which led Ricardo to refer to 'the laws of nature, which have limited the productive powers of the land', in pronouncing against the possibility of avoiding declining returns to capital and labour as the inevitable sequel to any period of growth. The land surface of the earth was a fixed quantity and formed a barrier to indefinite growth which it was impossible to surmount.

The escape from the constraints of an organic economy

An industrial revolution is physically impossible without access to energy on a scale which does not exist and cannot be secured in organic economies. It is thus reasonable to suppose that it was most unlikely to occur in a country without any coal. Water and wind power do not suffice. In principle it is conceivable, perhaps, that access to other fossil fuels such as oil or natural gas might provide an alternative route to success, but this can only be speculation. Nor does the presence of coal carry any guarantee that industrialisation will occur. It was known and used on a small scale in many other places than England, and notably in China where indeed for a time it was mined on a substantial scale.[19]

Coal measures occur in every continent. One question which is sometimes raised with this point in mind is the following. If coal was so important in the industrial revolution why were there not parallel developments to those taking place in England elsewhere in Europe or farther afield and perhaps at an earlier date? There can be no definitive answer to this question. It is reasonable to claim that *without* coal no industrial revolution was possible in the circumstances of an organic economy. The presence of coal measures, on the other hand, clearly carried no guarantee that it would be exploited. One consideration, however, should be borne in mind in this connection, since it strongly

[19] See, for example, Golas, 'Mining' and Hartwell, 'Chinese iron and coal industries'.

conditioned access to coal measures in the past. When pit drainage depended upon wind, water, and horse power it was impracticable to mine coal at depths greater than 100–150 feet.[20] Most of the world's richest coalfields are concealed fields covered by an overburden of rock, often many hundreds of feet thick. The great bulk of the Ruhr field, for example, existed as a geological fact but not as an economic possibility before steam drainage. Indeed the same was true of coal in the huge coalfield which extended, with some gaps, from the Pas-de-Calais in the west, through the Sambre–Meuse valley, to Aachen and the Ruhr. The coal in the concealed fields was inaccessible (and often unknown) at the beginning of the nineteenth century.[21] The bulk of the reserves in British coalfields were similarly inaccessible before steam drainage but coal outcropped to the surface more widely than in many other countries, making initial exploitation simpler.

The steadily rising production of coal in England had a dual importance. Not only did it foster sustained growth by solving one *old* and fundamental problem experienced by all organic economies, the limited availability of heat energy derived from wood, but it also posed a series of *new* problems whose gradual solution was also instrumental in fostering growth by transforming other aspects of economic life. The difficulty of pit drainage affected coal mining from an early date and offered a very strong incentive to find a means of capturing the energy in coal to overcome the problem, solved initially by the Newcomen engine. Or again, the character of coal as a very heavy and bulky raw material created novel problems and novel investment opportunities in moving it from the point of production to market. It encouraged radical improvements in both road and water transport.[22] And once it had become clear that coal could provide heat energy on a scale and at a price which had no previous precedent, it was not surprising that attention turned to the parallel problem with mechanical energy. One early solution was simple. Use the pumping engines which had solved the pit drainage problem to recycle water from the mill race to the header pond of a water mill. But this was a clumsy and limited expedient. Watt's steam engine captured far more of the energy released by burning coal than any earlier device, and it

[20] Flinn, *British coal industry*, II, p. 114.
[21] Wrigley, *Industrial growth and population change*, pp. 31–7.
[22] See above pp. 101–7.

was not long before the translation of the energy in the movement of pistons into rotary motion generalised the applicability of fossil fuel energy to an immensely wide range of productive purposes in manufacturing industry.

Initially the growth which took place in England had been little different from comparable periods in other European economies and for centuries England was a follower rather than a leader. England lagged well behind the Netherlands in the sixteenth and seventeenth centuries and was heavily dependent upon the Netherlands and other countries in western Europe both in acquiring more advanced productive technology and in developing more sophisticated commercial practices. Though an essential springboard to the later, distinctive phase of growth, there were few aspects of English development which set the country apart from the more advanced areas of the continent before the mid-eighteenth century other than the high and rising output per head in agriculture and the sustained and relatively rapid growth in coal output and consumption. Thereafter the effects of achieving liberation from what had been a universal constraint upon growth, and the significance of the new source of energy in making this possible, became more and more apparent. An unprecedented expansion in economic activity became possible. Rapid growth today no longer meant a brisk deceleration tomorrow.

The marginal cost of production must rise in an organic economy beyond a certain level of output. In contrast, in energy-rich, mineral-based economies it normally fell with increasing output. Increased output did not make further progress more difficult but rather the reverse. For example, the ability to produce iron upon a hitherto unparalleled scale and the discovery of ways of working metal to very fine tolerances changed production possibilities in novel ways. Goods could be produced with well-nigh perfectly uniform characteristics. A nut chosen at random from a pile of its identical copies would fit any bolt similarly chosen, a feat to challenge the powers of even the most skilled of craftsmen working by hand. Or again, the proportion of the potential energy of steam which could be captured by the movement of a piston in a cylinder rose steadily as the precision of metal working improved and the nature of the physical processes involved became better understood. Such examples could be multiplied almost indefinitely. Falling production costs encouraged a rapid growth in demand, and a virtuous circle became established, a set of circumstances which had been very difficult to secure in earlier centuries, and, even if temporarily secured, could not be long maintained.

The classic period of the industrial revolution was the key time of trial in England. National population growth rates reached a peak then and numbers were rising even in agricultural hundreds, but growth rates in these areas remained modest and the resulting stresses, though worrying to contemporaries, could be contained because of the exceptionally rapid growth of employment in a limited number of commercial centres, industrial towns, and industrial or mining villages. Towards the end of this period population growth rates eased and many more sectors of the economy acquired greatly extended productive capacities by the direct and indirect effects of the replacement of the organic economy by its mineral-based and energy-rich successor. In the decades which followed, in the Victorian era, living standards could rise as the new power to produce began to benefit the population generally.

The changing character of the growth surge

Few aspects of the development of the English economy in the early modern period can be quantified with any precision but the general character of the changes taking place can be described with fair confidence. The first point to emphasise is the remarkable achievement of English agriculture in securing a very large increase in agricultural output while at the same time increasing output per head in the agricultural labour force in a similar ratio. Enough is known about the changing occupational structure of the country to make it clear that, although agriculture remained the backbone of the economy and increased its output markedly, it occupied a steadily declining proportion of the labour force. Whereas in Tudor times agriculture employed about three-quarters of the workforce, by the early eighteenth century the comparable figure was only one half, and in the course of the eighteenth century it declined further; in 1800 it was less than two-fifths. This implies that there was a rapid growth in other types of employment. Secondary and tertiary employment more than doubled its share of those in employment, and, since the population of the country also more than doubled, the absolute size of the non-agricultural labour force by the end of the eighteenth century had soared to at least four times its number at the end of the sixteenth century.

Yet agriculture continued to meet the bulk of the food needs of the population until the end of the eighteenth century. In addition, most of the raw materials used in industrial production remained home-produced, and a high percentage of these raw materials were produced on farms. Given that the change in the structure of the labour force implies that industrial demand must have been rising substantially faster than the demand for food, this underlines the scale of the rise in agricultural production during the seventeenth and eighteenth centuries, and of the achievement which this rise implies.

Urban growth can be traced with confidence and, as might be expected, runs in parallel with the changes just outlined. In the early sixteenth century only a twentieth of the national population lived in towns with 5,000 or more inhabitants. By 1800 this figure had risen to more than a quarter, and England had become one of the two most heavily urbanised of all European countries.[23] If the definition of 'urban' is made less restrictive, and any settlement with more than 2,500 inhabitants is treated as a town, the urban percentage would be increased substantially, probably to more than a third.[24] The great majority of town dwellers were engaged in industrial or service pursuits. An earlier chapter portrayed the stimulus which urban demand gave to agricultural production and the feedback between the two. Each was dependent upon the other if growth were to be able to continue.

The behaviour of indicators such as these provides a testimony to the growth possibilities which existed in organic economies. In many ways England was repeating with a time lag the features which had been visible in the Dutch economy a century earlier. It was the type of growth which Adam Smith described and analysed in *The wealth of nations*. Writing in the later eighteenth century, he was very well placed to appreciate the scale and importance of what had been achieved, especially as his early memories of Scotland had given him direct experience of the severity of the poverty which was the lot of a majority of the population in less favoured organic economies. This knowledge, however, did not make him optimistic about the future. On the contrary, he found it difficult to believe that present good fortune could

---

[23] Wrigley, 'Urban growth and agricultural change', tab. 7.2, p. 162.

[24] De Vries, *European urbanization*, tab. 4.4, p. 59 estimates that at this time English towns of between 2,500 and 5,000 inhabitants contained 6.7 per cent of the national population.

continue, since every country, however successful during a happy inter-
lude, must eventually approach the stationary state.[25]

It deserves to be remarked that it is in the progressive state, while society
is advancing to further acquisition, rather than when it has acquired its
full complement of riches, that the condition of the labouring poor, of the
great body of the people, seems to be the happiest and the most comfortable. It is hard in the stationary, and miserable in the declining state.[26]

He was in no doubt that, although England had enjoyed a prolonged
period of growth with substantial benefit to the poor, there was no
prospect that this happy state of affairs could continue. Because he
provided persuasive arguments concerning the benefits of a capitalist
economy, he has often been assumed to have anticipated the advent of
the industrial revolution. Rostow, for example, wrote: 'Adam Smith
and Karl Marx implanted in all our minds the notion that, somehow,
the industrial revolution flowed in an automatic way from the commercial revolution, via the expansion of markets in the one case, the
enlargement of a middle class in the other.'[27] Yet Smith could hardly
have been more explicit in rejecting it as a possibility.

Eppur si muove.[28] Growth did not grind to a halt. Adam Smith's
forebodings proved unjustified, even though in the half-century after
the publication of the *Wealth of nations* the rate of population growth
accelerated, just the circumstance to guarantee misery in the reasoning of the classical economists. Why their forebodings proved mistaken has already been discussed at length. What can be said about the
nature of the emerging successor to the regime of organic economies?

Why the growth surge continued

A first point to stress is that an initially small but increasingly significant part in the expansion of the English economy while it was
still principally an organic economy was played by elements which

[25] See also quotation on p. 11 above.
[26] Smith, *Wealth of nations*, I, pp. 90–1.
[27] Rostow, *How it all began*, p. 225. And Himmelfarb wrote that the industrial
revolution was 'presumably reflected' in the *Wealth of nations*: Himmelfarb,
The idea of poverty, p. 44.
[28] The remark (and yet it moves) is said to have been made, perhaps under his
breath, by Galileo when forced by the Inquisition to renounce his view that
the sun rather than the earth was the centre of the solar system.

foreshadowed the character of its successor. In particular, the relative importance of different sources of energy had already changed radically well before the conventional dating of the industrial revolution. Table 4.2 shows that whereas in the mid-sixteenth century coal provided only 11 per cent of energy consumed, by the mid-eighteenth this figure had increased to 61 per cent, and the overall scale of energy consumption per head in England dwarfed that of her neighbours, with the partial exception of the Netherlands. The presence of a cheap and abundant source of heat energy in the form of coal played a major part in facilitating expansion in a range of industries by holding down production costs as production volumes increased; brick making, glass manufacture, lime burning, brewing, dyeing, salt boiling, and soap and sugar manufacture all benefited. The traditional dependence upon wood as a heat source had vanished in almost all branches of industry apart from iron manufacture by the early eighteenth century.[29] It is probable, if not conclusively demonstrable, that London would not have grown so freely but for the east coast coal shipments from Tyneside. Jones, commenting on a possible food/fuel tension over the use of land 'serious enough, perhaps, to have impeded the growth of London', added a line from an eighteenth-century versifier which captures a point of great importance crisply: 'England's a perfect world! has Indies too! correct your maps! Newcastle is Peru.'[30] Wilson stressed the vulnerability of London to any interruption in coal supplies such as occurred in time of war.

When Newcastle was blockaded in the Civil War, it was observed how many of those 'fine-nosed Dames' who had been in the habit of objecting to the smell of sea-coal 'now cry, would to God we had Seacoal, O the want of fire undoes us, O the sweet Seacoal we used to have, how we want them now, no fire to your Seacoal ... etc.' [31]

And if the growth of London had been constrained, the stimulus which its growth gave to agricultural production and specialisation would, of course, have been reduced.

It is true that industries which used heat on a large scale employed only a small fraction of those engaged in secondary occupations.

---

[29] See above p. 41.
[30] Jones, *Agriculture and the industrial revolution*, p. 8.
[31] Wilson, *England's apprenticeship*, p. 81.

There were many industries in which production methods scarcely changed. In these industries productivity per worker was probably little different in the early nineteenth century from what it had been a couple of centuries earlier. This is likely to have been true, for example, of trades such as carpenter, bricklayer, mason, tailor, shoemaker, cooper, cabinetmaker, or wheelwright. Even as late as 1841, when the census for the first time provided detailed information about occupation, men in occupational categories in which productivity had probably changed very little for centuries were substantially more numerous than those in industries in which increased productivity was probably widespread. Table 7.2 illustrates the point. It covers the whole of the secondary sector of employment.

The distinction between 'traditional' and 'modern' industries is arbitrary. There were, no doubt, 'progressive' elements in the first group and 'laggard' elements in the second group, but the table is suggestive nonetheless. The total in the 'traditional' group of industries is almost exactly twice as large as in the 'modern' group.

The 'modern' industries as a group were energy-intensive and many of them were largely or entirely dependent on mineral sources of raw material supply. Their increasing prominence is reflected in the changing balance of capital formation in different sectors of the economy during the conventional period of the industrial revolution. The increasing proportion of national income devoted to capital investment has attracted much attention in discussions both of economic growth generally and of the industrial revolution in particular. The scale of gross domestic fixed capital investment and its division between different sectors is the subject of table 7.3.

Table 7.3 is based on the work of Feinstein and Crafts in constructing estimates of capital investment during the later eighteenth and early nineteenth centuries. These estimates are subject to very wide margins of error. Setting them out in a table with figures to one place of decimals suggests a degree of accuracy which is spurious. Yet, where change is sweeping, an exercise of this type may give a notion of its nature and scale. Two of the categories in the table need little discussion. Agriculture and dwellings are not ambiguous. The other two are less clear cut. Feinstein provided estimates for seven occupational groups other than agriculture and dwellings: mining and quarrying; manufacturing; gas, water, and electricity; railways; distribution and other services; other transport and communication; and public and

Table 7.2 Men employed in 'traditional' and 'modern' industries in 1841 (males aged 20 and over)

'Traditional' industries		'Modern' industries	
Food and drink	106,931	Textiles	250,941
Clothing and footwear	277,562	Papermaking	7,090
Building and construction	257,986	Boat, barge, and ship building	17,986
Leather, bone, fur, hair, etc.	29,170	Printing and publishing	25,288
Woodworking	52,758	Pottery, glass, brick, lime	34,313
Cart, carriage, coach building	30,712	Brass, tin, copper, lead, zinc	27,397
Instrument making	13,969	Iron and steel	109,150
Furniture and furnishing	9,083	Engineering	43,208
Gold, silver, jewelry	9,250	Gunmaking	4,529
Rope making	7,064	Chemical industries	3,976
Straw and rush	5,194	Gas, coke, water	2,528
Minor trades	8,201		
Secondary, general	274,155		
Total	1,082,017	Total	526,406

Source. Wrigley, Poverty, progress, and population, tab. 5.8, pp. 166–9.

Table 7.3 Gross domestic fixed capital investment 1761–1860

Gross domestic fixed capital formation as a percentage share of gross domestic product

	1761–70	1771–80	1781–90	1791–1800	1801–10	1811–20	1821–30	1831–40	1841–50	1851–60
Agriculture	1.9	2.0	2.2	2.5	2.1	2.4	2.0	1.6	1.7	1.4
'Modern' sector	0.6	0.6	1.0	0.9	1.1	1.5	2.5	3.7	6.3	4.7
'Traditional' sector	2.4	2.6	2.5	2.8	3.0	3.3	3.7	3.3	2.5	2.5
Dwellings	1.3	1.6	1.6	1.6	2.0	2.7	3.3	2.9	1.6	1.7
Total	**6.3**	**6.8**	**7.2**	**7.7**	**8.2**	**9.9**	**11.5**	**11.5**	**12.1**	**10.3**

Proportionate share of gross domestic fixed capital formation

	1761–70	1771–80	1781–90	1791–1800	1801–10	1811–20	1821–30	1831–40	1841–50	1851–60
Agriculture	31.0	29.3	30.9	32.1	26.2	24.3	17.1	14.1	13.7	13.5
'Modern' sector	10.2	9.6	13.4	11.4	13.8	14.9	22.2	31.8	52.0	46.1
'Traditional' sector	38.1	38.0	34.2	35.9	36.1	33.9	31.9	29.1	20.7	24.2
Dwellings	20.7	23.1	21.5	20.6	23.9	26.9	28.7	25.0	20.7	16.2
Total	**100.0**	**100.0**	**100.0**	**100.0**	**100.0**	**100.0**	**100.0**	**100.0**	**100.0**	**100.0**

Notes. The proportions in the lower section of this table were derived from the first Feinstein table quoted below. The upper section of the table involved applying the proportions in the lower section of the table to GDP estimates in the second Feinstein table, modified in the period up to 1830 by taking into account Crafts's estimates of the slower growth of GDP over this period.

Source. Feinstein, 'National statistics, 1760–1920', app. tab. IX, pp. 444–5 and 'Capital formation in Great Britain', tab. 28, p. 91. Crafts, *British economic growth*, tab. 4.1, p. 73.

social services. Feinstein's table covered a very long period from 1760 to 1920, and some of his groupings have little relevance to a period ending in the mid-nineteenth century. Gas, water, and electricity, for example, were of limited consequence before 1860. I have chosen to group the first four of these as 'modern' and the last three as 'traditional'. Once again, this is crude and arbitrary. In the earlier decades of this period some types of manufacturing, which are categorised as 'modern' in table 7.3, were primarily traditional in character. Equally, and partially offsetting this distortion, a part of 'other transport and communication' was modern rather than traditional in character. For example, steamships were included in this grouping and were of increasing importance by the middle of the nineteenth century. Other types of transport, such as tramways and motor vehicles, only began to enter into estimates for this grouping after 1860 and do not therefore distort estimates in the period covered by table 7.3. An additional limitation of the table is that Feinstein's estimates related to Great Britain rather than to England. Despite such limitations, however, it is reasonable to hope that neither a better breakdown between traditional and modern, nor more complete and exact information about the scale of investment taking place, would cause a radical alteration to the picture presented by the table.

The first point to note is that investment roughly doubled as a percentage of gross domestic product over the century covered by the table. This suggests an acceleration in the creation of productive capacity and it explains some of the contrasts between the upper and lower sections of the table. For example, agriculture's *share* of investment declined steeply between 1760 and 1830 but it was only after 1830 that there was a clear fall in the *percentage* of domestic product invested in agriculture. The most striking feature of the table is the massive rise in the percentage of domestic product devoted to investment in the 'modern' sector, that is to the sector where the bulk of the raw materials used was mineral. As a proportion of all investment the 'modern' sector claimed only a tenth of the total at the beginning of the period, but this had risen to a half by its end; and whereas in 1761–70 investment in the sector represented only 0.6 per cent of domestic product, the comparable figure in the last two decades of the period averaged more than 5 per cent. Crucially, expansion in this sector, because of its nature, did not increase pressure on the land.

Almost equally striking was the absence of marked change in the combined percentage for agriculture and 'traditional' sectors of the economy. The proportion of domestic product invested in these two sectors averaged 4.8 per cent over the ten decades in the table. The lowest level was 3.9 per cent in the last decade, closely similar to its level in the earliest decades of the period. The highest level came in the middle decades 1811–20 and 1821–30, when it reached 5.7 per cent. As a proportion of all investment the share of these sectors declined sharply, but in absolute terms any change was relatively minor. The land was not neglected as an object of investment but the vast acceleration in overall production did not cause acute pressure on the land as a source of raw materials in contrast to what would have occurred in an organic economy.

One further point to be borne in mind in considering trends is fixed capital investment. Investment in dwellings appears to have been heavily influenced by changes in population growth rates, rising to a marked peak between 1811 and 1840 before declining thereafter to a level similar to that prevailing at the start of the period. But the significance of an increased rate of population growth extends well beyond domestic construction. It should be regarded as, in a sense, a deflator of investment rates generally during a period of acceleration in population growth, since an increased rate of investment is needed simply to make provision for rising numbers. In order to maintain the same ratio of capital stock to population and so to preserve living standards, the rate of investment must rise. The rate of growth of the capital stock depends upon the share of national income devoted to net investment divided by the capital/output ratio. For example, if the rate of population growth rises by 1 per cent per annum, and with a capital/output ratio of 3:1, in order to maintain the same ratio of capital stock to population the proportion of national income devoted to net investment would need to rise by 3 per cent compared with what was required before the rise in the population growth rate. If there were no increase during a period of more rapid population growth the consequence would be a decrease in real incomes compared with earlier times. A part of the rise in gross domestic fixed capital investment shown in table 7.3 should be, so to speak, discounted since it is making provision for increased numbers rather than improving the output or the living standards of the average person. In presenting his estimates of capital investment, Crafts was very conscious of this issue. He assumed a capital/output ratio of 2.5:1 and remarked that 'the rises in the home investment rate obtaining before 1821 were only just sufficient to cope with the extra population growth'.[32] He therefore concluded that it was only in the 1820s and later that the rate of investment was likely to have affected income per head positively.[33]

A summary of the character and timing of the changes which took place

The classical economists provided a formal framework to describe something which was widely understood intuitively in all organic economies. They held that three components were essential in all material production; capital, labour, and land. The first two could be expanded as necessary to match increased demand, but the third could not, and rising pressure on this inflexible resource arrested growth and depressed the return to capital and the reward of labour.

The truism concerning the fixed supply of land may obscure the underlying point which makes it so telling. The key variable, which translates the observation about the land constraint into an immediate reality, is the process of photosynthesis in plants. This was the bottleneck through which men and women, in common with all other animate creatures, gained access to the energy without which life is impossible. Every living thing is constantly expending energy in order simply to remain alive. This is as true of mankind as of any other animal species. Additional energy was needed if a man or woman was to make an active contribution to production. To be economically active in the past, whether in wielding an axe, thrusting a shuttle, or pushing a wheelbarrow, required additional energy inputs over and above what was needed simply to sustain life. The useful energy secured might be in the form of food for the individual or fodder for draught animals, or it might consist of the production of a wide range of organic raw materials needed for manufacture, but in every case the basic problem was the same. A fixed supply of land meant an upper limit to the quantity of energy which could be tapped as long as the dominant means of securing it was from the conversion, by plant photosynthesis, of a tiny fraction of the flood of energy reaching the

[32] Crafts, *British economic growth*, p. 76.
[33] *Ibid.*, pp. 77–8.

earth in the form of sunlight. Unless this restriction could be overcome, no exercise of ingenuity could do more than alleviate the problem; a solution was out of reach.

The problem was finally overcome by breaking free from dependence upon photosynthesis, or more accurately by finding a way of gaining access to the photosynthesis of past geological ages. Capital and labour remained as essential as ever if output was to expand, but for wider and wider swathes of the economy land was no longer a factor of central importance. Energy was still needed in every aspect of the production process and an adequate supply of raw materials remained essential, but the land could be by-passed in securing the first, and to an increasing degree the second. Land was losing its place in the trinity of factors determining production possibilities.

Coal provided the escape route. But there is a paradox in this story. There was no revolutionary change in the amount of coal a miner could dig in the course of the working day. At the coal face the tools employed and the nature of the work involved did not change greatly for long periods of time. A seventeenth-century coal miner could dig about 200 tons in the course of a year.[34] When coal production in the UK peaked in 1913 with a total of 287.5 million tons, the number of coal miners was 1,095,200, implying an annual output per man-year of just 260 tons, hardly a dramatic rise in manpower productivity, and possibly a lower figure than half a century earlier.[35] But this is to miss the point of the rise in coal use. The amount of energy made available by one man's effort in a coal mine was huge in relation to the energy which he expended. Cottrell provides a vivid illustration of the point:

A coal miner who consumes in his own body about 3,500 calories a day, will, if he mines 500 pounds of coal, produce coal with a heat value 500 times the heat value of the food which he consumed while mining it. At 20 per cent efficiency he expends about 1 horsepower-hour of mechanical energy to get the coal. Now, if the coal he mines is burned in a steam engine of even 1 per cent efficiency it will yield about 27 horsepower-hours of mechanical energy. The surplus of mechanical energy gained would thus

---

[34] Only scattered estimates are available and they refer primarily to the north-east coalfield where manpower productivity may have been atypically high. Hatcher, *British coal industry*, I, pp. 344–6; Nef, *British coal industry*, II, p. 138.

[35] Church, *British coal industry*, III, tab. 1.12, p. 86 and tab. 3.1, p. 189.

be 26 horsepower-hours, or the equivalent of 26 man-days per man-day. A coal miner, who consumed about one-fifth as much food as a horse, could thus deliver through the steam engine about 4 times the mechanical energy which the average horse in Watt's day was found to deliver.[36]

This is a very conservative estimate of the multiplier involved, since the average coal miner produced considerably more than 500 pounds of coal a day and the efficiency of steam engines commonly dwarfed the figure used in the illustration. Even on Cottrell's figures, however, the energy-magnifying effect of the use of coal was so large that the fact that the quantity of coal mined could be expanded at will, in contrast to the problem of expanding land area as a source of energy, created the possibility of escaping from the age-old constraints which had frustrated all earlier generations. However, in many industries the possibility of securing a massive increase in production because of a far more abundant energy supply could only be realised by finding ways of harnessing it effectively. The problems in many cases were far from trivial.[37] Nevertheless tapping into the new energy source changed the production horizon in a fundamental fashion that had happened only once previously in human history, at the time of the neolithic food revolution.

If, to emphasise once again a main theme of this work, the key question regarding the industrial revolution is not why and when it started but why it did not stop, the answer must lie in gaining access to a different source of energy. In this context the *timing* of the industrial revolution appears in a different light. It had its slight beginnings in the sixteenth century, gradually becoming a dominant element in the expansion of the English economy over the next two centuries. It was an almost imperceptible revolution to contemporaries but with the benefit of hindsight its importance is inescapable. Conscious recognition of coal as the arbiter of industrial success came only in the later nineteenth century, symbolised when Jevons published *The coal question*, in which he wondered anxiously about the brevity of British industrial supremacy given that other parts of the world had much

---

[36] Cottrell, *Energy and society*, p. 86.
[37] See, as an apparently minor example, which has a much wider relevance, the intriguing discussion of 'learning to heat a house with coal' in Allen, *The British industrial revolution*, pp. 90–3.

larger reserves of coal and were already beginning to take advantage of their good fortune. When the first edition of *The coal question* was published in 1865, little was known about the scale of the coal resources in other countries and Jevons was relatively optimistic about the future, but by the time of the third edition in 1906 it was clear that several countries, and especially China and the United States, possessed far larger reserves, and his tone changed: 'When coalfields of such phenomenal richness are actively developed, countries in which there no longer remain any large supplies of easily and cheaply mined coal are likely to feel the effect of the resulting severe competition.'[38]

Against this background, if the traditional question concerning timing is again raised, there is much to be said in favour of the older view of what constituted the critical phase in the transition to a new age. It is difficult to overstate the severity of the challenge posed by the rapidity of population growth between, say, 1780 and 1840 when viewed in terms of the limitations of an organic economy in a land long settled. In the sixty years in question the population of England more than doubled, a challenge of epic proportions.[39] All past experience suggested that there must be a catastrophic decline in living standards. That this did not occur is proof enough of the emergence of an economy with capacities of a new kind which had been gradually acquired over the two preceding centuries.

The increase in the productive powers of an industrialised society were such that for the first time in human history the miseries of poverty, from which previously only a small minority were exempt, could be put aside for whole populations. Success in escaping from the constraints which affected all organic economies did not, however, mean a swift and uninterrupted move towards greatly improved material circumstances for all. The *potential* for such a change existed. Realising it proved to be another matter. Economic structures which divided the benefits of increasing productive power very unevenly; political ineptitude, prejudice, or mismanagement; various kinds of discrimination; and the destruction of war – all were still capable of depriving much of the population of this benefit. Even so, the nature of the case had changed. Before the change a modest sufficiency was the most which could be hoped for, the kind

---

[38] Jevons, *The coal question*, p. 362.
[39] The population of England rose from 7.21 to 14.94 million between 1781 and 1841. Wrigley *et al.*, *English population history*, tab. A9.1, pp. 614–15.

of model which Goldsmith had in mind in describing the life of his 'bold peasantry',[40] but the commonest case was a constant uncertainty for much of the population even about securing enough food to stay healthy. Organic economies necessarily operated within strict limits. The industrial revolution made it possible to escape them. But for the country in which an industrial revolution first took place the definitive release from poverty was long in arriving for much of the population. If the industrial revolution did indeed occur between c.1780 and c.1840, and if the possibility of abolishing the traditional concomitants of poverty is one of its defining characteristics, then the realisation of the promise was long delayed for much of the population, as the social investigations of Mayhew, Booth, Rowntree, and others in the decades before and immediately after the First World War make clear.[41]

Many contemporaries were bitter about the sufferings of the urban poor where others were triumphalist about the achievements of the Victorian age. Both views have had able, at times passionate, advocates, sometimes influenced by a general conviction about the nature of capitalism or the dynamics of world history.[42] And there is a sense in which both views are justified, but with the elapse of time a somewhat different perspective seems more persuasive. Progress was not absent but for long it was limited. From mid-Victorian times the level of real incomes was rising, and in most respects the circumstances of life for the bulk of the population were better in 1900 than they had been in 1850. Further progress for half a century was delayed and at times reversed by the effects of two world wars and the Great Depression. Only in the second half of the twentieth century was improvement in health, education, and general welfare widespread, substantial, and sustained.

Looking back over the last century-and-a-half it is perhaps unsurprising that progress was initially limited and spasmodic. In part this was due to 'external' factors, the impact of major wars and the

---

[40] For the relevant verse of his poem see above p. 77.

[41] Mayhew, *London labour and the London* poor; Booth, *Life and labour*; Rowntree, *Poverty*.

[42] Capitalism is an elusive concept, variously defined. In an essay on economic growth, Jones, seeking agreed terms as a basis for his discussion, and irritated by this elusiveness, remarked: 'Definitions of capitalism are misty where not merely rhetorical, and lie, like beauty, too much in the eye of the beholder.' Jones, *Growth recurring*, pp. 31–2.

great slump, but it reflected also the unfamiliarity of many both of the problems and of the opportunities which arose with the acquisition of unprecedented powers of production. The enormous and very rapid growth of cities and towns, for example, which reflected the changing importance of different sectors of the economy, posed massive problems which were initially difficult to resolve. Urban mortality was for many years much higher in cities than in small towns or the countryside, but limited progress in improving the health of the urban populations in many areas was unavoidable until the modes of transmission of many diseases were better understood. Cholera epidemics, for example, could not be eliminated until the importance of securing a supply of pure water had been appreciated. And even when the knowledge had been gained, the infrastructural investment needed to reduce and eventually overcome this problem took time. Securing educational provision for all children took place only over several decades. This was due in part to the nature of the politics of the day, but even without delay for this reason it could not have happened overnight. In other words, it is reasonable to suggest that the fact that the nature of the industrial revolution was so little understood at the time and that the changes which came in its train were so radical should lessen any surprise that its potential benefits were not realised instantly.

8 | Modernisation and the industrial revolution in England

Introductory comment

It is frequently the case that discussions of the industrial revolution embody the assumption, either explicitly or implicitly, that there was a close association between 'modernisation' and the industrial revolution. The second is sometimes portrayed as, in effect, an aspect of the first. Modernisation is a term widely used by sociologists, economists, and historians to describe the transitional process by which traditional, largely rural society was replaced by an industrialised and urbanised successor. Industrialisation is then often treated as that aspect of the modernisation process which brings into existence the capacity to secure exponential economic growth. This in turn creates confidence that real incomes will rise into the foreseeable future, replacing the expectation that poverty is the permanent lot of the mass of mankind. This characterisation of the relationship between modernisation and industrialisation is unlikely to command universal assent, but it provides a convenient preface to a discussion of several aspects of the industrial revolution, and in particular to the question of whether modernisation, which is often regarded as a *necessary* condition for an industrial revolution, is also a *sufficient* condition for it. It also affords a convenient background to a discussion of what was common to the experience of England and the Netherlands, which for so long provided an exemplar to England in matters economic, and in what respects the two countries differed. Discussion of this issue is helpful in identifying some important features of the English industrial revolution, and since the term 'modernisation' is not self-explanatory it is sensible to begin by offering a definition of it.

The two key notions underpinning the concept of modernisation are rationality and self-interest. Both have a semi-technical meaning. By rational behaviour is meant action which tends to maximise the economic returns to an individual or group when choosing between different possible courses of action. There are, of course, utilities which might be maximised other than those that are economic, and in traditional societies such utilities may be given preference, but in the course of modernisation such non-economic priorities become sub-ordinated to economic imperatives. For example, it may be perfectly rational, given the preferences prevailing in a traditional community, for a family to retain a son on their holding even though his marginal product is less than his consumption, because the preservation of the family as an integral unit is viewed as more important than maximis-ing the average income within the family, but in the technical sense to do so would qualify as an irrational decision.

Similarly, self-interest is held to be the guiding principle of action in a modernised society to a degree that might appear both aberrant and abhorrent in a traditional community, given the interpretation of what constitutes self-interest in modernisation theory. Once again, in the general sense of the term, self-interest may be as conspicuous a guid-ing principle of action in traditional society as in a modern, industrial society. Indeed, one might argue that it is difficult to imagine any indi-vidual actions which are not actuated in some sense by self-interest. In a traditional society a man may devote much of his time and energy promoting the well-being, security, and status of his lord or of his dependents and yet be acting from a regard for self-interest as clear-cut as any Scrooge. For example, Hart and Pilling describe the life strategy of a young man among the Tiwi in northern Australia. A man's status depended above all upon the number of his wives. No man could hope to achieve high status in this way until his later forties, but he had to lay the foundation of future success many years earlier by forming links with powerful men who were willing to promise their female children, whether born or yet to be born, as his future wives in return for present services.[1] This was a risky strategy since the early death of young girls or an unfortunate run of male offspring might leave the older man unable to keep his side of the bargain. Given the circum-stances of his life, however, the young Tiwi man in following this strat-egy might be said to be acting from self-interest as clearly as a young Londoner in joining a merchant bank. In the context of of modernisa-tion theory, however, self-interest has come to mean the adoption of a calculus of advantage in which the unit is the individual or, at the

[1] Hart and Pilling, *The Tiwi*, pp. 51–2.

widest, the nuclear family, and the accounting scale is pecuniary gain rather than number of wives, or any other criterion.[2]

To make it possible to act 'rationally' as this is understood in the context of modernisation, there must be a common measure of value, and a calculus by which alternative courses of action can be compared. Money provides a common measure of value where most goods and services are provided through the market and has the advantage of assessing value on an interval scale. Monetary accounting makes it possible to estimate the costs and returns of alternative possibilities; to balance present utility against some greater future utility; and to compare the returns on investing a capital sum in different ways.

Given such a view of rational action, modernisation theory is able to define pairs of polar opposites which exemplify 'rationality' and 'irrationality'. Each society can then in principle be located somewhere in the spectrum of possible positions between the two extremes. An industrialised society is expected to be located towards one end of the spectrum, a feudal society towards the other.

Two of the most important of the changes which represent movement in a modernising direction are the replacement of ascription by achievement as the basis for recruitment to office and the substitution of universalistic for particularistic criteria for membership of groups, societies, and associations of all kinds. The first change concerns the way in which an individual is recruited to discharge a given role in society. Where achievement rules, only the fitness of the candidate to carry out the task in question is considered. Parentage, kin, age, nationality, religion, race, and sex are not to be taken into account. Where ascription prevails, the choice may be restricted to a particular group within society who are regarded as the only proper persons to discharge the role. Open, competitive examination for a government administrative post is an example of recruitment by achievement. Entry into a guild where preference is given to the sons of present guild members is an example of ascription.

The second change is closely related to the first. Where universalistic principles prevail, for example, it is understood that all men should be equal before the law and that the law should be the same for all men.

---

[2] This description of modernisation theory is abbreviated to the point of caricature. It is set out in greater detail in Wrigley, 'The process of modernization'.

It is at odds with this principle that a priest in holy orders should be able, simply in virtue of his office, to invoke immunity from the purview of the civil courts. Or again, where the local community is able to set prices, or can prevent traders from outside from offering their wares in the local market, or subjects them to disadvantages in doing so, this represents a particularistic ethos. All franchises, liberties, and privileges which distinguish particular groups are to be deplored on universalistic principles. The trade in all commodities should be free for all to participate, with the market the sole arbiter of price.

When modernising change occurs it is likely to be associated with movement towards a characteristic form and mode of operation of the legal system; with a particular definition of the scope, nature, and stability of property rights; and perhaps also with the development of the nation-state, exercising sovereignty, employing bureaucratic techniques of government, and acting in harmony with the interest of the bourgeoisie.

The move from traditional to modern structures and attitudes of mind may also be pictured as the move from *Gemeinschaft* to *Gesellschaft*, convenient terms for which the nearest equivalent English terms are perhaps community and association. The former suggests tight-knit groupings in which the personality of the individual merges with the structure and interests of the larger unit, the latter an atomised world in which the individual is little influenced by any consideration other than his or her immediate advantage. Adam Smith captured the nature of the new world which had come into existence in a passage which is frequently quoted to illustrate the character of a 'modernised' society. He had first described the solitary life of almost all animals and then continued:

But man has almost constant occasion for the help of his brethren, and it is vain for him to expect it from their benevolence only. He will be more likely to prevail if he can interest their self-love in his favour, and show them that it is for their own advantage to do for him what he requires of them – It is not from the benevolence of the butcher, the brewer, or the baker that we expect our dinner, but from their regard to their own interest. We address ourselves, not to their humanity but to their self-love, and never talk of our own necessities but of their advantages. Nobody but a beggar chuses to depend chiefly upon the benevolence of his fellow-citizens.[3]

[3] Smith, *Wealth of nations*, I, p. 18.

Or again, Tönnies, an early and extreme protagonist of the view that modern and traditional societies differ profoundly, remarked: 'The will to enrich himself makes the merchant unscrupulous and the type of egotistic, self-willed individual to whom all human beings except his nearest friends are only a means and tools to his ends or purposes; he is the embodiment of *Gesellschaft*.'[4] He thought the pressure towards an atomic individualism was so acute when *Gesellschaft* replaced *Gemeinschaft* that 'The family becomes an accidental form for the satisfaction of natural needs, neighbourhood and friendship are supplanted by special interest groups and conventional society life.'[5]

One further aspect of modernisation is widely held to have been important in easing the process of industrialisation and in serving the interests of capitalism. Max Weber stressed the close connection between rationality and bureaucratic method. But this is only one facet of the stimulus afforded by the nation-state to the modernisation process. The state provides the sanctions for the enforcement of contractual obligations and the maintenance of order without which accurate calculation of the consequences of alternative courses of action is not possible. The state is apt to encourage recruitment to the state bureaucracy by achievement rather than ascription. It opposes particularistic interests and provides an administrative framework within which rational action can flourish. In modernisation theory the bourgeois and the nation-state are held to be congenial to one another. Impediments to commerce, to the free movement of capital, to an unrestricted discretion in the use of private property, and to the treatment of labour simply as a production factor, impediments which inhibit the growth of a pure form of capitalism and which may display a notable persistence in the face of change, can all be reduced radically be a vigorous state acting in the bourgeois interest, which is also its own. Such at least is a 'pure' model of the part played by the nation-state in the process of modernisation. It is an open question, indeed, in some discussions of modernisation whether, given the central role played by the nation-state, it is achievable in any other context.

The foregoing is intended as a preliminary to a discussion of a question of the first importance to understanding the advent of the industrial revolution. If modernisation, the advent of capitalism, and a

---

[4] Tönnies, *Community and society*, p. 165.
[5] *Ibid.*, p. 168.

degree of industrialisation sufficient to warrant being called an industrial revolution are all aspects of a single phenomenon, it follows that the progressive modernisation of a society will in due course lead to an industrial revolution. If modernisation is in train in a range of different countries, the fact that an industrial revolution first occurs in country *a* rather than in country *b* is ultimately of limited interest because if it did not occur in country *a* it must sooner or later occur in country *b* or in some other modernising country. If, on the other hand, modernisation should be viewed as a necessary but not a sufficient condition for an industrial revolution, the circumstances of the latter's first appearance hold an added interest. The issue has not always been addressed directly by those writing about the industrial revolution since it may have little relevance to their immediate concerns, or may be viewed as necessarily an indeterminate question. The latter point must be regarded as ultimately valid since history cannot be re-run to test the outcome of alternative scenarios. Yet it is frequently the case that the issue is addressed implicitly and the stance adopted may colour conclusions drawn about the nature of the industrial revolution as a transformative event.

England and the Netherlands

It is in this context that comparison of England and the Netherlands holds a special interest, not least because de Vries and van der Woude, in their massive study of the Dutch economy between 1500 and 1815, are explicit in claiming that it became a modern economy during this period, but also that the case of the Netherlands shows clearly that modernisation is not necessarily a prelude to sustained economic growth of the type associated with the term 'industrial revolution'. They defined their position without ambiguity:

the presumption of sustained, even unending, growth adheres to the definitions of modern economic growth, while the economic history of the Republic was clearly one of growth followed by stagnation, something approximating an S-shaped, or logistic, curve. Instead of persisting exponential growth, our study describes a society whose growth eventually moved asymptotically toward a limit, rather as the classical economists predicted.[6]

[6] De Vries and van der Woude, *The first modern economy*, p. 718.

To avoid any danger of misunderstanding, they later added: 'This formulation harbors an implicit claim about modern economic growth. It is not self-sustained, exponential and unbounded.'[7] Their discussion of the evidence that the Netherlands displayed social, economic, and political characteristics which leave no room for doubt that the country had 'modernised' is authoritative and seems conclusive. Precocious modernisation occurred and was, indeed, the foundation of Dutch prominence in rivalry with much larger countries during the seventeenth century, but modernisation in the Netherlands did not result in sustained growth after the end of the 'golden age'.[8] Indeed de Vries and van der Woude make the intriguing assertion that 'the nineteenth-century industrial development of the Netherlands was not held back by its backwardness but rather by its very modernity'.[9]

In predicting that the process of growth which he analysed so effectively could not continue indefinitely, Adam Smith was heavily influenced by his reading of Dutch experience. He considered that the exhaustion of opportunities for profitable investment which was already clearly visible in the Netherlands was beginning to appear also in England and that the nature of material production rendered this sequence of events inevitable.[10] De Vries and van der Woude have shown that the 'stagnation' which supervened in the Netherlands was compatible with the maintenance of a relatively high standard of living. Smith's pessimism about the possibility of sustained growth was so profound that he was dubious about this even as a possibility.[11]

How similar was the experience of the Netherlands and England in the early modern period? And after apparently converging for so long, why did their paths later diverge?

Although there were notable similarities in their economic histories, there were also some important differences between England and the Netherlands. It may be helpful to list several major aspects of economic change in the two countries, their similarities and differences, before attempting answers to the two questions.

Consider first the growth of towns and cities in the two countries. In the early sixteenth century the Netherlands was already quite heavily

[7] *Ibid.*, p. 720.
[8] *Ibid.*, p. 720.
[9] *Ibid.*, p. 713.
[10] See above pp. 197–8.
[11] See the quotation on p. 11 above.

urbanised, while England languished towards the foot of a comparative table of European countries. But it is arguable that appearances are somewhat deceptive. Rather than being evidence of flourishing secondary and tertiary activity, the Dutch towns owed much of their early growth to rural distress brought about by the severity of the problems encountered by the farming community which induced many families to leave the land and seek refuge in small towns.[12] The further surge of urban growth in the second half of the sixteenth century and throughout most of the seventeenth, in contrast, was the result of the triumphant successes of the Dutch golden age. The Dutch urban system was changing in nature while also increasing in size. However, the structure of the urban hierarchy which developed in the Netherlands differed markedly from the emerging English system. Throughout the whole early modern period London was a dominant colossus in England, for much of the time containing more people than the combined population total of the rest of the urban sector.[13] In the Netherlands there was a much flatter urban pyramid, especially in the first half of the period when there were many substantial cities within a limited size range. The Dutch urban hierarchy also differed strikingly from the English in that its composition was remarkably stable; as already noted, nineteen of the twenty largest towns in 1550 were still in the top twenty in 1800. In England, in contrast, only seven of the top twenty in 1600 were still in the comparable list in 1800.[14] Both countries in 1800 had a high proportion of their population living in towns, and the level of urbanisation was similar.[15] The

---

[12] On town growth de Vries and van der Woude comment: 'Their fifteenth-century growth seems to have been related more to the growing crisis in the countryside than to any real urban prosperity. The decline of arable production, the shift to labor-saving livestock farming, and the rising costs of protecting the land led to a substantial migration to the towns. The fact that the urbanization of this era expressed itself more in the large *number* of cities than in their large *size* speaks to the importance of the "push" force of rural crisis relative to the "pull" of vigorous urban economies.' De Vries and van der Woude, *The first modern economy*, p. 19.

[13] If a 'town' is defined as any settlement with 5,000 or more inhabitants, London housed more than half the national urban total in the seventeenth century, and this was still the case in 1750, when 55 per cent of all urban dwellers lived in London, but in 1801 the share of London had fallen to 40 per cent. Wrigley, 'Urban growth and agricultural change', tab. 7.2, p. 162.

[14] See above pp. 61–4.

[15] De Vries, *European urbanization*, tab. 3.7, p. 39.

Netherlands, however, had seen a slight decline in urbanisation over the preceding century, the century during which stagnation supervened, whereas England only approached the Dutch level in the later decades of the century.

Notwithstanding the many contrasts in the history of urbanisation in the two countries, there was in one respect an uncanny similarity in the urban histories of the two countries. Their leading cities moved in lock step in relation to national population totals. In c.1550 both Amsterdam and London contained about 2 per cent of the populations of the Netherlands and England respectively. By the end of the sixteenth century in both cases the figure had risen to about 5 per cent; in 1700 to 11 per cent; but in both countries in the next century further progress was limited, with little or no change in their percentage shares of the national total (Amsterdam 10 per cent; 11 London per cent).[16] How far this similarity reflects common causation and how far it is coincidence might well repay further study.

In response to strong urban demand in both countries agriculture became increasingly market-orientated, moving away from a 'peasant' focus on local self-sufficiency. The Netherlands was clearly in advance of England in methods of cultivation and variety of crops until some point in the eighteenth century. Most of the innovations which gradually transformed English agriculture – a reduction in the proportion of arable land fallowed, new types of crop rotation, new crops such as turnips or lucerne – were well established in parts of the Netherlands and more generally in the Low Countries before becoming commonplace across the North Sea. The frequency with which England turned to Dutch expertise across broad swathes of agricultural, industrial, and commercial practice in order to narrow the gap between the two countries is abundantly clear and has often been emphasised. As Wilson remarked, 'One does not have to read much of the abundant economic literature of the century, nor to examine many of the advances in technology, commercial methods or public and private finance to realize that much of England's progress had been achieved by the simple process of borrowing from the Dutch.'[17]

---

[16] For London see tab. 3.2, p. 61 above. For Amsterdam, de Vries, *European urbanization*, app. 1, p. 271, and de Vries and van der Woude, *The first modern economy*, tab. 3.1, p. 50.

[17] Wilson, *England's apprenticeship*, p. 361. He was, of course, referring to the seventeenth century.

In some respects, however, the agricultures of the two countries were significantly different. The increasing prominence in the south and east of England of the system under which the land was owned by substantial landlords, and worked by tenant farmers employing a large workforce of landless labourers, was less evident in the Netherlands, though widespread in the Guelders river area and in the province of Holland. In other provinces there was a variety of different tenurial systems and associated differences in farm size. It is also probable that the marked rise in output per head in the agricultural labour force which occurred in England was less universal in the Netherlands, where the western part of the country was generally in advance of the eastern part. There were substantial differences in labour productivity in agriculture between the different provinces. At the beginning of the nineteenth century it was twice as high in the maritime zone as inland.[18]

The character of the English and Dutch agricultural systems was also fundamentally affected by another aspect of their functioning. England was essentially self-sufficient in temperate zone foodstuffs until the end of the eighteenth century. The government in Westminster made the assumption that this was both the norm and highly desirable. It was periodically thrown into something approaching panic by the prospect of a seriously defective grain harvest, which gave rise to restrictions on the use of grain, notably the malting of barley to produce beer, and to desperate endeavours to secure supplies from overseas. The Netherlands imported Baltic grain on a large scale routinely, since there was no prospect of local self-sufficiency. The import of food was balanced by a large export trade in foodstuffs, notably fish (the scale of Dutch fish exports was remarkable, especially in the seventeenth century[19]), but also dairy produce. During the later eighteenth century, exports of dairy produce grew rapidly and by the beginning of the nineteenth century accounted for half of all agricultural exports.[20] English agriculture improved its efficiency by an increasing regional specialisation in, say, beef cattle, dairy produce, or barley for malting, but the specialisation was predominantly in relation to demand within the country. Dutch agriculture, reflecting a

---

[18] De Vries and van der Woude, *The first modern economy*, pp. 230–1.
[19] About three-quarters of the herring catch was exported. *Ibid.*, p. 419.
[20] *Ibid.*, pp. 226–7.

salient feature of the Dutch economy in its golden age, specialised, so to speak, internationally rather than just nationally.

Industrial production in the two countries displays some striking similarities as well as differences. Since in earlier chapters the history of energy usage in England was given great prominence, it is interesting to note the close parallels between peat usage in the Netherlands and coal consumption in England. The scale of peat production and consumption in the Netherlands was truly remarkable. De Zeeuw has made estimates of the quantity of peat consumed annually. In the seventeenth century he suggests that this figure averaged 6,000 x 10⁹ kilocalories in heat equivalent.[21] Warde's estimates suggest that the English coal consumption provided about 40 petajoules of energy annually, averaged over the century.[22] The Dutch population in the mid-seventeenth century was about 1.85 million; that of England about 5.3 million.[23] Reducing the energy estimates to a common base, the quantity of energy from peat available per person in the Netherlands was 13.6 megajoules annually. The comparable English figure from coal is 7.5 megajoules, barely half the Dutch figure. It should occasion no surprise, therefore, that the Dutch industries which enjoyed a marked comparative advantage at this time, because they were all in need of heat energy on a large scale, were almost identical to the English industries whose prospects improved markedly with the availability of coal on a large scale and at a competitive price. De Vries and van der Woude remark:

And in the seventeenth century, numerous export-oriented industries (bricks, tile and ceramics, pipes, beer, spirits, sugar, salt, whale oil, glass – the list is a long one) shared a pronounced energy intensity, which suggest their common debt to the Republic's uniquely low-cost energy supplies. It appears that energy use in the Republic, both household and industrial, stood far above the levels common to the rest of Europe until the end of the eighteenth century.[24]

This claim closely matches the observation by Hatcher when commenting on the same industries in England.[25] The situation had

---

[21] De Zeeuw, 'Peat and the Dutch golden age', tab. III, p. 16.
[22] Warde, *Energy consumption in England and Wales*, app. I, pp. 115–17.
[23] De Vries and van der Woude, *The first modern economy*, tab. 3.1, p. 50; Wrigley *et al.*, *English population history*, tab. A9.1, pp. 614–15.
[24] De Vries and van der Woude, *The first modern economy*, pp. 338–9.
[25] See above p. 41.

changed greatly by the end of the eighteenth century. Dutch peat production declined after the mid-seventeenth century. This was balanced in some degree by increasing coal imports but at the end of the eighteenth century per caput energy consumption probably did not equal the level achieved a century and a half earlier.[26] Meanwhile coal consumption in England increased roughly ninefold over the same period, while the population rose by about two-thirds, suggesting that per caput consumption increased more than fivefold.

The history of peat production in the Netherlands and coal production in England produced other similarities. The exploitation of peat 'depended more on the cost of transportation than on the cost of gathering the resource itself'.[27] Peat was first exploited in the low-lying bogs of the alluvial areas which were close to navigable waterways. But exploitation of peat in the *hoogveen*, where the land was higher above sea level, depended upon a heavy prior capital expenditure on canal construction, without which the peat was economically inaccessible. This is a distinction very similar to that between the early exploitation of the coal pits close to the Tyne whence coal could be taken cheaply by sea to London and the later development of inland fields which could only be fully exploited when canals, or later railways, had been constructed to cut transport costs per ton-mile to the point which gave them access to a regional and eventually a national rather than a local market.[28]

A comparison of the similarities and differences between the economies of England and the Netherlands produces little to detract from the view that the latter was the more 'modernised' of the two during the bulk of the early modern period. Extending the comparison beyond economic matters would reinforce this view. Whereas English

---

[26] De Vries and van der Woude, *The first modern economy*, pp. 37–40 and 709–10.

[27] *Ibid.*, p. 37.

[28] In commenting on the nature of the changes which had transformed the Netherlands by the middle of the seventeenth century, de Vries and van der Woude note that the urban network was 'now connected by a system of inland waterways that overcame some, but by no means all, of the medieval obstacles to the efficient circulation of goods and persons. A highly capitalized peat digging and distribution sector replaced the informal and small-scale industry to supply urban industries with a level of per capita energy consumption unsurpassed until the British industrial revolution.' *Ibid.*, p. 40.

political life continued to be heavily influenced by a landed aristocracy, a commercial elite played the same part in the Netherlands. 'Rational' behaviour and the determination of self-interest by reference to a scale of pecuniary advantage were at least as prominent in decision making in the Dutch society as in English, and arguably more so. Until at least the end of the seventeenth century average incomes were higher in the Netherlands than in England and the structure of aggregate demand therefore offered strong encouragement to secondary and tertiary activity.[29] Yet the Netherlands did not generate what might be termed a home-grown industrial revolution. De Vries and van der Woude included a final chapter in their book in which they attempted to distil the lessons to be learnt from their survey of Dutch economic history in relation to the concept of modernisation. Their conclusions are clear-cut. 'The society of the Netherlands', they wrote, 'distinguished itself – by its advancement of processes that assisted those rational actors in increasing the efficiency of economic activity. Those modernizing, dynamic processes included urbanization, education, mobility, monetization, and political and legal development.'[30] There follows a discussion of the role played by the Dutch state in furthering these processes. 'These features of Dutch society in the seventeenth and eighteenth century', they added, 'placed the rational actor, the *homo oeconomicus*, in a dynamic setting conducive to innovation.'[31]

The Netherlands, perhaps paradoxically, nevertheless lost economic momentum progressively during the late seventeenth and early eighteenth centuries. In the analysis of de Vries and van der Woude this was not due to the type of limitations which normally arrested growth in organic economies. There was, for example, no problem of energy supply. There remained large deposits of peat to be dug and coal could be imported readily from Britain. The Dutch economy:

did not decelerate because of the supply constraints of inelastic energy sources, but because of economic circumstances that limited demand. The Netherlands was, in fact, an early adopter of the seminal industrial invention, the steam engine. Already in the 1780s, drainage boards had acquired

[29] A comparison of real wages of craftsmen in southern England and the western Netherlands suggests that the Dutch advantage lasted regionally, if not nationally, throughout the eighteenth century. *Ibid.*, fig. 12.6, p. 631.

[30] *Ibid.*, p. 713.

[31] *Ibid.*, p. 715.

them for pumping purposes. However, they remained conspicuously rare in the industrial sector, where the high costs of production could not be undone by the introduction of steam engines alone.[32]

For many decades high production costs severely limited the advantages to be gained from adopting new technologies like the steam engine. They offered insufficient savings to justify the necessary investment. When it came, 'the transition was not one from a traditional, supply-limiting economy to sustained economic growth; it was a demand-delayed transition from a first to a second cycle of modern economic growth'.[33] This analysis arises naturally from their more general thesis that an economy may embody all the chief distinguishing features of modernisation without necessarily experiencing the transformation of productive capacities which characterise an industrial revolution.

The Dutch case repays close attention because it provides an illuminating background to any discussion of the course of events in England. That the Netherlands was indeed a thoroughly modernised society is perhaps most convincingly shown by considering life in the remote countryside rather than in a town or city. Some years ago I took advantage of an elegant study by Roessingh based on a set of tax records relating to the Veluwe in 1749 to illustrate the point:

The Veluwe lies in central Holland south of the Zuider Zee. – It was an agricultural area with no large town, where the soils were at best of moderate quality. Yet Roessingh's study shows that even small settlements from 400 inhabitants upwards almost invariably had a village shop (at a time when shops were still rare in England in places of similar size), a tailor, a shoemaker and very often a weaver and baker as well. All were frequently found in much smaller villages too, and the hierarchical pattern of service function by settlement size was very well ordered. This was an economy in which division of labour had been pushed very far; in which money and the market entered into the lives of small men to a degree which supported shops in small villages and caused wives to cease baking at home. The villages of the Veluwe were far removed from the type of communities which Tönnies had in mind in describing the nature of *Gemeinschaft*, even though theirs was largely an agricultural economy in a strictly rural setting.

[32] *Ibid.*, pp. 719–20.
[33] *Ibid.*, p. 720.

The Veluwe was part of an economy which had been modernized but not industrialized. – When rationality prevails and men's actions are informed by self-interest, there must be gains in efficiency, but there is no certain and permanent rise in living standards for the bulk of the population.[34]

A consideration of the Dutch case should call in question the view that institutional change can be regarded as an adequate explanation of an industrial revolution. It may well be a sufficient explanation of modernisation but the link between modernisation and industrialisation is too uncertain to sustain the view that the advent of the former results in the occurrence of the latter.

The relationship between industrialisation and modernisation

Industrialisation may quite reasonably be regarded not as the culmination of modernisation but as a disruptive event which for a period tends to reverse trends which are normally associated with modernisation. The vast increase in productive capacity which defined the industrial revolution in England had by the middle decades of the nineteenth century made it clear that the limits to growth which were integral to the world of Adam Smith had melted away, but many contemporaries thought it doubtful whether the upshot should be counted gain. Novels such as George Eliot's *Adam Bede* or Disraeli's *Sybil* (given, revealingly, the alternative title of *The two nations*) emphasise both the lack of mutual comprehension between the 'old' world and the 'new' and the horror which some aspects of industrialisation evoked among contemporaries.

Das Kapital is, in a sense, a commentary on the severity of the tensions produced by the uneasy marriage of industrialisation and modernisation. Later events have demonstrated the marriage could be for the most part both stable and successful for long periods, though not universally, but the initial price was high. Marx attempted to categorise the lessons to be learned from the turmoil of events in England in the previous half-century. The marriage, he concluded, was intolerable and must be dissolved if the benefits made possible by the industrial revolution, but denied to the masses by the capitalist system set

---

[34] Wrigley, 'The process of modernization', p. 251. The article to which reference is made is Roessingh, 'Village and hamlet'.

in a bourgeois state, were ever to be distributed more equitably, a view that had much in common with that of the youthful Toynbee.[35] A capitalist system based on 'rationality' and 'self-interest' would condemn the workers to a living standard little better than bare subsistence: 'the value of labour-power is the value of the means of subsistence necessary for the labourer',[36] a definition essentially similar to that favoured by the classical economists but now rendered intolerable in Marx's view. In the new circumstances of an energy-rich era, with Prometheus unbound, justice required that labour should be better rewarded. The marriage has proved more durable than Marx expected. What had seemed inconceivable to Adam Smith and intolerable to Karl Marx became an acceptable commonplace. National product proved able to increase without apparent limit but was so divided that all major groups in society benefited in material terms, though not necessarily in equal proportion, and subject periodically to recessions and at times to more serious disruptions as 'irrational exuberance' and inadequate regulation resulted in imbalance followed by collapse.

The reality of an apparent inconsistency between modernisation and industrialisation is reflected in some of the quantifiable attributes of those contrasting parts of England which best typified the two concepts. The growth of London had been a major factor in the 'modernisation' of England. The existence of the London market was a prime factor in transforming English agriculture both by ensuring a rising demand for food and industrial raw materials and by underwriting regional specialisation. The London of Defoe was modernised but not industrialised (there was a very large employment in industry, but the production units were usually tiny, often the home itself, and much of the energy input in a wide range of London's industries was from human muscle) and this was still largely true in Dickens's day. Literacy was substantially higher than in the rest of the country, and in its economic and social functioning London conformed well to a checklist of the features of modernisation: rationality and self-interest were eminently visible.

In contrast to London, the large urban sprawls which unrolled across the industrial North and Midlands from the end of the eighteenth

---

[35] See above pp. 48–9.
[36] Marx, *Capital*, I, p. 149.

century might almost be described as industrial but not modern. In these areas, for example, literacy was very low. In the early 1840s the two counties in which the level of female illiteracy was highest, measured by the percentage of women who signed the marriage register with a mark rather than a signature, were Lancashire and the West Riding, where the figures were 67 and 63 per cent respectively. The two lowest were Middlesex and Surrey, where the figures were 23 and 28 per cent (London was not separately distinguished, but it is safe to assume that in London itself the figure would have been slightly lower). It is illustrative of the serious impact that industrialisation had upon the attainment of literacy that in both the East and North Ridings the proportion of women unable to sign their name on marriage was only 38 per cent, little more than half the level in the West Riding (the national average was 49 per cent). Industrial counties fared somewhat better in regard to male literacy. The national figure for male illiteracy was 33 per cent. Lancashire and the West Riding were in the middle of the pack, roughly half-way down the ranking list at 38 and 37 per cent respectively. London, however, was once again a leader. The male figure for Middlesex was 12 per cent, the lowest for any county, while Surrey was third lowest at 17 per cent. For men the area of lowest literacy was East Anglia and its neighbours. The five worst counties for male literacy were agricultural rather than industrial: they were Hertfordshire, Bedfordshire, Cambridgeshire, Essex, and Suffolk, with the following percentages of illiteracy: 50, 49, 47, 47, and 47.[37]

In the new centres of industrial and mining activity the dimming of features held to symbolise modernisation was by no means confined to education. For example, the free play of the market and the universal use of money as a means of exchange were threatened by practices such as truck systems of payment and the tying of employees to the company shop. Langton noted that 'the fastest growing industrial towns had far fewer shops per inhabitant than long-established towns in rural areas, and therefore, it may be surmised, fewer other tertiary activities, too'.[38] Recruitment by 'achievement' rather

---

[37] The county percentages of men and women unable to sign their names in the marriage register were taken from *1841 Census*, Occupation abstract, Preface, pp. 10–11.

[38] Langton, 'Urban growth and economic change', p. 486.

than 'ascription' was gravely hampered not merely by inadequate and uneven access to education but by the development of tightly knit communities inhabited almost exclusively by working-class people, communities which exhibited many of the features associated with *Gemeinschaft* rather than *Gesellschaft*. Some of the traits which characterised these communities lasted for several generations. The industrial revolution brought with it some markedly regressive features judged by the measuring rods of modernisation.[39]

Perhaps the lesson to be drawn from the above is that although concepts such as modernisation and industrialisation may provide stereotypes which are helpful in the initial stages of discussion, historical reality is apt to prove recalcitrant if pressed to conform to any simple patterns. Both the particular example of the Netherlands and the general considerations advanced by the classical economists show that it is mistaken to suppose that modernisation necessarily implies industrialisation. It may be true that it is difficult to imagine an industrial revolution occurring unless in a setting in which many of the key characteristics of the modernisation process were in evidence, but beyond this one should perhaps look to coincidence rather than causation.

National entities and lopsided growth

It is common practice to discuss economic history in the same framework as political history, embodying the assumption that the geographical unit which matters is the nation-state. That the nation-state is the appropriate unit is frequently taken for granted, so obviously correct as to need no discussion. There are notable exceptions to this rule. Sidney Pollard, for example, never tired of stressing the limitations of a focusing on a 'national' approach to issues related to the industrial revolution. He remarked that he would argue:

that, useful as the 'national' approach has been in the past, particularly by evolving testable models, it was based on faulty observation. The industrialization of Europe did not proceed country by country. On a map of Europe

---

[39] This is reflected, though not directly addressed, in studies such as Hoggart, *The uses of literacy* or Young and Willmott, *Family and kinship in east London*.

in which industrialization was coloured, say, red, it would by no means be the case that an area corresponding to a country within its boundary would turn uniformly pale pink, dark pink, and so on to deepest crimson. On the contrary, industrialization would appear as red dots, surrounded by areas of lighter red diminishing to white, and with the spread of industrialization these dots would scatter across the map with little reference to political boundaries. It would also follow that the dynamic of the infection of this rash of red dots, crossing frontiers while by-passing large areas of the home country, must clearly have a largely non-political explanation.[40]

That Pollard's comment is justified is in one sense beyond dispute. The very nature of secondary, manufacturing activity ensured that it would be concentrated in particular localities and that in this respect it would contrast sharply with agricultural production which was, again by its nature, widely and thinly spread in conformity with the distribution of farmland. And it is salutary to be reminded that industrialising districts on either side of a national frontier might have more in common with each other than with other areas in their respective countries.[41] A robust exploration of the limitations of narrowly national perspectives was certainly to be welcomed; an unquestioning assumption that the state is the natural unit for analysis results in a failure to do justice to the complexity of change and the frequency with which the initiatives taken by individual actors were heavily influenced by international contacts. Yet this is not an either/or issue. Many of those who did not live in the 'red dots' were nevertheless as much a part of the new age as workers in a cotton factory or a coal mine. Turnpike gate keepers, to take a trivial example, were scattered widely throughout England but their work arose from developments which played a central role in the emergence of an industrialised economy. The same was true at a later date of permanent way workers on the railway, many postal workers, and a host of those engaged in retail trading. The gradual extension of educational and medical services into rural areas illustrates the same point.

[40] Pollard, 'Industrialization and the European economy', pp. 636–7.
[41] This, indeed, was a feature of the industrial growth in the middle and later nineteenth century in the belt of coalfields stretching from the Pas-de-Calais in the north of France through the Sambre–Meuse valley to the Aachen area and the Ruhr which formed the central thesis of an earlier book of mine: Wrigley, *Industrial growth and population change*.

The bulk of the labour force in the 'white' areas which were apparently untouched by the new developments were, of course, working on the land, but eighteenth-century agriculture was greatly changed from its Tudor predecessor. Agriculture had become much more a business than a way of life. The very fact that the term 'farmer' had replaced 'husbandman' and 'yeoman' symbolises the increasing dominance of market-orientated decision making. In later centuries, when the governments of countries where peasant agriculture still predominated became determined to foster rapid industrialisation, both the circumstances and the solutions were very different from the course of change during the industrial revolution in England. In England there was change in all the main sectors of the economy and feedback between them. The changes were less eye-catching in rural areas where a substantial fraction of each rising generation was leaving its parish of birth to move to industrial or commercial centres than in the towns which were providing them with work. But the changes taking place were visible in 'rural backwaters' as well as the new urban sprawls.

Or the same point can be put differently. It was intrinsic to the nature of the growth taking place that it was 'lopsided'. With the change in the structure of aggregate demand there was necessarily a matching change in occupational structure, a shift from primary to secondary and tertiary employment. Many types of secondary production could be carried out most efficiently in plants producing on a large scale, which were few in number and clustered close together. In other words, 'red dots' were bound to emerge from the nature of the change taking place. But it does not follow that there was little change in the 'white' areas of the map. During the seventeenth and much of the eighteenth centuries it is probable that output per head in agriculture was rising more rapidly than in manufacture. Equally, there were industrial sectors employing large numbers of men in which labour productivity probably changed little. Tailors, shoemakers, carpenters, masons, bricklayers, and handloom weavers, for example, formed a large part of the industrial labour force but it is unlikely that their productivity rose as markedly as that of their counterparts working on the land in the early modern period. Rapid gains in manpower productivity in manufacturing only became widespread with the advent of factory production and with the steep rise in the quantity of heat and mechanical energy at the disposal of each worker, best symbolised by the spread of the steam engine.

Indirectly, Pollard's thesis might be said to be directing attention once again to the importance of bearing in mind the distinction between modernisation and industrialisation. Only a limited number of places will provide the sites for new forms of industrial production when an industrial revolution takes place but its occurrence may still be contingent upon the society in which these changes occur having experienced modernisation, at least in the case of the first country to experience an industrial revolution. It is true that employment in the major manufacturing industries will be heavily concentrated in a few locations because of the economies associated with the production of standard articles on a large scale and because of the advantages of agglomeration, that is of the benefits of a ready access to a large supply of labour possessing a wide variety of skills, and to capital and technical expertise. In England's case these general incentives to industrial concentration were strongly reinforced by advantages of a coalfield location. As Aikin remarked in 1795, 'Cheap and plentiful coal is an advantage inestimable to a manufacturing district.'[42] But, though it is mistaken to suppose that industrialisation arises naturally out of modernisation, it is very difficult to suppose that it would have occurred in England unless England had first followed the Dutch example and acquired the characteristics of a modernised society. In pointing out that industrialisation took place much earlier in south Lancashire than in Lincolnshire, therefore, Pollard was singling out a feature of industrialisation which was intrinsic to its nature. It would have been deeply surprising if there had not been massive regional differences of this sort in industrialisation. These indeed were structural features of industrialisation. There was no reason to expect that counties like Lincolnshire would ever become industrialised to the degree that mirrored what took place in Lancashire or the west Midlands. But it is not paradoxical to suggest that some areas which did not industrialise, or which industrialised later and to a lesser extent than the major industrial agglomerations, were nonetheless more modernised than the latter.

Pollard's chief concern in stressing the limitations of discussions of the industrial revolution which focus exclusively on the national unit was to draw attention to interactions across national boundaries rather than to a lack of uniformity in the timing of change within

---

[42] Aikin, *A description of the country*, p. 96.

individual countries. He did note that 'we shall miss much of the actual dynamic of industrialization if we neglect the fact that the "industrial revolution" came much earlier, say, to South Lancashire and the Black Country than it did to Lincolnshire or Kent'.[43] But he was primarily interested in demonstrating that 'European industrialization should not be seen as the repetition of a model, but as a single, if complex, process.'[44] Following the appearance of 'red dots' on Manchester and Birmingham, he insisted, others would be visible at, say, Charleroi or Liège much sooner than in Devon or Suffolk. His warning about the limitations of a purely national framework of description and analysis is well taken.

Conclusion

Events in the twentieth and twenty-first centuries have made it difficult to argue that modernisation is a necessary let alone a sufficient condition for an industrial revolution. The rapid, if wasteful industrialisation of the Soviet Union in the seven decades of its existence leave little room for doubt that modernisation is not a prerequisite of rapid industrial growth. More recently the course of change in China might be said to suggest that modernisation may be the child of industrialisation rather than the reverse. The massive growth of the 'middle class', the emergence of rapacious individualism, and the spread of a consumerist mentality in China were made possible by very rapid industrial growth and the associated increase in individual incomes, rather than the reverse. But many European scholars a century ago, looking back two or three generations, found much to encourage the belief that only a prior set of linked changes which could be labelled 'modernisation' had made it possible to bring about the novel situation, both exciting and troubling, in which economic growth was far more rapid than in the past and held out the promise of continuing indefinitely. And further, they were apt to argue that the nature of modernisation ensured that an industrial revolution must occur.

The example of the Netherlands during and after its golden age suggests strong links between modernisation and the achievement of major gains in economic efficiency which produced unusually rapid

---

[43] Pollard, 'Industrialization and the European economy', p. 637.
[44] *Ibid.*, p. 646.

growth. It does not, however, suggest that a modernised society can necessarily expect to experience an industrial revolution. Other conditions must also be met if this is to happen. The issue can perhaps be understood better by being expressed differently. There can be a wide difference between an advanced organic economy such as the Netherlands in the seventeenth century which displays all the key features of a modernised society and an organic economy which lacks such features, as was the case for Europe in medieval times. But it remains a fact that both the Netherlands and medieval Europe were bound by the limits attaching to all organic economies. Access to peat to provide plentiful supplies of heat energy and to the resources of other countries by conducting brilliantly successful international trading alleviated the basic problem in the Dutch case. A long-lasting solution was possible, however, only by escaping from a 'fungible' world, where the size of the annual growth of vegetable matter set an upper limit to the scale of raw material production and to the amount of energy which could be harnessed to productive activity, and entering a 'consumptible' world where energy stored up over millions of years became available, a new situation of great promise and commensurate dangers.

When Dutch growth lost momentum, Dutch population growth decelerated in parallel, so that during the eighteenth century living standards remained well in advance of the bulk of the continent. England had followed in Dutch footsteps for more than a century and Adam Smith, well informed and of penetrating intelligence, expected that England would experience the same problems, brought about in particular by the exhaustion of opportunities for profitable investment. He viewed the past two centuries as a period of marked progress: 'Since the time of Henry VIII the wealth and revenue of the country have been continually advancing, and, in the course of their progress, their pace seems rather to have been gradually accelerated than retarded.'[45] But alarmed by the level to which the rate of interest had fallen in Holland, which he took as a reliable indicator of the opportunity for profitable investment, he foresaw an approaching stagnation.[46] The period of growth and prosperity would shortly end. A sharply increasing rate of population growth might be expected to

[45] Smith, *Wealth of nations*, I, p. 100.
[46] *Ibid.*, pp. 101–10.

be the harbinger of disaster in such circumstances, as was implied in Malthus's model of the interplay of population and production. Yet not only did the population of England increase at an unprecedented rate in the half-century following the publication of the *Wealth of nations* but it did so without a collapse in living standards. Furthermore the new momentum of economic growth which was achieved took a form which fostered further growth at a comparable rate.

As population growth rates moderated in the later decades of the nineteenth century, real incomes were able to rise more rapidly than during the decades of fastest population growth. The stresses which accompanied rapid growth produced much misery and dislocation, but by the end of Victoria's reign it would have seemed anachronistic to argue as Arthur Young had done that 'everyone but an idiot knows that the lower classes must be kept poor or they will never be indus-trious'.[47] The existence of an enormous stock of energy in the form of coal deposits and the invention of a means of using it not only to provide energy in the form of heat but also to convert heat energy into mechanical energy, combined with the substitution of mineral for organic raw materials across an increasingly wide spectrum of human needs, created a novel situation, which came to be termed an industrial revolution.

One way of characterising the changes which had made it pos-sible to overcome the limitations of an organic economy is to talk of the conjunction of two capitalisms. The economy and society of the Netherlands was transformed during the sixteenth and seven-teenth centuries by a range of linked changes which enabled a much increased population to secure a standard of living well in advance of the rest of Europe. It became the first 'modern' society and there-fore developed as a capitalist economy. Its economic success sprang from the ability of a capitalist system to marshal and deploy resources more effectively than the system it replaced. Agriculture, commerce, and industry alike were conducted in a manner which raised output per head sufficiently to improve income levels across the board and render the traditional threat of famine a remote rather than an ever present danger. It was able to achieve this progress because, as Adam Smith put it:

---

[47] Quoted in Ashton, *An economic history of England*, p. 202.

As the accumulation of stock is previously necessary for carrying on this great improvement in the productive powers of labour, so that accumulation naturally leads to this improvement. The person who employs his stock in maintaining labour, necessarily wishes to employ it in such a manner as to produce as great a quantity of work as possible. He endeavours, therefore, both to make among his workmen the most proper distribution of employment, and to furnish them with the best machines he can either invent or afford to purchase. His abilities in both respects are generally in proportion to the extent of his stock, or to the number of people whom it can employ. The quantity of industry, therefore, not only increases in every country with the increase of the stock which employs it, but, in consequence of that increase, the same quantity of industry produces a much greater quantity of work.[48]

But although this type of capitalism could make better use of the resources of an organic economy than its predecessors had been able to achieve, it could not of itself break free from the constraints which limited the possibility of progress in all such economies. The most significant single constraint was energy supply. As long as the sun rose in the heavens energy would cascade down to the earth's surface in abundance, but the human access to this energy flow was governed by plant photosynthesis, which was incapable of capturing more than a tiny fraction of the energy in incident sunlight. The energy flow was insufficient to underwrite increased output on the scale associated with an 'industrial revolution'. Only by gaining access to a vast *store* rather than a limited *flow* of energy could this problem be solved. Coal measures provided the answer. They represented a capital stock, a second type of 'capitalism', which in conjunction with the more conventional type of capitalism enabled England to avoid the deceleration which afflicted the Dutch republic and to cope with a burst of population growth at a speed which would otherwise have meant desperate impoverishment. One might say that the presence of one type of capitalism was not enough; it needed access to a second type to achieve a breakthrough.

[48] Smith, *Wealth of nations*, I, p. 292.

Part IV

Retrospective

9 | *The industrial revolution and energy*

The energy revolution

One of the best ways of defining the essence of the industrial revolution is to describe it as the escape from the constraints of an organic economy. Civilisations of high sophistication developed at times in many places in the wake of the neolithic food revolution: in China, India, Egypt, the valleys of the Tigris and Euphrates, Greece, and Rome, among others. Their achievements in many spheres of human endeavour match or surpass those of modern societies; in literature, painting, sculpture, and philosophy, for example, their best work will always command admiration. Some built vast empires and maintained them for centuries, even millennia. They traded over great distances and had access to a very wide range of products. Their elites commanded notable wealth and could live in luxury. Yet invariably the bulk of the population was poor once the land was fully settled; and it seemed beyond human endeavour to alter this state of affairs.

The 'laborious poverty', in the words of Jevons, to which most men and women were condemned did not arise from lack of personal freedom, from discrimination, or from the nature of the political or legal system, though it might be aggravated by such factors. It sprang from the nature of all organic economies. The neolithic food revolution had restricted the vegetable cover of much of the earth's surface to a limited range of plants which men could eat, feed to their animals, or treat as raw materials for conversion into a useful product. It meant the annexation solely to human use of plant growth which had previously been shared with all other living creatures, and made possible an immense increase in human populations. But it also meant that the plant growth in question represented the bulk of the sum total of energy which could be made available for any human purpose. The other energy sources which were accessible, chiefly wind and water, were, comparatively speaking, of minor importance.[1] The

[1] See above tab. 4.1, p. 92.

239

ceiling set in this fashion to the quantity of energy which could be secured for human use was a relatively low limit because only a tiny fraction of the energy reaching the surface of the earth from the sun was captured by plant photosynthesis. Since all productive processes involved the consumption of energy, and plant growth was the predominant energy source, the productivity of the land conditioned everything else.

At first sight, however, the existence of a ceiling of this kind need not involve 'laborious poverty' for most people. Put arithmetically, even if the maximum of energy which could be secured from a plot of land were only 1,000 units, the amount available to each person would be 1,000 divided by the population total in question. If the population were 100, each person could make use of 10 units of energy. If the population were only 50, however, each person would have 20 units available. And since available energy can be regarded as equivalent to an income measure, the standard of living need not be reduced close to subsistence level. But matters were not so simple. There was first the problem whose exposition made Malthus at once famous and widely loathed, the problem which was embodied in figure 1.1. In easy circumstances, population will tend to rise because mortality will be lower than fertility and therefore living standards will come under pressure. It does not follow that they must fall to subsistence level, as Malthus himself insisted as his empirical knowledge grew, but both logic and experience proved that his point had substance. Even if this were not the case, however, the arithmetic example is misleading. The productivity of the individual in an organic economy is limited by his or her access to energy. In the simplest case, the 'engine' whose work results in useful output is only as powerful as the muscles of the individual in question, as when a man digs a potato patch. This may be supplemented by the muscular output of draught animals, as in the case of a ploughman, but it is still a limited quantity. In most organic economies a man labouring on the land can produce only sufficient food to sustain himself and his family and at best a little more, so that, for example, three families may produce sufficient to support themselves and one other family, but this still implies 'laborious poverty' for most families.

There is a revealing passage in St Matthew's gospel describing an event in the house of Simon the leper.

There came unto him a woman having an alabaster box of very precious ointment, and poured it on his head as he sat at meat. But when his disciples saw it, they had indignation, saying, To what purpose is this waste? For this ointment might have been sold for much, and given to the poor. When Jesus understood it, he said unto them, Why trouble ye the woman? for she hath wrought a good work upon me. For ye have the poor always with you; but me ye have not always.[2]

To a modern ear Jesus's remark about the poor may seem somewhat unfeeling, or, in modern jargon, not politically correct, but it was so obviously true of a world restricted by the limits inherent in an organic economy as to pass without objection. The incident epitomises the contrast between the circumstances of life in the world before the industrial revolution and those which prevail today. Routine and widespread poverty implied for most individuals constant worry about securing each day their 'daily bread' and made it certain that only a privileged few could live in comfort.

Jonathan Swift, in a chapter satirising the attitudes and actions of European governments, caused the king in Brobdingnag to express a sentiment which must have been widely shared. Gulliver had offered to teach the king how to manufacture gunpowder and construct cannon and so make royal power absolute. The king was revolted by what he heard and replied that 'whoever could make two ears of corn, or two blades of grass to grow upon a spot of ground where only one grew before, would deserve better of mankind, and do more essential service to his country, than the whole race of politicians put together'.[3] Given the nature of all organic economies, what the king claimed must have seemed almost self-evident. Improvement in the general lot required access to more energy, which in turn meant raising output from the land. Periods of success in this regard were possible in organic economies since the ceiling set by the productivity of the land was not fixed. Better systems of crop rotation, dressing the land with marl, securing improved farm animals by selective breeding, and a host of comparable innovations could substantially improve gross output and in some cases also output per head. And there were other, if minor, ways of securing more energy from insolation. For example,

---

[2] St Matthew, 26, vv. 7–11.
[3] Swift, *Gulliver's travels*, p. 176.

more energy could be captured from the wind both by improving windmill technology and by changing the number, arrangement, and operation of sails on ships. The changes taking place in Dutch and English agriculture and in their economies more generally in the early modern period show very clearly that substantial advance in raising energy capture on the land and elsewhere was possible in organic economies. But periods of success were bound to be followed by deceleration and stagnation, because of dependence on the land as the source of energy and the problems associated with this dependence which were identified by the classical economists. The declining return on local investment in the Netherlands stressed by Adam Smith exemplified the problem.[4] England escaped it, but only by gaining access to a different energy source, present in mineral deposits rather than in growing plants.

The process of escape was slow but progressive. It was summarised in figure 4.1. From being a minor contributor to energy supply in Tudor times, coal increased steadily in importance, reaching a position of almost total dominance by the mid-nineteenth century. The rate of growth in coal consumption varied only slightly over the whole period, averaging about 1.3 per cent per annum, which implies a doubling roughly every half-century.[5] With organic raw materials, a rate of growth as high as this would very soon cause intolerable pressure upon the land and a sharp rise in price. If, for example, wood use were to rise at a similar rate, it would require sixteen times as much land to be devoted to forest after two centuries of growth as had been needed at the start of the period, since a doubling every half-century implies this scale of expansion. In organic economies growth of this kind is physically impossible. Once again, the significance of the distinction between a fungible and a consumptible is clear. Over a period of centuries, though not indefinitely, the massive size of coal deposits meant that a high rate of growth could be maintained, with the marginal cost of coal remaining stable or even declining. If the energy obtained from burning coal could be successfully adapted to a wider and wider range of production activities, the economy could expand in a manner which had previously been prohibited by the character of organic economies.

[4] See above pp. 55–6.
[5] See above tab. 4.2, p. 94.

Coal was cheap to mine but expensive to transport overland before the construction of canals and railways. Where it could be made available at a moderate cost because the existing transport facilities made this possible, it was quickly adopted as the prime energy source for heating purposes. It is striking that the annual coal consumption per head of population in London was already c.0.7 tons at the beginning of the seventeenth century and had risen only modestly to c.1.25 tons two hundred years later.[6] The fact that there were coal mines close to the Tyne and that sea transport was relatively cheap meant that the price of coal landed in London was competitive with wood, even when London was a comparatively small city, and coal was rapidly adopted as a fuel in consequence since its price changed little whereas the price of wood and charcoal tended to rise. Much of the steady and rapid growth in coal use nationally reflected the effect of improved inland transport facilities, especially during the eighteenth and early nineteenth centuries, which allowed an increasing proportion both of English industry and of the English population to enjoy the benefit of coal use.

It took a quarter of a millennium for coal to change from supplying a tenth of the energy consumed in England and Wales to nine-tenths (table 4.2). Its increasing importance reduced the pressure on other energy sources, and notably on forest land (since until a late date coal was a source of heat energy but not of mechanical energy). Its role in facilitating the occurrence of an industrial revolution is widely recognised, and appears using a variety of analytic methods.[7] One aspect of its importance deserves particular emphasis when considering its role in relation to economic growth and change during the three centuries which separated the reign of Elizabeth from that of Victoria. Achieving a scale of growth to merit being termed an industrial revolution required access to a matching growth in energy use. The proportion of the rise in energy use which could be secured from 'traditional' sources was bound to decline as growth continued, since the quantum of energy which could be secured in an organic economy was limited. The potential gap between the energy required and the energy available was met by increasing coal use in England, which in turn implies

[6] See above p. 106.
[7] See, for example, Allen, *The British industrial revolution*, chs. 4 and 5.

that its relative importance rose as time passed. In the later stages of the transition it was of much greater significance than in the early stages. Above all, access to coal meant that the rate of growth could be maintained or even accelerated rather than having to slow down, as was otherwise unavoidable. At a still later date other energy sources came to rival coal. Oil and natural gas in the twentieth century, and towards its end nuclear power, became major sources of energy, but the initial achievement of prolonged exponential growth in material production, the central feature of the industrial revolution, was based on coal as an energy source. The coalfields indeed were the site of much of the most spectacular industrial growth in this period.

One way of picturing the difference between the new mineral source of energy and the older sources which depended on the productivity of the land is to note that there were 128,086 coal miners in England and Wales at the time of the 1851 census and 1,135,833 men engaged in agriculture, or roughly nine times the coal mining total (both totals refer to men aged 20 and over[8]). In the decade 1850–9 coal contributed 1,689,100 terajoules per annum to the consumption of energy in England and Wales, so that on average each coal miner produced 13 terajoules of energy annually. The annual energy consumption of people and of draught animals combined in the same decade was 117,890 megajoules.[9] If this combined figure for these two classes of energy consumption is taken to capture the energy output of agriculture, then the average contribution to energy consumption of each man working in agriculture was 0.10 terajoules, less than one hundredth of the equivalent figure for a coal miner. It is probably fair to claim that to make this comparison is only superficially to compare like with like. Yet the scale of the difference in the two figures is huge and would survive any plausible adjustment. It helps to give substance to the point that access to a new and different energy source from those which were the basis of material production in organic economies was essential if a promising period of growth was to culminate in an industrial revolution. The energy needed to achieve the continued growth in total output at a rate which exceeded, say, 1 per cent

[8] I excluded the small number of land proprietors from the total for agriculture. *1851 Census*, II, Ages, civil condition, occupations, etc., vol. I, Summary tables, tab. xxv, pp. ccxxii–ccxxvii.
[9] The energy totals are taken from tab. 4.2, p. 94 above.

annually could not be secured from 'traditional' sources. Much higher rates of growth were achieved and maintained by many countries which experienced an industrial revolution, but I have used 1 per cent per annum as an illustration, since even this very modest level of growth would mean that, over two centuries, output would expand roughly eightfold, something which no organic economy could manage, except perhaps when new land was being settled. In this case, if the area of new territory was large in relation to the area settled at the beginning of the period, the energy base (agriculture) could grow quickly for a time, but only as long as this condition held true.

In the Victorian period, harvest festival services were often held in parish churches in the autumn, with the church decorated with sheaves of corn and baskets of fruit. The harvest festival service was in a sense the celebration of acquisition of a store of energy which could be used to 'fuel' people and farm stock, or to provide the raw material for industries such as straw plaiting for the forthcoming year. Earlier the hay harvest had provided a similar food source for cattle and sheep and so, indirectly, for the production of wool and hides. To hold a celebration once the harvest had been safely gathered in was highly appropriate. For many generations the stock of energy acquired in the wake of a season of plant growth had provided the basis for both life and work between one harvest and the next. At the level of the local community it exemplified dependence upon the annual cycle of insolation and its conversion into a form which was useful to man by photosynthesis. The mining of coal was not subject to a similar annual rhythm. It was a store which could be drawn down at any time and in any required quantity, at least for a period of centuries. The local parish church in a mining community was not decorated annually with coal, and indeed might well celebrate the getting in of the harvest in the traditional fashion, but the new mineral source of energy had come to dwarf older sources by the Victorian age even though its significance was not celebrated in a comparable fashion.

Pandora's jar again

When Epimetheus opened the jar which Pandora gave him on their marriage neither he nor she had any idea of its contents. Opening it released a multitude of mighty forces whose effects were both unpredictable and inescapable. In this respect the industrial revolution

echoes one of the central features of the Greek myth. The consequences of the industrial revolution were more evenly balanced than
in the story of Pandora's jar; indeed the predominant view must be
that the beneficial changes which have taken place in its wake out-
weigh any drawbacks. Yet there remain instructive parallels between
the myth and the historical event.

Like Pandora and Epimetheus, those who were alive during the
central decades of the 'classic' period of industrial revolution did not
appreciate either the scale or the nature of the change which was in
train. No doubt it took some time for Pandora and her husband to
recognise what his action had brought about. It is, almost by definition, intensely difficult to identify the nature of a truly novel situation.
Countless generations of living with the limitations of an organic economy had conditioned everyone to suppose that they were unchange-
able. It is notable, for example, that John Stuart Mill, an intellectual
phenomenon, familiar with the views of the leading thinkers of his
day, and writing in the middle decades of the nineteenth century after
the end of the 'classic' period of the industrial revolution, was uncertain about the character of the new age. He echoed the pessimistic
conclusion of Ricardo and paraphrased his analysis:

The materials of manufacture being all drawn from the land, and many of
them from agriculture, which supplies in particular the entire material of
clothing; the general law of production from the land, the law of diminishing return, must in the last resort be applicable to manufacturing as well as
to agricultural history. As population increases, and the power of the land
to yield increased produce is strained harder and harder, any additional
supply of material, as well as of food, must be obtained by a more than
proportionally increasing expenditure of labour.[10]

It is true that Mill then went on to express the hope that the drag
upon labour productivity which this implied might by matched by
rising productivity in some types of manufacture, leaving the overall
situation in doubt, but his discussion shows vividly how long it took to
appreciate the nature of the new world of the industrial revolution.

A few years later the uncertainty was removed. Men such as Marx,
Toynbee, and Jevons gained a clearer insight into the completeness of

[10] Mill, *Principles of political economy*, I, p. 182

the break with the past which had occurred, but they were uncertain about its implications. If, for example, most of the benefit was to be confined to a small minority and the bulk of the population was to live a life of Marxian bare subsistence, this must result in intolerable tensions. It was precisely his appreciation of the very different nature of the new capitalist age which both gave Marx a basis for his analysis of its character and provoked his dismay and anger. Toynbee in large measure agreed with the view Marx expressed, while advocating a different remedy. Jevons, while very conscious of the advantages attainable only because of the vastly greater energy supplies provided by the use of coal, was disturbed by the problems associated with the finite nature of fossil fuel resources. Though not using the same terminology, he understood the distinction between a fungible and a consumptible and was keenly aware of the long-term dangers of dependence upon a consumptible.

Subsequent events justified in some measure both the hopes and the forebodings of such men. Though living standards were rising for most groups in the population, the dangers of the new age were also sobering. In the first half of the twentieth century the First World War showed what slaughter on an industrial scale was like, and barely a decade later at the time of the Great Depression many millions throughout the industrial world were forced to go without employment for years on end through no fault of their own. The second half of the twentieth century, on the other hand, seemed for a time to show that, whatever the transitional stresses, the long-term upshot of the industrial revolution was benign. More recently, new and potentially devastating problems have surfaced. For example, is relative prosperity for all only attainable at the cost of radical and destructive climate change? Is the Sahara going to move north a thousand miles?

We have been given an interval, brief in comparison with earlier periods of human history, in which to find a new balance. Access to fossil fuels has brought unexampled prosperity to three continents and is rapidly transforming two more. Continued dependence on fossil fuels, however, is a recipe for disaster for two reasons. Since they are consumptibles they will become exhausted. The scale of the remaining reserves of coal, oil, and natural gas has been the subject of much examination but remains uncertain. These energy sources are, however, unlikely to be able to meet prospective energy demand for more than, say, two or three more generations, especially if the rate of energy consumption continues to grow. But there is a more immediate problem. The release of gases which occur when a fossil fuel is burnt causes temperatures to rise and may make conditions of life intolerable for much of the globe in decades rather than generations, especially if there proves to be a 'tipping point' in the process. Of course, greater success than has been achieved to date in tapping solar or geothermal energy, combined with resolute and co-ordinated action to minimise the emission of carbon dioxide, may make these fears shortlived, but at present the problem remains pressing and the outcome unsure.

The benefits which have flowed in the wake of the industrial revolution are great and universal. Expectation of life at birth has more than doubled in England over the past three centuries and many infectious ailments which once killed on a large scale have virtually disappeared. The plea in the Lord's Prayer, 'Give us this day our daily bread', may well seem quaint in an age when in advanced economies superabundant nutrition is a greater threat than malnourishment. For a large majority of the population of England and other industrialised countries, homes are warm and dry even in midwinter; and they are rarely over-run with vermin, a state of affairs beyond attainment for most families in earlier times. Literacy was once the privilege of a tiny minority of the population and formal education played no part in the upbringing of most children. Today school and other types of formal education form a major part of the lives of children for anything between a dozen and twenty years. A list of this sort could be greatly extended, and all such changes can be said to have been made possible by the creation of wealth and plenitude of resources which lie downstream from the industrial revolution.

Opening Pandora's jar has brought great benefits; but also countervailing dangers in addition to those associated with the use of fossil fuels. The new dangers are most acutely felt in relation to warfare. A conflict conducted with nuclear weapons or germ warfare is capable of destroying life on a scale which was not within the capacity of states in the past, however bloodthirsty their leaders may have been. Even individual terrorists may prove capable of a scale of destruction for which there was no parallel in earlier times. And the interconnectedness of life in modern society carries dangers which were largely absent in the past. The present turmoil in credit markets and the spectacular collapse of merchant banks, insurance companies, and mortgage lenders have produced traumas across the whole spectrum of production and commerce of a kind which was unknown when local communities might suffer severely from a deficient harvest but were largely untroubled by distant events.

I have argued as if the industrial revolution should be both credited for the benefits and blamed for the dangers just listed. At one level this may seem ridiculous. The medical advances which have played a major role in increasing expectation of life, for example, unlike the improvement in nutrition which has occurred, might seem only distantly related to economic events, if related at all. Atom bombs are very expensive to make and for this reason if no other were beyond the capacity of any pre-industrial economy, but the discoveries in physics and engineering which made possible their construction have more to do with the so-called scientific revolution beginning in the seventeenth century than with the industrial revolution.

Yet realising the benefits which are implicit in scientific discovery may often prove impossible without exploiting the new capacity to produce on a scale which was beyond attainment in organic economies. It is possible to calculate with tolerable accuracy the scale of energy supplies which could be tapped in an organic economy.[11] This constraint set severe limits to the feasible scale of material production. The type of infrastructural investment which underwrites a wide range of the activities taking place in modern societies could not have been provided in the organic era. This is readily demonstrable in some contexts. The quantity of iron and steel needed to build a railway network or to construct bulk carrier ships, for example, could not have been produced even if all the forested land had been denuded of timber. But it holds true across a much broader spectrum of social and economic life, even if this is less simply demonstrable. The quantity of energy needed to build a large hospital complex or to construct hundreds of miles of motorway is, by the standards of the past, huge. Constructing a modern city involves producing bricks, mortar, concrete, steel, and other construction materials on a massive scale, and then transporting them to construction sites. These are all activities which require the expenditure of much energy. They produce facilities from which everyone benefits but which could not have been realised previously. Even forms of human endeavour and achievement which

[11] See above p. 14.

may appear at first sight not to be closely dependent on the new power to produce might prove hard to pursue in their absence. They are feasible only with access to facilities which organic economies could not provide. They rely upon the existence of the infrastructure of contemporary industrial societies today and could not have been created or sustained without access to energy on a scale which was unattainable before the industrial revolution.

The world today faces both opportunities and dangers very different from those faced in the past. In large measure, both have been the offspring of the ability which mankind now possesses to produce goods and services on a scale beyond the imaginings of people in earlier generations. The validity of the analogy between the occurrence of the industrial revolution and the opening of Pandora's jar hinges on two points: that in both cases the changes which followed were unforeseen by those whose actions initiated them, and that the changes were of sufficient magnitude for it to be fair to say that there was hardly any aspect of life which was not greatly altered as a result.

Appendix

The three tables in this appendix are fuller versions of tables 5.1, 5.2, and 5.3 which appear in an abbreviated form in the main text.

Table 5.1 *Number of males in agriculture per 1,000 acres in 1841*

	Males in agriculture	County acreage	Males per 1,000 acres		Males in agriculture	County acreage	Males per 1,000 acres
Middlesex	15,445	182,040	84.8	Norfolk	47,483	1,304,471	36.4
Essex	47,618	982,754	48.5	Gloucestershire	28,199	798,125	35.3
Bedfordshire	14,193	297,484	47.7	Rutland	3,261	97,245	33.5
Kent	46,167	995,853	46.4	Lincolnshire	56,283	1,681,533	33.5
Hertfordshire	18,718	406,233	46.1	Huntingdonshire	7,849	236,854	33.1
Suffolk	41,832	945,573	44.2	Hampshire	33,460	1,039,445	32.2
Buckinghamshire	20,813	474,297	43.9	Leicestershire	16,551	521,350	31.7
Worcestershire	20,200	464,053	43.5	Shropshire	27,381	865,632	31.6
Lancashire	51,499	1,183,797	43.5	Devon	51,587	1,662,237	31.0
Surrey	20,734	484,549	42.8	Yorkshire, ER	24,350	805,476	30.2
Warwickshire	23,548	578,812	40.7	Yorkshire, WR	50,254	1,719,984	29.2
Berkshire	18,721	461,049	40.6	Cornwall	25,032	866,703	28.9
Staffordshire	30,266	755,250	40.1	Herefordshire	15,423	541,302	28.5
Oxfordshire	19,054	476,812	40.0	Dorset	17,730	632,835	28.0
Somerset	41,658	1,044,666	39.9	Derbyshire	17,654	663,262	26.6
Cambridgeshire	21,191	546,641	38.8	Durham	14,072	706,582	19.9
Northamptonshire	24,433	640,571	38.1	Yorkshire, NR	25,507	1,348,880	18.9
Cheshire	24,743	655,142	37.8	Cumberland	13,889	969,123	14.3
Wiltshire	33,051	885,211	37.3	Northumberland	15,977	1,232,593	13.0
Nottinghamshire	19,981	540,219	37.0	Westmorland	6,201	499,479	12.4
Sussex	34,042	927,628	36.7	England	1,086,050	32,121,741	33.8

Notes. The totals of males in agriculture are the combined totals of farmers and graziers and agricultural labourers for each county in the 1841 census.

Sources. Males in agriculture: *1841 Census, Occupation abstract.* Acreages: Wrigley, *The early English censuses,* tab. A1.1.

Table 5.2 *County population densities (persons per 1,000 acres)*

	Population densities					Densities indexed to 1601 (100)				
	1600	1700	1750	1801	1851	1600	1700	1750	1801	1851
Middlesex	1,556.0	2,869.7	3,211.2	4,685.0	10,523.5	100.0	184.4	206.4	301.1	676.3
Surrey	176.5	255.8	310.8	576.1	1,428.0	100.0	144.9	176.1	326.3	808.8
Metropolitan group	**552.5**	**968.3**	**1,101.4**	**1,696.1**	**3,907.1**	**100.0**	**175.2**	**199.3**	**307.0**	**707.1**
Cheshire	114.1	139.5	190.6	306.4	706.0	100.0	122.3	167.1	268.7	619.0
Lancashire	155.2	196.4	267.9	593.9	1,743.1	100.0	126.6	172.7	382.7	1123.3
Staffordshire	104.6	153.2	201.2	339.8	826.9	100.0	146.4	192.3	324.7	790.3
Warwickshire	114.9	151.7	229.9	374.6	837.3	100.0	132.1	200.1	326.1	729.0
Yorkshire, WR	113.1	136.9	183.1	334.2	757.2	100.0	121.1	161.9	295.6	669.8
Industrial group	**122.2**	**155.8**	**212.7**	**398.4**	**1,007.0**	**100.0**	**127.4**	**174.0**	**326.0**	**823.9**
Bedfordshire	146.4	168.6	178.5	222.5	425.0	100.0	115.2	121.9	152.0	290.3
Buckinghamshire	119.2	142.5	182.7	236.6	348.4	100.0	119.5	153.3	198.5	292.3
Cambridgeshire	134.0	153.4	134.8	170.6	344.3	100.0	114.5	100.6	127.4	256.9
Essex	159.5	167.7	191.9	242.2	382.0	100.0	105.2	120.3	151.9	239.6
Herefordshire	116.6	126.5	138.1	172.8	219.2	100.0	108.5	118.4	148.2	187.9
Hertfordshire	145.3	169.4	207.9	252.0	421.6	100.0	116.6	143.1	173.5	290.2
Huntingdonshire	120.6	138.0	138.1	169.4	282.2	100.0	114.5	114.5	140.5	234.1
Lincolnshire	104.3	116.3	97.4	129.7	246.3	100.0	111.6	93.4	124.4	236.2
Northamptonshire	142.7	163.0	179.8	213.1	334.0	100.0	114.3	126.0	149.3	234.1
Oxfordshire	139.9	161.2	196.2	239.4	355.0	100.0	115.3	140.2	171.2	253.8
Rutland	118.3	143.2	136.3	175.1	240.2	100.0	121.1	115.2	148.1	203.1
Suffolk	147.7	168.1	176.0	236.4	361.8	100.0	113.8	119.1	160.0	244.9

Table 5.2 (cont.)

	Population densities					Densities indexed to 1601 (100)				
	1600	1700	1750	1801	1851	1600	1700	1750	1801	1851
Wiltshire	132.6	155.7	189.9	220.1	297.1	100.0	117.4	143.2	165.9	224.0
Yorkshire, NR	75.5	86.0	87.8	121.0	159.6	100.0	113.9	116.2	160.3	211.3
Agricultural group	123.9	140.1	149.8	189.6	298.3	100.0	113.1	120.9	153.1	240.9
Berkshire	124.7	158.0	199.7	250.4	373.2	100.0	126.7	160.2	200.9	299.4
Cornwall	120.1	139.3	150.3	231.0	415.6	100.0	116.0	125.2	192.4	346.2
Cumberland	79.0	83.4	86.0	126.1	204.9	100.0	105.6	108.9	159.7	259.4
Derbyshire	107.0	144.3	159.6	255.9	457.0	100.0	134.8	149.1	239.2	427.1
Devon	157.1	194.2	176.2	213.8	346.3	100.0	123.6	112.2	136.1	220.4
Dorset	119.9	136.7	145.8	188.8	296.0	100.0	114.0	121.6	157.5	246.9
Durham	119.7	179.3	197.6	259.6	645.8	100.0	149.8	165.0	216.8	539.3
Gloucestershire	128.8	175.3	259.8	328.7	585.9	100.0	136.2	201.7	255.3	455.0
Hampshire	101.6	111.2	139.5	221.1	397.1	100.0	109.4	137.2	217.5	390.7
Kent	154.3	161.6	184.7	324.2	629.1	100.0	104.7	119.7	210.2	407.8
Leicestershire	121.5	141.5	184.7	258.3	443.7	100.0	116.5	152.0	212.7	365.3
Norfolk	132.8	177.2	179.2	219.0	345.1	100.0	133.4	134.9	164.9	259.8
Northumberland	57.2	88.9	104.3	127.0	224.0	100.0	155.6	182.4	222.2	392.0
Nottinghamshire	146.3	170.6	163.7	271.4	508.4	100.0	116.6	111.9	185.5	347.6
Shropshire	92.8	130.0	159.8	212.4	292.4	100.0	140.1	172.1	228.8	315.1
Somerset	164.0	198.0	222.5	274.0	433.0	100.0	120.8	135.7	167.1	264.1
Sussex	110.7	111.3	105.6	178.6	366.9	100.0	100.5	95.4	161.3	331.3
Westmorland	85.4	84.2	71.0	85.2	118.6	100.0	98.6	83.1	99.8	138.7
Worcestershire	138.4	195.7	228.7	303.3	543.4	100.0	141.4	165.3	219.2	392.7
Yorkshire, ER	89.6	98.7	104.2	188.5	361.0	100.0	110.2	116.3	210.5	403.0
Other counties group	118.3	144.8	159.5	221.8	389.3	100.0	122.5	134.9	187.5	329.2
England	129.6	162.2	184.4	270.0	530.2	100.0	125.2	142.3	208.4	409.2

Population totals

	1600	1700	1750	1801	1851
Metropolitan group	369,024	646,668	735,586	1,132,767	2,609,449
Industrial group	602,823	768,190	1,048,822	1,964,973	4,966,482
Agricultural group	1,185,241	1,340,802	1,433,419	1,814,404	2,854,826
Other counties group	2,004,696	2,454,962	2,704,078	3,759,213	6,599,390
England	4,161,784	5,210,623	5,921,905	8,671,357	17,030,147
Percentage share					
Metropolitan group	8.9	12.4	12.4	13.1	15.3
Industrial group	14.5	14.7	17.7	22.7	29.2
Agricultural group	28.5	25.7	24.2	20.9	16.8
Other counties group	48.2	47.1	45.7	43.4	38.8
England	100.0	100.0	100.0	100.0	100.0

Sources. Population totals and acreages: Wrigley, *The early English censuses*, tab. A2.1.

Table 5.3 *Estimated county net migration totals 1600–1851*

	Net migration				
	1600–1700	*1700–50*	*1750–1801*	*1801–51*	*1600–1851*
Bedfordshire	−5,430	−4,879	−15,063	−6,014	−31,386
Berkshire	−524	7,873	−25,442	−59,044	−77,138
Buckinghamshire	−4,610	8,584	−20,443	−59,483	−75,952
Cambridgeshire	−9,634	−23,280	−19,491	1,077	−51,328
Cheshire	−4,024	19,269	9,708	60,812	85,766
Cornwall	−12,124	−9,230	874	−40,514	−60,993
Cumberland	−16,868	−10,080	−5,320	−46,032	−78,300
Derbyshire	5,079	−4,758	7,765	−36,391	−28,305
Devon	−10,580	−80,323	−92,910	−135,758	−319,571
Dorset	−10,319	−7,743	−21,663	−51,779	−91,504
Durham	17,098	−6,253	−27,626	81,629	64,848
Essex	−35,232	−1,899	−50,533	−100,834	−188,498
Gloucestershire	8,718	45,418	−54,651	−57,251	−57,766
Hampshire	−19,223	11,359	7,913	−46,941	−46,891
Herefordshire	−12,051	−4,361	−20,720	−68,132	−105,264
Hertfordshire	−6,475	4,875	−26,731	−33,470	−61,801
Huntingdonshire	−3,687	−4,962	−9,707	−13,171	−31,527
Kent	−35,166	−2,053	41,438	−19,685	−15,467
Lancashire	−1,968	48,397	217,763	656,528	920,720
Leicestershire	−7,125	11,099	−12,740	−38,537	−47,303
Lincolnshire	−28,209	−62,253	−32,378	−22,391	−145,230
Middlesex	239,151	62,166	268,287	531,425	1,101,029
Norfolk	9,934	−33,322	−72,009	−120,929	−216,326
Northamptonshire	−12,340	−5,569	−40,048	−59,678	−117,635
Northumberland	20,579	1,930	−42,006	−38,817	−58,314
Nottinghamshire	−8,703	−18,134	11,314	−18,696	−34,220
Oxfordshire	−8,382	4,733	−29,379	−60,016	−93,044
Rutland	−756	−2,844	−3,247	−10,723	−17,571
Shropshire	9,912	8,175	−27,629	−114,019	−123,561
Somerset	−11,764	−6,619	−69,305	−120,270	−207,958
Staffordshire	14,738	18,043	23,931	110,203	166,915
Suffolk	−19,337	−17,377	−31,141	−105,388	−173,243
Surrey	38,493	26,752	128,894	133,606	327,745
Sussex	−27,992	−21,488	15,843	8,897	−24,739
Warwickshire	2,931	31,406	13,184	50,561	98,082
Westmorland	−12,416	−13,155	−11,696	−25,980	−63,247
Wiltshire	−11,977	8,784	−61,956	−125,860	−191,008
Worcestershire	9,144	1,217	−22,380	−30,506	−42,525

Table 5.3 *(cont.)*

	Net migration				
	1600–1700	*1700–50*	*1750–1801*	*1801–51*	*1600–1851*
Yorkshire, ER	–11,767	–7,399	21,838	–12,227	–9,554
Yorkshire, NR	–14,082	–15,897	–18,084	–112,405	–160,468
Yorkshire, WR	–13,014	43,798	95,547	156,203	282,534

Notes. For an account of the method of calculation see accompanying text. Positive figures represent net in–migration; negative figures net out–migration. Due to rounding of the county totals to produce whole numbers, the cumulative total for all counties does not exactly sum to zero.

Sources. The county totals underlying the results set out in the table were taken from Wrigley, *The early English censuses*, tab. A2.6.

Bibliography

Aikin, J., *A description of the country from thirty to forty miles around Manchester* (London, 1795).

Allen, R. C., 'Agriculture during the industrial revolution', in R. Floud and D. McCloskey, eds., *The economic history of Britain since 1700*, 2nd edn, I, 1700–1860 (Cambridge, 1994), pp. 96–122.

'Real wages in Europe and Asia: a first look at the long-term patterns', in R. C. Allen, T. Bengtsson, and M. Dribe, eds., *Living standards in the past: new perspectives on well-being in Asia and Europe* (Oxford, 2005), pp. 111–30.

The British industrial revolution in global perspective (Cambridge, 2009).

Ashton, T. S., *The industrial revolution 1760–1830* (Oxford, 1948).

An economic history of England: the 18th century (London, 1955).

'The relation of economic history to economy theory', in N. B. Harte, ed., *The study of economic history: collected inaugural lectures 1893–1970* (London, 1971), pp. 161–79.

Bagwell, P. S., *The transport revolution from 1770* (London, 1974).

Booth, C., ed., *Life and labour of the people in London*, 4 vols. (London, 1889–91).

Brunt, L., 'Where there's muck, there's brass: the market for manure in the industrial revolution', *Economic History Review* **60** (2007), pp. 333–72.

Campbell, B. M. S., *English seigniorial agriculture 1250–1450* (Cambridge, 2000).

Chartres, J. A., 'The marketing of agricultural produce', in J. Thirsk, ed., *The agrarian history of England and Wales*, V, pt II, 1640–1750 (Cambridge, 1985), pp. 406–502.

Chartres, J. A. and Turnbull, G. L., 'Road transport', in D. H. Aldcroft and M. J. Freeman, eds., *Transport in the industrial revolution* (Manchester, 1983), pp. 64–99.

Church, R., *The history of the British coal industry*, III, 1830–1913: Victorian pre-eminence (Oxford, 1986).

Clapham, J. H., *An economic history of modern Britain*, 2nd edn., reprinted, 3 vols. (Cambridge, 1950–2).

Clark, C., *The conditions of economic progress*, 2nd edn (London 1951).

Clark, G., 'Labour productivity in English agriculture, 1300–1860', in B. M. S. Campbell and M. Overton, eds., *Land, labour and livestock: historical studies in European agricultural productivity* (Manchester, 1991), pp. 211–35.

Clarkson, L. A., 'The manufacture of leather', in G. E. Mingay, ed., *The agrarian history of England and Wales*, VI, *1750–1850* (Cambridge, 1989), pp. 466–83.

Coleman, D. C., *Myth, history and the industrial revolution* (London, 1992).

The economy of England 1450–1750 (Oxford, 1977).

Collins, D., *An account of the English colony in New South Wales with remarks on the dispositions, customs, manners, etc. of the native inhabitants of that country*, 2 vols. (London, 1798).

Cottrell, F., *Energy and society: the relation between energy, social change, and economic development* (New York, 1955).

Crafts, N. F. R., *British economic growth during the industrial revolution* (Oxford, 1985).

Cressy, D., 'Literacy in context: meaning and measurement in early modern England', in J. Brewer and R. Porter, eds., *Consumption and the world of goods* (London, 1993), pp. 305–19.

Deane, P. and Cole, W. A., *British economic growth 1688–1959: trends and structure* (Cambridge, 1962).

Defoe, D., *The history and remarkable life of the truly honourable Colonel Jack*, The Novel Library (London, 1947) [first published 1722].

Dejongh, G. and Thoen, E., 'Arable productivity in Flanders and the former territory of Belgium in a long-term perspective (from the middle ages to the end of the Ancien Régime)', in B. J. P. van Bavel and E. Thoen, eds., *Land productivity and agro-systems in the North Sea area (middle ages–20th century)*, CORN publications ser. 2 (Turnhout, 1999), pp. 30–64.

de Vries, J.*European urbanization 1500–1800* (Cambridge, Mass., 1984).

'Between purchasing power and the world of goods: understanding the household economy in early modern Europe', in J. Brewer and R. Porter, eds., *Consumption and the world of goods* (London, 1993), pp. 85–132.

'The industrial revolution and the industrious revolution', *Journal of Economic History* 54 (1994), pp. 249–70.

The industrious revolution: consumer behaviour and the household economy 1650 to the present (Cambridge, 2008).

de Vries, J. and van der Woude, A., *The first modern economy: success, failure, and perseverance of the Dutch economy, 1500–1815* (Cambridge, 1997).

de Zeeuw, J. W., 'Peat and the Dutch Golden Age. The historical meaning of energy-attainability', *A.A.G. Bijdragen* **21** (Wageningen, 1978), pp. 3–31.

Dobson, M. J., *Contours of death and disease in early modern England* (Cambridge, 1997).

Eltis, W., *The classical theory of economic growth* (London, 1984).

Eversley, D. E. C., 'The home market and economic growth in England, 1750–80', in E. L. Jones and G. E. Mingay, eds., *Land, labour and population in the industrial revolution: essays presented to J. D. Chambers* (London, 1967), pp. 206–59.

Farr, W., *Vital statistics* (London, 1885).

Feinstein, C. H., 'Capital formation in Great Britain', in P. Mathias and M. M. Postan, eds., *The Cambridge economic history of Europe*, I, pt I (Cambridge, 1978), pp. 28–96.

'National statistics, 1760–1920', in C. H. Feinstein and S. Pollard, eds., *Studies in capital formation in the United Kingdom, 1750–1920* (Oxford, 1988), pp. 257–471.

'Pessimism perpetuated: real wages and the standard of living in Britain during the industrial revolution', *Journal of Economic History*, **58** (1998), pp. 625–58.

Fisher, F. J., 'The sixteenth and seventeenth centuries: the dark ages of English economic history?', in N. B. Harte, ed., *The study of economic history: collected inaugural lectures 1893–1970* (London, 1971), pp. 181–200.

Flinn, M. W., *The history of the British coal industry*, II, *1700–1830: the industrial revolution* (Oxford, 1984).

Foster, C. F., *Capital and innovation: how Britain became the first industrial nation* (Northwich, 2004).

Galloway, J. A., Keene, D., and Murphy, M., 'Fuelling the city: production and distribution of firewood and fuel in London's region, 1290–1400', *Economic History Review*, **49** (1996), pp. 447–72.

Geertz, C., *Agricultural involution: the process of ecological change in Indonesia* (Berkeley, Calif., 1963).

Gerhold, D., 'Productivity change in road transport before and after turnpiking, 1690–1840', *Economic History Review*, **49** (1996), pp. 491–515.

Golas, P. J., 'Mining', in J. Needham, ed., *Science and civilisation in China*, V, pt XIII (Cambridge, 1999), pp. 186–201.

Goldstone, J. A., 'The demographic revolution in England: a re-examination', *Population Studies* 40 (1986), pp. 5–33.

Goubert, P., *Beauvais et le Beauvaisis de 1600 à 1730*, 2 vols. (Paris, 1960).

Gough, R., *The history of Myddle*, ed. D. Hey (London: Folio Society, 1983).

Grantham, G., 'The growth of labour productivity in the production of wheat in the *Cinq Grosses Fermes* of France, 1750–1929', in B. M. S. Campbell and M. Overton, eds., *Land, labour and livestock: historical studies in European agricultural productivity* (Manchester, 1991), pp. 340–63.

Hajnal, J., 'European marriage patterns in perspective', in D. V. Glass and D. E. C. Eversley, eds., *Population in history: essays in historical demography* (London, 1965), pp. 101–43.

Hammersley, G., 'The charcoal iron industry and its fuel, 1540–1750', *Economic History Review*, 2nd ser., **26** (1973), pp. 593–613.

Hart, C. W. M. and Pilling, A. R., *The Tiwi of north Australia* (New York, 1960).

Hartwell, R., 'A revolution in the Chinese iron and coal industries during the northern Sung, 960–1126 A.D.', *Journal of Asian Studies* **21** (1962), pp. 153–62.

Hatcher, J., *The history of the British coal industry, I, Before 1700: towards the age of coal* (Oxford, 1993).

Himmelfarb, G., *The idea of poverty: England in the early industrial age* (London, 1984).

Hoggart, R., *The uses of literacy: aspects of working class life, with special reference to publications and entertainments* (London, 1967).

Jackson, R. V., 'What was the rate of economic growth during the industrial revolution?', in G. D. Snooks, ed., *Was the industrial revolution necessary?* (London, 1994), pp. 79–95.

Jevons, W. S., *The coal question: an inquiry concerning the progress of the nation, and the probable exhaustion of our coal mines*, 3rd edn rev. 1906 (ed. A. W. Flux, Reprints of Economic Classics, New York, 1965).

Jones, E. L., *Agriculture and the industrial revolution* (Oxford, 1974).

'Agriculture 1700–1800', in R. C. Floud and D. N. McCloskey, eds., *The economic history of Britain since 1700*, I (Cambridge, 1981), pp. 66–86.

Growth recurring: economic change in world history (Oxford, 1988).

Kitson, P. M., '*Family formation, male occupation and the nature of parochial registration in England, c. 1538–1837*', unpub. Cambridge Ph.D. thesis (2004).

Kussmaul, A., *Servants in husbandry in early modern England* (Cambridge, 1981).

Langton, J., 'Urban growth and economic change: from the late seventeenth century to 1841', in P. Clark, ed., *The Cambridge urban history of Britain*, II, *1540–1840* (Cambridge, 2000), pp. 453–90.

Laslett, P., 'Mean household size in England since the sixteenth century', in P. Laslett and R. Wall, eds., *Household and family in past time* (Cambridge, 1972), pp. 125–58.

'Family, kinship and collectivity as systems of support in pre-industrial Europe: a consideration of the "nuclear hardship" hypothesis', *Continuity and Change* **3** (1988), pp. 153–75.

Levasseur, E., *La population française*, 3 vols. (Paris, 1889).

Livi-Bacci, M., *The population of Europe: a history* (Oxford, 2000).

Malanima, P., 'Urbanisation and the Italian economy during the last millennium', *European Review of Economic History*, **9** (2005), pp. 97–122.

Energy consumption in Italy in the 19th and 20th centuries: a statistical outline (Rome, 2006).

Pre-modern European economy: one thousand years (10th–19th centuries) (Leiden, 2009).

Malthus, T. R., *An essay on the principle of population as it affects the future improvement of society* [1798], in *The works of Thomas Robert Malthus*, ed. E. A. Wrigley and D. Souden (London, 1986), I.

An essay on the principle of population, or a view of its past and present effects on human happiness, 6th edn [1826], 2 vols., in *The works of Thomas Robert Malthus*, ed. E. A. Wrigley and D. Souden (London, 1986), III.

Principles of political economy considered with a view to their practical application, 2nd edn [1836], in *The works of Thomas Robert Malthus*, ed. E. A. Wrigley and D. Souden (London, 1986), V and VI.

Marx, K., *Capital: a critical analysis of capitalist production*, ed. F. Engels, translated from the 3rd German edn by S. Moore and E. Aveling, 2 vols. (London, 1887).

Mathias, P., 'The social structure in the eighteenth century: a calculation by Joseph Massie', *Economic History Review*, 2nd ser., **10** (1957), pp. 30–45.

The first industrial nation: an economic history of Britain 1700–1914, 2nd edn (London, 1983).

Mayhew, H., *London labour and the London poor*, 2 vols. (London, 1851).

McKendrick, N., 'The commercialization of fashion', in N. McKendrick, J. Brewer, and J. H. Plumb, *The birth of a consumer society: the commercialization of eighteenth-century England* (London, 1982), pp. 34–99.

'The consumer revolution of eighteenth-century England', in N. McKendrick, J. Brewer, and J. H. Plumb, *The birth of a consumer society: the commercialization of eighteenth-century England* (London, 1982), pp. 9–33.

Mill, J. S., *Principles of political economy with some of their applications to social philosophy*, ed. J. M. Robson, 2 vols. (Toronto, 1965).

Mitchell, B. R., *British historical statistics* (Cambridge, 1988).

European historical statistics 1750–1975, 2nd rev. edn (London and Basingstoke, 1981).

Mokyr, J., *The lever of riches: technological creativity and economic progress* (New York, 1990).

'Editor's introduction: the new economic history and the industrial revolution', in J. Mokyr, ed., *The British industrial revolution: an economic perspective* (Boulder, Colo., 1993), pp. 1–131.

Musson, A. E., 'Industrial motive power in the United Kingdom, 1800–70', *Economic History Review*, 2nd ser., **29** (1976), pp. 415–39.

Nef, J. U., *The rise of the British coal industry*, 2 vols., first pub. 1932 (reprinted, New York, 1972).

North, D. C., *Structure and change in economic history* (New York, 1981).

O'Brien, P. K. and Toniolo, G., 'The poverty of Italy and the backwardness of its agriculture before 1914', in B. M. S. Campbell and M. Overton, eds., *Land, labour and livestock: historical studies in European agricultural productivity* (Manchester, 1991), pp. 385–409.

Overton, M., *Agricultural revolution in England: the transformation of the agrarian economy 1500–1850* (Cambridge, 1996).

Overton, M. and Campbell, B. M. S., 'Productivity change in European agricultural development', in B. M. S. Campbell and M. Overton, eds., *Land, labour and livestock: historical studies in European agricultural productivity* (Manchester, 1991), pp. 1–50.

'Statistics of production and productivity in English agriculture 1086–1871', in B. J. P. van Bavel and E. Thoen, eds., *Land productivity and agro-systems in the North Sea area (middle ages–20th century)*, CORN publication ser. 2 (Turnhout, 1999), pp. 189–208.

Overton, M., Whittle, J., Dean, D., and Hann, A., *Production and consumption in English households, 1600–1750* (London, 2004).

Pimentel, D., 'Energy flow in the food system', in D. Pimentel and C. W. Hall, eds., *Food and energy resources* (London, 1984), pp. 1–24.

Pollard, S., 'Industrialization and the European economy', *Economic History Review*, 2nd ser., **26** (1973), pp. 638–48.

Pomeranz, K., *The great divergence: China, Europe, and the making of the modern world economy* (Princeton, 2000).

Pounds, N. J. G., 'Barton farming in eighteenth-century Cornwall', *Journal of the Royal Institution of Cornwall*, new ser., 7 (1973), pp. 55–75.

Rappaport, S., *Worlds within worlds: structures of life in sixteenth-century London* (Cambridge, 1989).

Redford, A., *Labour migration in England 1800–1850*, 3rd edn (Manchester, 1976).

Ricardo, D., *On the principles of political economy and taxation* in *The works and correspondence of David Ricardo*, I, ed. P. Sraffa with the collaboration of M. H. Dobb (Cambridge, 1951).

Roessingh, H. K., 'Village and hamlet in a sandy region of the Netherlands in the middle of the eighteenth century', *Acta Historiae Neerlandica* 4 (1970), pp. 105–29.

Rostow, W. W., *How it all began: origins of the modern economy* (London, 1975).

Rowntree, B. S., *Poverty: a study of town life* (New York, 1971).

Schofield, R. S., 'The relationship between demographic structure and environment in pre-industrial western Europe', in W. Conze, ed., *Sozialgeschichte der Familie in der Neuzeit Europas* (Stuttgart, 1976), pp. 147–60.

'English marriage patterns revisited', *Journal of Family History* 10 (1985), pp. 2–20.

Shammas, C., *The pre-industrial consumer in England and America* (Oxford, 1990).

Smith, A., *An inquiry into the nature and causes of the wealth of nations*, ed. E. Cannan, 5th edn, 2 vols. (London, 1961).

Söderberg, J., Jonsson, U., and Persson, C., *A stagnating metropolis: the economy and demography of Stockholm, 1750–1850* (Cambridge, 1991).

Stobart, J., *The first industrial region: north-west England, c. 1700–60* (Manchester, 2004).

Swift, J., *Gulliver's travels* [1726], ed. P. Dixon and J. Chalker (Harmondsworth, 1967).

Szostak, R., *The role of transportation in the industrial revolution: a comparison of England and France* (Montreal and Kingston, 1991).

Thomas, B., 'Escaping from constraints: the industrial revolution in a Malthusian context', *Journal of Interdisciplinary History* 15 (1985), pp. 729–53.

The industrial revolution and the Atlantic economy: selected essays (London, 1993).

Timmins, G., *Made in Lancashire: a history of regional industrialization* (Manchester, 1998).

Tönnies, F., *Community and society*, ed. C. P. Loomis (East Lansing, 1957).

Toynbee, A., *Lectures on the industrial revolution of the eighteenth century in England* (5th impression: London, 1919).

Turnbull, G., 'Canals, coal and regional growth during the industrial revolution', *Economic History Review*, 2nd ser., **40** (1987), pp. 537–60.

Turner, M. E., Beckett, J. V., and Afton, B., *Farm production in England 1700–1914* (Oxford, 2001).

van der Woude, A., Hayami, A., and de Vries, J., eds., *Urbanization in history: a process of dynamic interactions* (Oxford, 1990).

Ville, S., 'Total factor productivity in the English shipping industry: the north-east coal trade, 1700–1850', *Economic History Review*, 2nd ser., **39** (1986), pp. 355–70.

'Transport', in R. Floud and P. Johnson, eds., *The Cambridge economic history of modern Britain*, I, *Industrialisation, 1700–1860* (Cambridge, 2004), pp. 295–331.

Voth, H.-J., 'Time and work in eighteenth-century London', *Journal of Economic History* **58** (1998), pp. 29–58.

Warde, P., *Energy consumption in England and Wales 1560–2000* (Rome, 2007).

Weatherill, L., *Consumer behaviour and material culture, 1660–1760* (London, 1988).

Weir, D. R., 'Rather never than late: celibacy and age at marriage in English cohort fertility', *Journal of Family History* **9** (1984), pp. 340–54.

White, L. P. and Plaskett, L. G., *Biomass as fuel* (London, 1981).

Wilson, C. H., *England's apprenticeship 1603–1763* (London, 1965).

Woods, R., 'The effects of population redistribution on the level of mortality in nineteenth-century England and Wales', *Journal of Economic History* **45** (1985), pp. 645–51.

Wrigley, E. A., *Industrial growth and population change: a regional study of the coalfield areas of north-west Europe in the later nineteenth century* (Cambridge, 1961).

'The process of modernization and the industrial revolution in England', *Journal of Interdisciplinary History*, **3** (1972), pp. 225–59.

'Marriage, fertility and population growth in eighteenth-century England', in R. B. Outhwaite, ed., *Marriage and society: studies in the social history of marriage* (London, 1981), pp. 137–85.

'Men on the land and men in the countryside: employment in agriculture in early nineteenth-century England', in L. Bonfield, R. M. Smith, and K. Wrightson, eds., *The world we have gained: histories of population and social structure* (Oxford, 1986), pp. 295–336.

'Some reflections on corn yields and prices in pre-industrial economies', in E. A. Wrigley, *People, cities and wealth: the transformation of traditional society* (Oxford, 1987), pp. 92–130.

'Urban growth and agricultural change: England and the continent in the early modern period', in E. A. Wrigley, *People, cities and wealth: the transformation of traditional society* (Oxford, 1987), pp. 157–93.

'A simple model of London's importance in changing English society and economy, 1650–1750', in E. A. Wrigley, *People, cities and wealth: the transformation of traditional society* (Oxford, 1987), pp. 133–56.

Continuity, chance and change: the character of the industrial revolution in England (Cambridge, 1988).

'Two kinds of capitalism, two kinds of growth', *L.S.E. Quarterly* 2 (1988), pp. 97–121.

'Explaining the rise in marital fertility in England in the "long" eighteenth century', *Economic History Review* 51 (1998), pp. 435–64.

'Energy availability and agricultural productivity', in B. M. S. Campbell and M. Overton, eds., *Land, labour and livestock: historical studies in European agricultural productivity* (Manchester, 1991), pp. 323–39.

'Country and town: the primary, secondary, and tertiary peopling of England in the early modern period', in P. Slack and R. Ward, eds., *The peopling of Britain: the shaping of a human landscape* (Oxford, 2002), pp. 217–42.

'British population during the "long" eighteenth century, 1680–1840', in R. Floud and P. Johnson, eds., *The Cambridge economic history of modern Britain*, I, *Industrialisation, 1700–1860* (Cambridge, 2004), pp. 57–95.

Poverty, progress, and population (Cambridge, 2004).

'The transition to an advanced organic economy', *Economic History Review* 59 (2006), pp. 435–80.

'English county populations in the later eighteenth century', *Economic History Review* 60 (2007), pp. 35–69.

'Rickman revisited: the population growth rates of English counties in the early modern period', *Economic History Review* 62 (2009), pp. 711–35.

The early English censuses, British Academy, Records of Social and Economic History (Oxford, 2011).

'Coping with rapid population growth: how England fared in the century preceding the Great Exhibition of 1851', in D. Feldman and J. Lawrence, eds., *Structures and transformations in modern British history: essays for Gareth Stedman Jones* (in press),

Wrigley, E. A., Davies, R. S., Oeppen, J. E., and Schofield, R. S., *English population history from family reconstitution 1580–1837* (Cambridge, 1997).

Wrigley, E. A. and Schofield, R. S., *The population history of England 1541–1871* (London, 1981).

Young, A., *Travels in France and Italy during the years 1787, 1788 and 1789*, Everyman's Library (London and Toronto, n.d.).

Travels in France during the year 1787, 1788, and 1789, ed. J. Kaplow (New York, 1969).

Young, M. and Willmott, P. *Family and kinship in east London* (Harmondsworth, 1957).

Official sources

1841 Census, Occupation abstract, *PP* 1844, XXII.

1851 Census, II, Ages, civil condition, occupations, etc., vol. I, *PP* 1852–3, LXXXVIII, pt I.

Index